Frontier
Development Policy
in Brazil

Frontier Development Policy in Brazil
A Study of Amazonia

Dennis J. Mahar

PRAEGER PUBLISHERS
Praeger Special Studies

New York • London • Sydney • Toronto

Library of Congress Cataloging in Publication Data

Mahar, Dennis J
   Frontier development policy in Brazil.

   Rev. translation of Desenvolvimento econômico da
Amazônia, published in 1978.
   Bibliography: p.
   1. Regional planning--Amazon Valley. 2. Tax credits
--Amazon Valley. 3. Amazon Valley--Economic policy.
I. Title.
HC188.A5M3313 1979   309.2'5'09811   78-19750
ISBN 0-03-047091-9

This book was originally published in Portuguese by IPEA (Instituto de Planejamento Economico e Social) under the title *Desenvolvimento Ecônomico da Amazonia: Uma Análise des Políticas Governamentais*, as No. 39 in its Research Series (Rio de Janeiro, 1978). The responsibility for opinions expressed in this volume rests solely with the author, and publication does not necessarily constitute an endorsement of the views expressed in them by IPEA, or by the Brazilian Government.

PRAEGER PUBLISHERS
PRAEGER SPECIAL STUDIES
383 Madison Avenue, New York, N.Y. 10017, U.S.A.

Published in the United States of America in 1979
by Praeger Publishers,
A Division of Holt, Rinehart and Winston, CBS, Inc.

9 038 987654321

For Helga, Lisa, and James

I'd be an Indian here, and live content
To fish, hunt, and paddle my canoe,
And see my children grow, like young wild fawns,
In health of body and peace of mind,
Rich without wealth, and happy without gold.

>   —Alfred Russell Wallace
>   (Travels on the Amazon and Rio
>   Negro, 1889)

The green area of Amazonia should be totally devastated
. . . because the forest represents the paralyzation of
the country's development.

>   —Brazilian Congressman
>   (Quoted in O Globo, October 19,
>   1977)

The present course of road building, settlement, and destruction of the forest can only end in disaster.

>   —Betty J. Meggers
>   ("Man in the Amazon" Conference,
>   University of Florida, 1973)

Preface

Until the past few decades, Amazonia was the forgotten region of Brazil. Although public and private initiatives in the region date from the colonial period, they were primarily geared to the predatory exploitation of forest products. These sporadic intrusions did create periods of prosperity, but their long-run effects were mostly negligible. The first attempts at comprehensive socioeconomic planning started only in the 1950s when the federal government established an agency for this purpose. While these initial attempts were not entirely successful, they did provide the necessary background for the massive efforts of the 1960s and 1970s.

Since the mid-1960s, the development and human occupation of Amazonia have become high-priority goals for policy makers. To these ends, the federal government has directly financed new transportation and communications networks, agricultural colonization, and research on natural resource potentials. In addition, private capital has been attracted to the region through an array of fiscal and credit incentives. The interim results of these policies are mixed, but it is clear that Amazonia is finally becoming integrated with the rest of Brazil.

Surprisingly, there have been few published accounts of these recent developments. My original purpose was to partially fill this gap through a study of the fiscal incentives legislation affecting Amazonia. Fiscal incentives have been important tools of regional development in recent decades and obviously merited special attention. Moreover, I also reasoned that a study of fiscal incentives in Amazonia would provide some useful comparisons with parallel research on the Brazilian Northeast.* In general, the final version incorporates these initial intentions. As in most projects of this sort, however, a number of modifications were made as the work progressed.

For example, soon after beginning I decided that an exclusive emphasis on fiscal incentives would be of limited instructive or practical value. That is, fiscal incentives do not operate in isolation, but rather as part of the overall regional development process. This pro-

---

*The most complete work on fiscal incentives in the Northeast is D. E. Goodman and R. Cavalcanti de Albuquerque, Incentivos à Industrialização e Desenvolvimento do Nordeste, Coleção Relatórios de Pesquisa, no. 20 (Rio de Janeiro: IPEA/INPES, 1974).

cess, in turn, is conditioned by a unique set of economic, cultural, political, and physical (natural) variables. With this fact in mind, I expanded my original research agenda to include complementary studies of the history, demography, ecology, and general economic structure and performance of Amazonia.

Even in its present, expanded version, this study purports to be neither a complete nor even balanced treatment of the realidade Amazônica. The emphasis (or lack of emphasis) given to various subtopics was governed by two factors: the availability of statistical information and my professional interests. Of these two factors, the first was by far the most limiting; generally, socioeconomic data on Amazonia are still as undeveloped as the region itself. As a result, some parts of the study are necessarily brief, especially in such important areas as trade flows, internal migration, agriculture, colonization, and land tenure.

Although the scarcity of basic data was always a serious problem, considerable information was generated during the course of my research. This gathering of information was greatly facilitated by the many people who generously shared their time and special "knowledges" of Amazonia. Indeed, without their help this study could never have been completed. In this respect, I owe a large debt of gratitude to the faculty and students of the Nucleus of Amazonian Studies (NAEA) of the Federal University of Pará. Paraense hospitality, plus welcome advice and criticism, was always offered by José Marcelino M. da Costa and Paulo S. R. Cal, director and vice-director, respectively. Special thanks are also due Manoel Pinto da Silva, Jr., Constantino Ribeiro Otero, and Roberto da Costa Ferreira for their aid in collecting the data for Chapter 4.

I must thank both the Superintendency for the Development of Amazonia (SUDAM) and Radar Mapping in Amazonia (RADAM) for their collaboration. SUDAM enthusiastically supported my research efforts and provided a wealth of essential data. Its superintendent, Hugo de Almeida, and deputy-superintendent, Jacó Charcot Pereira Rios, gave me an excellent orientation to the public sector's role in the development of Amazonia. João Batista Ramos and Ivan Rickmann of the fiscal incentives department helped guide the data-collection process and resolved many complicated problems encountered at this stage. The staff of RADAM freely offered their unique, firsthand knowledges of Amazonia's natural resources and also arranged for a fascinating trip to one of their advanced bases in the interior. Here acknowledgments are due Otto Bittencourt Neto and Antonio L. Sampaio de Almeida, superintendent and executive secretary, respectively.

In Manaus, my research was facilitated by the Superintendency for the Manaus Free Trade Zone (SUFRAMA) and the State of Amazonas Development Commission (CODEAMA). Both organizations provided a general orientation to the special characteristics of western Amazonia, as well as much of the data employed in Chapter 5. The fiscal incentives department of SUFRAMA was particularly helpful owing to the cooperation of Marcílio R. de A. Junqueira, Clycério Vieira do N. e Sá, and Rômulo de Paula Nunes. At CODEAMA, thanks are due the executive secretary, José Fernando P. da Silva, as well as Benedito J. de C. Pinto and Samir Mamed Assi.

The technical staff of the Research Institute (INPES) of the Institute of Economic and Social Planning (IPEA) provided a stimulating intellectual environment in which to work, as well as many useful ideas in those areas where my professional background was weakest. Hamilton C. Tolosa, superintendent of IPEA/INPES, generously granted permission to reproduce extensive portions of an earlier, Portuguese-language version of this study (Desenvolvimento Econômico da Amazônia, Coleção Relatórios de Pesquisa, no. 39, Rio de Janeiro: IPEA/INPES, 1978). I must also acknowledge the efforts of colleagues who read preliminary drafts of the manuscript and who suggested many ways in which to improve the final version. The principal readers were Thompson A. de Andrade (IPEA/INPES), Werner Baer (University of Illinois), and Fernando A. Rezende (IPEA/INPES).

The arduous task of data processing was ably handled by Leila Maia, Antônio Carlos da Fonseca, Antônio Tércio de Freitas, and the research-assistant pool of IPEA/INPES. The equally arduous secretarial tasks were performed by Alzira da Silva Souza; Helga Bliwernitz Mahar was in charge of preparing the bibliography.

Though I am deeply grateful to all the individuals and organizations mentioned above—and to many who remain unmentioned—I assume full responsibility for all errors, misinterpretations, and points of view.

Contents

1

Development Planning
for Amazonia:
Past and Present

THE CHALLENGES

The Amazon Basin has always presented formidable challenges
to policy makers. In Brazil, government planning for the region dates
from the early decades of this century. Amazonia continues to be,
however, the most sparsely populated, unexplored, inaccessible, and
undeveloped part of the country.

Perhaps the most important historical challenge perceived by
policy makers has been the region's extremely low average population
density and its unequal spatial distribution. Even as of 1975, only
4.2 million persons (or about 4 percent of the national population) in-
habited the "classic Amazon." Since this population was distributed
over 3.5 million square kilometers (or over 40 percent of the national
territory), the average density was just over one inhabitant per square
kilometer—roughly equal to that of the Sahara Desert. Major settlements do occur in the state and territorial capitals, but the rural population tends to be highly dispersed along the main course of the Amazon River and its many tributaries. In general, these demographic
characteristics attest to the region's limited capacity to support human occupation and have, moreover, furthered the intraregional concentration of modern economic activity, impeded the provision of basic social services to the rural population, and made the maintenance
of Brazilian sovereignty in frontier areas a difficult task.

A second challenge to policy makers has been Amazonia's traditional dependence on the extraction of forest products (rubber, fruits,
and nuts, hides, and skins) as a source of income and employment.
This factor has been largely responsible for the dispersion of the rural
population and has retarded the formation of permanent settlements.
It has also delayed the introduction of modern production techniques to
the region's primary sector. Moreover, as a result of their direct
links with international markets, extractive activities have injected an
undesirable degree of instability into the regional economy.

1

A third barrier to effective policy making has been the rudimentary knowledge of the region's natural resources. Although important mineral and nonmineral resources are known to exist, systematic mapping and scientific research are very recent developments in Amazonia. Thus, the vision of Amazonia as a new "El Dorado" continues to be based more on myth than on fact. One such myth, no doubt conjured up by observations of the lush tropical forest, is that the region could be transformed into the world's "breadbasket." While technological breakthroughs may yet vindicate this belief, preliminary studies indicate that only a small proportion of the land (probably less than 5 percent) is suitable for annual crops, owing to poor soils and the delicate ecological balances that characterize a tropical rainforest.

A final challenge to policy makers stems from the region's long isolation from the rest of Brazil. Although Amazonia possesses one of the world's great river systems, the southern tributaries of the Amazon River are only navigable for relatively short distances. As a result, commerce has historically tended to flow in an east-to-west direction. Through these commercial flows, Amazonia has, through the centuries, developed economic and cultural ties with Europe, North America, and its South American neighbors, which have often been stronger than its ties with southern Brazil. These foreign ties have, during some historical periods, brought temporary prosperity to the region, but today its average per capita income is only about half that of the nation as a whole.

The purpose of the present chapter is to describe and evaluate the ways in which regional planners have reacted to the challenges presented in Amazonia. In doing so, emphasis will be placed on the changing government objectives in this region (as revealed in the formal national and regional development plans) as well as the major factors that have influenced the policy makers.

PLANNING THE RUBBER ECONOMY: 1912-45

From 1912 to the end of World War II, two major attempts were made at regional planning. The first, the Rubber Support Plan, was initiated in 1912 and lasted little more than a year. The second plan, the so-called Batalha da Borracha (Battle for Rubber), began in 1942 with the signing of the "Washington Accords" and lasted until 1947. Planning for Amazonia during the period from 1912 to 1945 was thus almost exclusively devoted to attempts to recuperate the regional rubber economy. By following this rather narrow concept of development, policy makers of the era mistakenly thought they could revive the prosperity of the 1870-1912 rubber boom.[1] Instead, they perpetuated a mentality based on the extraction of forest products that practically assured a long-term economic stagnation of the region.

The Rubber Support Plan
(Plano de Defesa da Borracha)

By 1912, Amazonia was nearing the end of a boom based on the exportation of wild rubber that had brought an unprecedented prosperity to the region for almost half a century.[2] World rubber prices, which had peaked at 12s. 9d. on the London market in 1910, had already fallen to as low as 4s. 1d., and the rising (and more efficient) production of plantation-grown Asian rubber threatened to depress them even further.[3] In this foreboding environment, the government of Hermes da Fonseca decided to take immediate action to protect the regional economy. The result was the establishment of the Rubber Support Plan, codified by Decrees 2543-A (January 5, 1912) and 9521 (April 17, 1912). This plan, though mainly aimed at maintaining Brazil's position in the international rubber market, also sought to bring about general improvements in the region's economic and social conditions. Among other things, it called for the provision of cash premiums to persons planting rubber trees as well as to those building rubber-processing plants, hospitals, railroads, port facilities, or housing. In addition, taxes were abolished on the importation of merchandise utilized in rubber, livestock, fish, and fuel production. State export taxes on rubber, which were viewed as a major impediment to sales, were reduced by 50 percent.

To finance the plan, a special credit of 8,000 contos (approximately U.S. $2.6 million) was opened, and a superintendency was created to coordinate its expenditure. During the first year of the plan, over 4,000 contos were spent on office facilities, agricultural experiment stations, and research on regional health and transportation problems. Certain important factors, however, doomed the plan from its start. Among these were the precarious financial state of the nation, the scarcity of private capital and skilled technicians, the comprehensive objectives of the plan, the predatory and nomadic psychology that characterized the region, and the lack of a developed domestic market for rubber.[4] For these and other reasons, the national congress refused additional funding in 1914 and the support program was thus abolished. In retrospect, it is difficult to see how the plan could have succeeded even if additional funding had been available. Its fatal flaw was linking the prosperity and future development of Amazonia to the export of one forest product, a product sold on a market in which Brazil could not effectively compete.

The "Batalha da Borracha"

The debacle of the Rubber Support Plan and the rapidly increasing competition from Asian rubber caused the Amazonian economy to enter a 30-year period of collapse and stagnation, interrupted only briefly in the mid-1920s by British attempts to restrict their own production and thus raise world prices.[5] Rubber production, which had reached its maximum level at over 42,000 tons in 1912, fell to a low of 6,550 tons in 1932. Regional population growth also stagnated during this period as labor recruited during the rubber boom began to leave the region in search of more promising opportunities.[6] The population that remained reverted to the most primitive subsistence agriculture, supplemented by extractive activities (principally rubber and Brazil nuts) when market conditions permitted. Sporadic attempts by public and private interests to recuperate the regional economy through immigration and the establishment of rubber plantations (most notably by the Ford Corporation in Belterra and Fordlândia), produced negligible results.[7] On the eve of World War II, rubber production still remained at levels only slightly above those prevailing in the 1880s.

The entry of the United States into World War II provided temporary relief from these three decades of stagnation and neglect.[8] Through the "Washington Accords" of March 1942, Brazil agreed to cooperate with the Allied forces in supplying strategic raw materials, including rubber, and a major effort to mobilize production began.[9] To finance this undertaking, the Import-Export Bank offered Brazil a U.S. $100 million credit to facilitate a general mobilization of its economic resources. The Rubber Reserve Company (later the Rubber Development Corporation—RDC), in turn, created a fund of $5 million specifically to assist the Brazilian government in the development of Amazonian rubber production.

An administrative structure encompassing credit, shipping, health, and labor recruitment was rapidly assembled to implement the accords and placed under the general supervision of a federal commission. At the center of this administrative structure was the Banco de Crédito da Borracha (BCB), a forerunner of the present regional development bank. This bank—which was initially underwritten by the national treasury (87,500 shares), the Rubber Development Corporation (60,000 shares), and private interests (2,500 shares)—was given a monopoly over the purchase and sale of rubber as well as the responsibility for developing agricultural colonies, food production, transportation facilities, cooperatives, and rural credit. The Rubber Reserve Corporation obliged the BCB to export all rubber production in excess of domestic needs to the United States at a fixed price of 39 cents per pound, which was raised in steps to 60 cents by 1944, and offered cash premiums on exports of over 5,000 tons.

In order to comply with these production commitments, the Brazilian government was faced with the immediate problem of mobilizing a labor force. To do so, the Serviço Especial de Mobilização de Trabalhadores (SEMTA) was created in 1942 to assemble up to 50,000 workers in Belém. Between 1942 and 1945, this organization and its successor, the Comissão Administrativa do Encaminhamento de Trabalhadores para a Amazônia (CAETA), actually did transport over 32,000 workers and their dependents (in total, over 48,000 persons) to Amazonia.[10] This mass migration was facilitated, as it had been in the late 1870s, by a prolonged drought in the Northeast. Although significant in quantitative terms, government recruitment efforts were not without their defects. Potential workers were often misled as to the true nature of living conditions in Amazonia and arrived completely unprepared to deal with the rigors of rubber extraction. As a result, many ultimately refused to work or abandoned their jobs after only a few days.

For those workers who effectively became a part of the labor force, the government established agencies to deal with problems concerning health and basic supplies. The first of these areas was put under the jurisdiction of the Serviço Especial de Saúde Pública (SESP). This agency was to provide medical assistance to the regional population, promote general sanitation efforts, and control malaria. To this end, it initiated drainage programs in Manaus, Belém, Porto Velho, and other cities and operated a network of clinics and dispensaries in the rubber collection areas. The agency in charge of providing adequate food and other supplies was the Superintendência de Abastecimento do Vale Amazônico (SAVA). Through an agreement with the Rubber Development Corporation, SAVA was to create conditions through which newly arrived workers could cultivate enough food for their own subsistence. Through another agreement between these two entities, stockpiles of food were established at strategic points in the rubber-producing areas to be sold to workers at fixed prices.

Another crucial problem encountered during the war years was that of transportation. With the greatly expanded need to transport workers, equipment, and rubber, the existing infrastructure proved to be completely inadequate. Initially, this problem was surmounted by the increased use of air transport; new airports were established at Manaus and Iquitos (Peru)—two strategic cities in the rubber-producing areas. Later, in July 1943, the RDC signed a contract with the government-owned Serviço de Navegação na Amazônia e Administração do Porto do Pará (SNAPP), according to which the former would finance the modernization of fluvial transportation in return for guaranteed shipping facilities. During the period of this contract, the RDC acquired over 80 boats for SNAPP and subsidized the importation of coal from the United States.

In relation to the effort and costs involved, the production results of the Batalha da Borracha were quite modest. From 1941 to 1945, the annual output of natural rubber rose by only 10,000 tons (from 12,840 tons to 22,902 tons) to a level only slightly more than half that registered in the peak production year of 1912. Furthermore, due to the short-term "emergency" nature of the program, its impact on the region was almost purely transitory.[11]

THE RISE AND FALL OF SPVEA: 1946-64

The Creation of SPVEA

At the end of World War II, Asian rubber production once again entered world markets and Amazonia seemed destined to return to economic stagnation. Recognizing the failures of past programs aimed solely at recuperating the rubber economy, however, parliamentary representatives from the region argued for a more comprehensive, long-term development policy. This idea was well received in the Constituent Assembly and was subsequently formalized in the new national Constitution of 1946. Article 199 of this document provided for the establishment of a development program for Amazonia to be financed through a 3 percent share of total federal tax revenues for a period of 20 consecutive years. In addition, the regional, state, and municipal governments were to contribute a similar share of their tax revenues for this purpose.

With a long-term source of resources seemingly assured by this clause, a congressional committee was formed and charged with the responsibility of framing a law to implement this constitutional article. Studies, debates, and bureaucratic delays surrounding this topic, however, impeded the implementation of the legal directives for over six years.[12] Law 1806 (January 6, 1953), which regulated Article 199, was finally approved by Congress on February 11, 1953. Article 1 of this law called for the creation of a regional development plan (Plano de Valorização Econômica da Amazônia) broadly conceived as a system of services and public works designed to develop agricultural, mineral, and industrial production and to improve the social and economic well-being of the regional population.

To execute this plan, the congress created a central coordinating agency (Superintendência do Plano de Valorização Econômica da Amazônia—SPVEA) with headquarters in Belém. This organ was divided into a superintendency in charge of executive matters and a 15-member planning commission to elaborate plans and supervise their execution. Of the 15 members of the latter administrative organ, six were to be specialists in the general areas of interest of the plan (health, credit and commerce, natural resources, agriculture, cultural development and transportation, communications and energy) and nine were to be representatives of each of the states and territories under the jurisdiction of SPVEA.*

The question of geographical jurisdiction was much debated in the period leading up to the passage of Law 1806. The first concept adopted was that of the "classic Amazon" comprised of Amapá, Acre, Roraima (then Rio Branco), Rondônia (then Guaporé), Amazonas, and Pará. This area was successively enlarged so as to better conform to an economic, as opposed to a purely geographical, concept of Amazonia. When finally written into the law, SPVEA's area of jurisdiction (called the "legal Amazon") was to include all of the "classic Amazon" plus parts of Mato Grosso (north of the sixteenth parallel), Goiás (north of the thirteenth parallel), and Maranhão (west of the forty-fourth meridian). This legal concept of Amazonia was over one-third larger than the classic Amazon and covered almost 60 percent of the national territory.

The First Five-Year Plan
(Preimeiro Plano Qüinqüenal)

Article 13 of Law 1806 called for the overall regional development plan to be carried out in partial plans of five years each. In contrast to the delays encountered in the definitive version of Law 1806, however, the first partial plan was to be formulated by the planning commission within a period of nine months. While this was being prepared, public action in Amazonia continued with a transitional "Emergency Program" (Programa de Emergência) funded through the regular federal budget at Cr$ 330 thousand.[13] During 1954, practically all of these funds were spent, although major alterations were made in the original budgeting. In essence, the "emergency program" was not really a plan but rather a series of political decisions that had, after the fact, taken the form of a plan.

Problems with the First Five-Year Plan started almost at its inception. The origin of many of these problems was the comprehensive nature of its goals coupled with an extremely rudimentary knowledge of the region's socioeconomic structure and potential.[14] Article 7 of Law 1806 listed the 11 fundamental objectives of the plan. Included among these were the promotion of agriculture, industry, and mining as well as the formulation of programs dealing with flood control, transportation, communications, energy, social welfare (that is, nu-

---

*The particular structure of the planning commission would later lead to criticisms that the policies of SPVEA were more governed by political considerations than by economic considerations.

trition, health, sanitation, education, immigration, and colonization), banking and credit, and general research. On the basis of these objectives, the plan was prepared in the record time of five months and submitted to the president within the nine-month limit prescribed by law. The finished document, as a result, had little scientific foundation and was mainly an attempt to simply recognize the region's major problems.[15] It is perhaps for these reasons that the full plan was never approved by congress and development programs became funded on an annual basis.

In the original formulation of the First Five-Year Plan, the highest priority was given to agricultural development. In this sector, the objectives of SPVEA were to make the region self-sufficient in foodstuffs and to expand the production of raw materials for export and internal use. These goals were supposed to be accomplished through research, colonization, and various production incentives. Second in priority was the development of transportation, communications, and energy (especially the first). Emphasis was placed on the improvement of fluvial transportation through an expansion and modernization of the river fleet and port facilities. Third priority was afforded to the health problems of the region. In this area, the major goals were the construction, expansion, and improvement of hospitals and clinics as well as the assurance of adequate water supplies and sewer systems in the capital cities. Other concerns of the plan, in order of their original budget allocations, were credit and commerce, education, and natural resources.

Unfortunately for SPVEA and Amazonia, subsequent funding problems precluded the possibility that these rather grandiose objectives would ever be realized. First, annual budgeting made long-term planning a difficult, if not impossible, task. Second, SPVEA never had sufficient control over the allocation of its own resources. This was partially caused by the fact that 75 to 85 percent of its funds were spent through contracts with other organs in the region; moreover, about 25 percent of the total budget was earmarked for specific purposes. The net result of these arrangements was a geographical and functional fragmentation of expenditures that prevented a concerted effort in any of the major problem areas. Finally, and most important, large budget cuts by the national congress forced alterations of on-going projects and the postponement or cancellation of proposed projects.

The extent of these cuts may be appreciated by comparing the budgeted and actual revenues of SPVEA. As Table 1.1 indicates, only slightly more than 60 percent of the funds guaranteed by the Constitution of 1946 was actually received and spent during the period of the First Five-Year Plan. With the exception of Pará, the states and municípios within the jurisdiction of SPVEA apparently ignored the

TABLE 1.1

SPVEA: Budgeted and Actual Expenditures of First Five-Year Plan
by Sector, 1955-60
(Cr$ 1,000, 1978 prices)

Expenditure Category	Budgeted (1)	Actual (2)	Shortfall (1 - 2)	Percent (2 ÷ 1)
Transportation and com-munication*	4,890.2	2,840.0	2,050.2	58.1
Credit	4,290.6	2,742.1	1,548.5	63.9
Health	2,961.5	1,979.5	982.0	66.8
Electric energy	1,472.7	1,021.8	450.9	69.4
Agriculture	1,792.0	1,066.9	725.1	59.5
Education	1,100.8	556.3	544.5	50.5
Natural resources	661.9	398.2	263.7	60.2
Total	17,169.7	10,604.8	6,564.9	61.8

*Excludes expenditures on the Belém-Brasilia highway totaling
Cr$ 3.8 billion (as of June 1960).

Note: Excludes administrative expenditures and transfers.

Source: Superintendência do Plano de Valorização da Amazônia
(SPVEA), Política de Desenvolvimento da Amazônia: SPVEA, 1954-
1960 (Rio de Janeiro, 1961), vol. 1, p. 84.

constitutional law concerning their financial obligations to the plan.
Transfers of funds from the national treasury to SPVEA, moreover,
were often delayed and at irregular intervals, a practice made even
more detrimental by the 20 percent inflation that characterized the period. In an attempt to adjust to these revenue shortfalls, SPVEA was
obliged to establish a system of expenditure priorities. This policy
was especially harmful to programs in education and agriculture where
budgets were cut by over 40 percent.*
    In addition to making these direct expenditures, SPVEA also
supervised a fund aimed at supplying credit to agricultural and industrial enterprises. This fund (Fundo de Fomento à Produção) was orig-

---

*When the costs of the Belém-Brasilia highway are considered,
actual expenditures on transportation and communications exceed the
original budgeted amounts.

inally constituted in 1950 to finance the rubber monopoly of the Banco de Crédito da Amazônia (BCA), the successor to the now extinct Banco de Crédito da Borracha. Upon the establishment of SPVEA, however, the fund received 10 percent of this organ's budget to be utilized in accordance with the objectives of the Five-Year Plan.

Between 1954 and 1960, over Cr$ 1 billion were added to this fund of which about Cr$ 750 million were actually invested. Since the relationship between SPVEA and BCA was not sufficiently defined, however, the contribution of this fund to the overall development of Amazonia is debatable. The accounts of BCA indicate that a significant amount of credit was extended for developing modern agriculture and rural industry, but it was the suspicion of SPVEA that most of these funds ultimately flowed to the extractive rubber sector. Furthermore, the resources of the fund were often routed to the bank's more lucrative commercial operations; the result being that projects of a more "social" nature often went unfunded. [16]

OPERATION AMAZONIA: 1965-67

The defects and abuses that characterized public planning for Amazonia in the 1950s continued into the early 1960s, although some futile attempts were made to restructure SPVEA and reorient its planning goals and strategies. [17] At the end of ten years of operation, SPVEA could point to some successes such as supervising the construction of the Belém-Brasília highway, the modernization of SNAPP, and the financing of several major industries. Its general impact on the region, however, had been minimal. By 1964, SPVEA was described by its new superintendent as a failed and disorganized institution, incapable of performing its duties as the region's socioeconomic development agency. [18]

With the coming to power of a new national government in 1964, development planning for Amazonia started to take a new direction. The first hints as to what this new strategy would be were revealed in a 1965 speech by President Castello Branco. [19] The major themes of this speech were the promotion of greater efficiency in the regional planning apparatus and an increased development role for private enterprise. These objectives were to be formalized in a unified and harmonious regional development plan elaborated in a climate where technical orientation took precedence over partisan interests. To effect such a strategy, the president called for a sweeping transformation of the BCA and the greater use of special funds and fiscal incentives for attracting private capital to Amazonia. [20] Two days after this speech, a presidential decree created a five-member committee (Grupo de Estudos para a Reformulação da Política Econômica da

Amazônia) charged with defining the objectives of this new policy and the drafting of legislation for its subsequent implementation. The fruits of this committee's studies and recommendations were a series of laws passed in late 1966 and early 1967 and collectively known as "Operation Amazonia."[21]

The keystone of Operation Amazonia was Law 5173 (October 27, 1966). Article 4 of this document, which listed 13 objectives of government action in Amazonia, provided the basic orientation of the new policy; future policy for the region would be oriented toward establishing "development poles" and stable, self-sustaining population groups (especially in frontier areas), encouraging immigration, providing incentives to private capital, infrastructure development, and research on natural resource potentials. Within these specific objectives, one may distinguish two distinct, but interrelated approaches, one economic and the other geopolitical.

In the economic sphere, the approach amounted to the transferral to Amazonia of the development model previously applied with some success in the Northeast.[22] This model essentially involved the promotion of import-substitution industrialization that was to be financed by both foreign and domestic private capital. In the latter case, it was presumed that most of the investment capital would emanate from the dynamic industrial centers of the Center-South. The role of the public sector was to be that of attracting capital to the region through appropriate monetary and fiscal mechanisms as well as that of providing the necessary preinvestment infrastructure. In contrast to the objectives of SPVEA, which called for the realization of regional transportation, communications, energy, and flood-control plans, the new directives of infrastructure development were nonspecific.

The geopolitical content of Operation Amazonia is implied in those objectives that called for the effective occupation of the region through interregional and foreign immigration and the formation of permanent, self-sustaining settlements in the frontier areas. This settlement imperative is easily comprehended when one considers the low population density of Amazonia and the fact that it forms a part of seven nations other than Brazil. These two factors had been less important in the past when the entire region was practically devoid of human settlement. By the mid-1960s, however, it had become evident that several of the border states (particularly Peru and Venezuela) were already well advanced in programs designed to occupy and develop their respective Amazonias. Since it was (and still is) generally believed that vast quantities of natural resources still remained hidden in the region, the desire to assure Brazilian sovereignty appears to have been quite rational.[23]

The same legislation that enumerated these policy objectives also created the basic administrative structure through which they

would be carried out. Rather than continue with the unwieldy structure of SPVEA, a new agency, the Superintendência do Desenvolvimento da Amazônia (SUDAM), was established in its place. This
agency was molded along the lines of the previously successful planning
agency for the Northeast (Superintendência do Desenvolvimento do
Nordeste—SUDENE) and was linked to the Ministry of the Interior.
For its financial agent, Law 5122 (September 28, 1966) created the
Banco da Amazônia (BASA) and abolished the BCA. Unlike the BCA,
BASA was to function as a true regional development bank and was established with an administrative structure similar to that of the northeastern development bank (Banco do Nordeste do Brasil—BNB).

To implement the policy encouraging private initiative in the region, Operation Amazonia also resulted in legislation that widened the
scope of fiscal incentives. Through Law 5174 (October 27, 1966), private firms deemed of interest to the development of Amazonia could
qualify for up to a 100 percent exemption from their federal income
tax liability until 1982. Qualifying firms were also to be exempt from
duties on the export of regional products as well as on the import of
machinery and equipment. Finally, corporations were allowed income tax credits up to 75 percent of the value of BASA securities
(Obrigações da Amazônia) they acquired and 50 percent of their total
tax bill when the resulting savings were invested in agriculture, livestock, industry, and basic service activities approved by SUDAM.
This latter provision greatly increased the latitude of this mechanism
since fiscal incentive funds could previously only be invested in industrial ventures.

As an additional benefit to the private sector, SUDAM was to
supervise a new credit fund (Fundo para Investimentos Privados no
Desenvolvimento da Amazônia—FIDAM). It was to be constituted of
no less than 1 percent of federal tax revenues (later rescinded), the
proceeds of BASA securities, fiscal incentive funds not invested in
specific projects, the resources of the Fundo de Fomento à Produção, and the net revenues accruing from its own operation. The accumulated funds were to be invested by BASA in private firms and research considered essential to the development of Amazonia.

The culmination of Operation Amazonia was legislation passed
in early 1967 providing special tax incentives to private enterprises
operating in the states and territories of western Amazonia (Amazonas,
Acre, Rondônia and Roraima). This legislation, in part, represented
an effort to implement the objectives of creating "development poles"
and the occupation of the sparsely populated frontier zones. Perhaps
more important, however, it was an attempt to counterbalance the
policies of SPVEA that were alleged to have favored eastern Amazonia.
It was argued by proponents of western Amazonia that the eastern subregion (meaning the city of Belém and its environs), because of its su-

perior infrastructure and larger market, was attracting a disproportionate share of the investment funds made possible by SPVEA fiscal incentives.* As a result, it was further argued, the western subregion (the city of Manaus and its environs) was falling behind Belém and suffering high unemployment and an exodus of capital and human resources.[24]

The most important of this compensatory legislation was Decree-Law 288 (February 28, 1967), which established the Manaus Free Trade Zone (Zona Franca de Manaus—ZFM). The basic intent of this law was to create, through fiscal means, an industrial, commercial, and agricultural center in Manaus to serve as the "development pole" for western Amazonia. More specifically, firms locating within the confines of the ZFM were to be exempt from import and export duties as well as from the federal manufacturer's sales tax (IPI). All goods exported from the ZFM to domestic markets were completely free of the IPI, while goods with a foreign import content were subject to import duties at a rate reduced in proportion to the value added in the ZFM. The overall supervision of the ZFM was to be exercised by the Superintendência da Zona Franca de Manaus (SUFRAMA), an agency linked to the Ministry of the Interior, although not directly to SUDAM.

THE EXPERIENCE OF SUDAM: 1967-70

By early 1967, the main features of Operation Amazonia had already been enacted into law. The first priority of the new regional development agency was to formulate a coherent development plan to guide the implementation of these laws. During its initial years, SUDAM produced two plans: the First Five-Year Development Plan and the Primeiro Plano Diretor.† Both were designed to incorporate the spirit of Operation Amazonia and, at the same time, avoid the errors that had plagued SPVEA. In reality, however, neither plan was ever operative for essentially the same reason that caused the action of SPVEA to be so ineffectual, that is, the wide discrepancy between the plan's objectives and the means—both financial and technical—available to achieve them.

---

*During the 1964-66 period, less than 5 percent of the total investment approved for SPVEA fiscal incentives was located in western Amazonia.

†A plano diretor is, in effect, a plan within a plan. It is designed to provide interim direction to a larger, longer-term plan.

The First Five-Year Development Plan
(Primeiro Plano Qüinqüenal de
Desenvolvimento) of SUDAM

The First Five-Year Development Plan of SUDAM was approved
in 1967 through Decree 60,296 (March 3).[25] Although the plan had
eight specific objectives, they all generally conformed to the economic
model of regional import substitution and the geopolitical imperatives
of human occupation. These goals were to be attained by programming
projected public and private investment in the region by economic sector. In an attempt to free Amazonia from its historical dependence on
extractive commerce, the highest priority among the directly productive sectors was given to crops, livestock, and industry (Table 1.2).
While the regional economy was predicted to grow at a 9.4 percent
average annual rate during the 1967-71 period, the "leading sectors,"
modern agriculture and industry, were programmed at annual rates
of 11.5 and 11.9 percent, respectively. Extractive agriculture and
commerce, on the other hand, were expected to grow at the respective
rates of 1.7 and 5.4 percent.

Table 1.2 attests to the high priority given to expenditures on
basic economic infrastructure in the Five-Year Plan. This particular
emphasis would indicate that the planners visualized the immediate
needs of Amazonia to be essentially of an engineering nature. Within
the transportation sector, over 80 percent of the proposed investment
was allocated to the building or paving of roads. The objective of this
strategy was to connect selected regional "development poles" (Cuiabá
and Porto Velho, Manaus and Boa Vista, and the like) and thus foster
the growth of "development zones" (faixas de desenvolvimento) in the
intervening areas. By concentrating efforts in a few geographical subregions, it was hoped that the fragmentation of resources experienced
by SPVEA could be avoided. At the same time, this policy would also
further the geopolitical objectives of populating the region and physically integrating it with the rest of Brazil.

A crucial weakness of the Five-Year Plan was that its successful implementation was almost totally dependent upon the financial and
administrative cooperation of entities beyond the direct control of
SUDAM. In the financial sphere, the influence of SUDAM was weak-
ened by the fact that only 12 percent of the plan's total resources
emanated from its own budget, the other 88 percent being scattered
among various government agencies and the private sector. Judging
from the tone of the Primeiro Plano Diretor, the actual level of public
funds allocated to the Five-Year Plan fell far below expectations. Furthermore, although the new fiscal incentives legislation attracted a
significant amount of private savings to the region, the technical deficiencies of SUDAM prevented rigorous controls over its sectoral and

TABLE 1.2

SUDAM: Projected Sectoral Distribution of Investment
Expenditures in Regional Development Plans, 1967-79
(percent)

Sector	First Five-Year Plan (1967-71)	Primeiro Plano Diretor (1968-70)	PDAM I* (1972-74)	PDAM II (1975-79)
Extractive agriculture	0.1	0.1	0.0	0.5
Crops and livestock	16.4	24.3	1.9	11.7
Mining	—	—	—	15.4
Industry	12.6	13.4	0.0	13.0
Supply	1.4	0.0	10.1	0.0
Services	4.9	6.1	—	0.0
Government and urban development	1.3	—	0.1	1.3
Transportation	40.5	25.8	50.8	19.1
Energy	4.5	12.8	11.8	15.8
Communications	1.9	1.0	1.7	2.7
Natural resources	2.9	1.1	4.2	2.8
Housing	3.6	6.3	—	2.1
Health and sanitation	5.8	5.6	2.8	3.4
Education	2.7	1.0	5.1	2.0
Colonization	1.4	0.3	17.5	1.8
Other	—	2.5	3.1	8.6
Total	100.0	100.0	100.0	100.0

*Excludes fiscal incentive funds.

Note: Data based on constant prices. Dashes indicate nothing budgeted. Figures in tables may not total 100 due to rounding.

Sources: Primeiro Plano Qüinqüenal (SUDAM), p. 63; Primeiro Plano Diretor, vol. 1, pp. 54, 56; PDAM I, pp. 108-15; PDAM II, pp. 289-301.

spatial allocation. Finally, the effectiveness of the plan was lessened by a general breakdown of communications between its designers, who were outside consultants, and those entities charged with implementing it (SUDAM, federal ministries, state and municipal governments, and the like).

The Primeiro Plano Diretor

In an attempt to rectify the deficiencies of the Five-Year Plan, the Primeiro Plano Diretor was elaborated in 1968 by a team of six regional técnicos.[26] It was to be in effect for the 1968-70 period. The text was presented in three volumes comprising a draft of new legislation, a survey of the regional economy, and an explanation of the plan's basic goals and programs.

In general, the Plano Diretor was much less technically oriented than its immediate predecessor and was much more a "statement of position" on regional development strategy than a true plan. Its major argument was that the level of federal investment expenditures in Amazonia was becoming completely incompatible with regional needs. Private investment in the region, induced by fiscal incentives, could not be a substitute for this autonomous investment and, in fact, could be constrained in the future by a lack of basic infrastructure development. The proposed solution to this dilemma was perhaps the most novel aspect of the plan.

First, it was suggested that the federal government turn over to SUDAM all of its tax collections in the region for a period of three consecutive years. This special fund, although only representing about 1 percent of total federal revenues, would double the budget of the regional development agency.[27] Second, the Plano Diretor proposed a special regional electrification fund, based on one-tenth of a centavo surtax per kilowatt-hour on the national consumption of electricity. It was estimated that such a tax would add only 1 percent to electricity bills but would double the total resources available for electrification programs in Amazonia. The obvious message here was that the rate of development in Amazonia could be significantly accelerated without an undue burden on the rest of Brazil.

In addition to a plea for more federal resources, the Plano Diretor suggested some modifications in the goals and strategies of regional development. These proposals were based on the premise that certain past policies were producing results contrary to the best interests of Amazonia. One important theme in this respect was the concept of regional self-sufficiency. It was argued that previous strategies, which had concentrated on promoting extractive agriculture (especially rubber), had made the region highly vulnerable to price oscillations in the international market for primary products. Road-building programs, on the other hand, had increased the dependency of Amazonia on industrial and commercial interests in the Center-South. According to the Plano Diretor, regional self-sufficiency was the most promising way of solving these problems.

A second theme concerned the spatial aspects of regional development. Five years of experience with fiscal incentives had clearly shown that private investments in industry and agriculture continued to exhibit a marked locational preference for eastern Amazonia. This tendency, it was argued, was accentuating existing intraregional disparities and, hence, impeding efforts to achieve a balanced development of the region. Although private investment in the industrial and agricultural sectors was highly important in the proposed budget of the Plano Diretor (see Table 1.2), it was suggested that the project selection process be modified to give special consideration to entrepreneurs willing to locate in western Amazonia or in urban areas outside of state capitals.

In summary, the Plano Director was basically a call for immediate federal action in Amazonia through a significant increase in public investment spending and a correction of the distortions arising from previous regional policies. Perhaps because of its novelty and critical tone, however, the plan was never officially sanctioned. As a result, development efforts in Amazonia between 1967 and 1970 were largely the responsibility of the private sector. The increase in direct federal investment called for in the Plano Diretor did not materialize until the early 1970s.

SUDAM, SUFRAMA, AND THE POLICIES OF NATIONAL INTEGRATION: 1970-75

The early 1970s were characterized by a marked intensification of federal activity in Amazonia. Although economic development still remained an important policy concern, the objectives of occupation and physical integration became paramount. In this respect, there seemed to be a belated recognition that Amazonia was not a typical depressed region like the Northeast, but rather a "resource frontier," and that strategies appropriate to the one region did not necessarily apply to the other.[28] Indeed, regional policies during this period were based more on the socioeconomic complementarities of these two regions than on their similarities.

Since a fundamental aspect of the new strategies was their long-term nature, firm conclusions as to their efficacy are probably premature. The present discussion, therefore, is mainly concerned with the decision-making process and the interim results of the major programs.

The National-Integration Program (Programa de Integração Nacional)

The most important legislation of this era was undoubtedly Decree-Law 1106 (June 16, 1970), which established the National Inte-

gration Program (PIN). According to this law, the federal government was to reserve Cr$ 2 billion during 1971-74 for the financing of
an east-west (trans-Amazon) highway connecting Amazonia with the
Northeast, a north-south (Santarém-Cuiabá) highway linking it with
the Center-South, and an irrigation plan for the Northeast. Through
Decree-Law 1243 (October 30, 1972), the budget of PIN was raised to
Cr$ 2.8 billion and its duration extended to 1978. This legislation
also provided for the construction of an east-west (northern perimeter)
highway along the northern bank of the Amazon River. A number of
potential revenue sources were contemplated for the financing of PIN,
although the most important was to be a 30 percent share of the fiscal
incentive funds.

It is difficult to discern the single most important motive surrounding the creation of PIN. By most accounts, President Médici's
decision was precipitated by his visit to the Northeast in early June
1970 to observe the effects of a severe drought.[29] The construction
of an east-west highway, it was reasoned, would provide a short-run
solution to this problem by providing immediate employment opportunities to displaced workers. In the medium and long runs, moreover, planned and spontaneous settlements along the trans-Amazon
highway would tend to alleviate both population pressures and social
tensions in the Northeast while at the same time promoting the occupation of Amazonia.

An additional motive for the establishment of PIN involved considerations of national security and the threat of foreign domination
in the region. Although "international greed" (a cobiça internacional)
has always been a dominant theme in the literature on Amazonia, it
had received an inordinate amount of attention in the years immediately
preceding PIN.[30] First, a national debate had ensued over the suggestion that regional development could best be achieved by damming
the Amazon River to create a series of "great lakes." This idea was
originally formulated by a Brazilian engineer (E. P. Lopes) but was
later advocated by a group of Americans (led by Herman Kahn and
Robert Panero of the Hudson Institute). The major benefits of such a
scheme were supposed to be the creation of cheap electrical energy,
improved transportation, and various production advantages. Na-
tionalist factions, however, viewed it as entreguismo that would lead
to the "internationalization" of Amazonia.[31] This fear of undue external influence was further reinforced by the revelation that large
tracts of land in the region had been recently sold to foreign interests.[32]

For these and other motives (including the possibility of discovering new mineral deposits along the route), the actual construction
of the trans-Amazon highway hastily began on September 1, 1970,
less than three months after President Médici's visit to the Northeast.

At the time, the total cost of the highway construction program was estimated to be about Cr$ 400 million, or about 20 percent of the resources of PIN; the other 80 percent was allocated to agricultural colonization and irrigation.[33]

Although the decision to establish PIN was generally well received, it was not without its share of critics. Perhaps the most vocal of the early criticism emanated from northeastern political interests, which viewed PIN as a means of transferring fiscal incentive funds from their region to Amazonia. This policy, they argued, would severely limit the action of SUDENE and, hence, slow the process of regional industrialization. Another group of critics questioned the basic economic rationale of PIN. Their argument was based on the fact that highway construction was initiated with no previous recourse to detailed cost-benefit analyses or economic feasibility studies. Also questioned was the logic of physically linking the Northeast and Amazonia ("poverty with misery") when areas suitable for agricultural colonization were more accessible in the states of Maranhão and Pará.[34]

The Land Redistribution Program
(Programa de Redistribuição de Terras)

Complementing PIN was the Land Redistribution Program (PROTERRA), established by Decree-Law 1178 (June 1, 1971). The official objectives of this program were to facilitate land acquisition, improve rural labor conditions, and promote agroindustry in Amazonia and the Northeast. Initially, Cr$ 4 billion was allotted for the period 1972-74. This fund was to be constituted of federal budget allocations and transfers from PIN, as well as a 20 percent share of the fiscal incentive funds.* It was to be utilized for purchasing or appropriating large landholdings (for later resale to farmers with small-to-medium landholdings), supplying rural credit, financing agroindustry and its supporting infrastructure, subsidizing the use of modern agricultural inputs, supporting the prices of agricultural exports, and supervising the use of lands in the public domain.

The creation of PROTERRA, like that of PIN, was an attempt to reorient the previous strategy of regional development based on import-substitution industrialization. In his formal announcement of PROTERRA, President Médici directly criticized the system of fiscal incentives and its excessive concentration in the industrial sector.[35]

---

*This 20 percent was in addition to the 30 percent share already diverted to PIN.

The benefits of this system, he argued, had been almost entirely confined to urban areas, thus neglecting over half the population of Amazonia and the Northeast. PROTERRA would rectify this problem by attacking the major sources of rural poverty in these regions: the unequal distribution of landownership and the inefficient utilization of the land itself.

As might be expected, PROTERRA was also criticized by northeastern interests who feared the consequences of a further reduction of fiscal incentive funds at the disposal of SUDENE. The official response to this criticism was that total fiscal incentive funds destined for the Northeast would not fall as a result of PROTERRA, but would only be redirected more toward the agricultural sector.[36] Since this program was to be administered by the Ministry of Agriculture (through the Instituto Nacional de Colonização e Reforma Agrária—INCRA), however, the role of both SUDENE and SUDAM in the execution of regional policy was effectively lessened.

The First National Development Plan
(Primeiro Plano Nacional de Desenvolvimento)
and the Amazon Development Plan
(Plano de Desenvolvimento da Amazônia)

The First National Development Plan (PND I) placed great emphasis on the objectives implicit in PIN and PROTERRA. According to the PND I, the national goals with respect to Amazonia were integration (physical, economic, and cultural), human occupation, and economic development.[37] Referring to the first two objectives, the PND I continued to stress the alleged socioeconomic complementarities between Amazonia and the Northeast. The initial strategy utilized to achieve these goals was to be agricultural colonization along the trans-Amazon and Santarém-Cuiabá highways by northeastern immigrants. This aspect of the strategy was to be executed by the public sector through the PIN and PROTERRA budgets. In contrast, the objective of economic development continued to be delegated to private investment attracted by the fiscal incentives of SUDAM and SUFRAMA.

The Amazon Development Plan (PDAM) of SUDAM detailed the general guidelines of the PND I. The former abandoned the sophisticated models that characterized the Five-Year Development Plan and, instead, concentrated on surveying the regional economy and programming federal initiatives for the 1972-74 period.[38] Since the major policy decisions pertaining to Amazonia (that is, PIN and PROTERRA) had already been made at the national level, however, SUDAM was left little scope for innovation.

In terms of objectives, the PDAM reiterated the position of the PND I on combining the development of the Northeast with the occupation of Amazonia. It also stressed the advantages of integrating the economies of the North and the Center-South. The latter region's industry, it was argued, would tend to stagnate in the future if it did not have easy direct access to raw material-producing regions. Moreover, integration would also lead to an expansion of the domestic market for southern-produced goods. Here, as in other government documents, it was implicitly assumed that integration would have only positive economic and social repercussions on Amazonia.

The preoccupation of the PDAM with the objectives of integration and occupation is further revealed in its projected investment budget. Here, expenditures on transportation and colonization composed almost 70 percent of the total (see Table 1.2). With respect to colonization, the PDAM set the ambitious goal of settling 70,000 families (approximately half a million persons) during the 1972-74 period: 64,000 families along the trans-Amazon and Santarém-Cuiabá highways and the remainder in other areas of Amazonia.[39]

With regard to economic development strategy, it was implied that modern agriculture and livestock would receive the highest priorities. In contrast to earlier plans, the PDAM exhibited some pessimism concerning regional import-substitution industrialization. After noting the serious obstacles to industrialization (for example, the scarcity of entrepreneurial ability and limited local markets), the plan recommended that future development in this sector be oriented toward processing those regional primary products for which there was demand in international markets.

An additional aspect of the development strategy stressed in the PDAM was the need for natural resource surveys. Although this objective had received considerable attention since the period of SPVEA, the PDAM approached it in a highly sophisticated manner. The plan called for the aerial mapping of 1.5 million square kilometers of Amazonia during the 1972-74 period, initially covering the area south of the Amazon River. Mapping was to be subsequently extended to the entire region. This undertaking was to be financed through PIN and executed by "Projeto RADAM" (Radar na Amazônia) of the Ministry of Mines and Energy. Through photointerpretation and complementary field studies, RADAM was thus entrusted with elaborating the first systematic inventory of minerals, soils, and vegetation ever attempted for the entire Brazilian Amazon.

INTERIM RESULTS

Although basically of a long-term nature, the programs initiated in the early 1970s have already had a profound socioeconomic impact on Amazonia. While some old problems have been ameliorated by these programs, others have been exacerbated. Still other problems have been created that did not previously exist. In contrast to the fanfare that accompanied the inauguration of the "national integration" era, however, few evaluations have yet appeared in its immediate aftermath. Such an evaluation can be obtained from available official reports, supplemented by the published impressions of journalists, scientists, businessmen, government employees, and others.

For clarity of exposition, the objectives of integration and occupation (exemplified by the road-building and agricultural colonization programs of PIN and PROTERRA) are combined and considered separately from the objective of economic development (exemplified by the fiscal incentives of SUDAM and SUFRAMA). This is done so as to differentiate between the two more or less distinct approaches to the challenges presented by Amazonia. The interdependencies of these approaches (both complementarities and conflicts), however, are also noted.

Integration and Occupation

As previously discussed, the objectives of integration and occupation received the highest priority during the early 1970s. The first concrete result in this direction was the completion of the initial 1,200 kilometers (Estreito to Itaituba) of the trans-Amazon highway in late 1972.* The Estreito-Itaituba stretch of the trans-Amazon highway, which intersected with both the Belém-Brasilia and Santarém-Cuiabá highways, was to be the site of INCRA's first experiment with agricultural colonization based on the expected immigration of "excess" northeastern population. To execute this strategy, INCRA designed a network of planned communities (agrovilas, agrópoles, and rurópoles—in ascending order of predicted population) at predetermined intervals along the highway's route.[40] Each community was to be equipped with basic urban services (electricity, water, medical and dental facilities, schools) and the prospective colonist was reserved an agricultural plot of 100 hectares. INCRA was to select and transport the colonists from their regions of origin and guarantee their subsistence for a period of from six to eight months. In addition, colonists were offered attractive terms of credit for the purchase of plots, the construction of housing, and the acquisition of implements and other basic necessities.

---

*An additional 1,000-kilometer stretch (Itaituba to Humaitá) was inaugurated in early 1974. The Santarém-Cuiabá highway was completed in late 1976; construction of the northern perimeter highway is currently (1979) stalled owing to technical and financial difficulties.

With the initiation of the joint integration-occupation strategy, it thus appeared that public policy had finally begun to surmount one of the fundamental challenges to development planning for Amazonia. Previously inaccessible land was now available for economic exploitation and its human settlement was being facilitated in an aggressive and innovative manner. For a number of reasons, however, the initial results of this strategy have fallen far short of expectations. Although available sources of data are not completely consistent, it appears that only slightly more than 6,000 families (approximately 42,000 persons) were actually settled along the trans-Amazon highway by the end of 1974.[41] This total represented less than 10 percent of the number of colonists projected in the PDAM and less than 2 percent of the "excess" rural population of the Northeast estimated for 1970.[42]

The explanations of this rather poor performance are both varied and complex. The core of the problem, however, seems to lie in the naive premise that northeastern migrants could be readily transformed into prosperous farmers in a region ecologically much different from that of their origins.[43] Compounding this fundamental misconception was the fact that the network of planned communities was designed with little regard for either terrain or suitability for agriculture. Since the first agrovilas were established in an area of relatively fertile soils, however, high first-year crop yields obscured the reality that most soils along the route of the trans-Amazon highway are unsuitable for traditional agriculture.[44] In fact, specialists on tropical agriculture are in almost total agreement that the cultivation of annual crops such as manihot, rice, corn, and beans in the uplands of Amazonia is both ecologically damaging and ultimately unproductive.[45]

Factors other than poor soils have also been blamed for the initial failures of planned agricultural colonization. Among those most frequently cited in the literature are a lack of sufficient technical assistance to the colonists, difficulties in storing and distributing production, and the excessive paternalism of the supervisory agencies. As a result, there have been persistent reports of colonists abandoning their plots, either to return to their origins or to locate employment in other activities (for example, mining and agriculture, wage labor on corporate agricultural enterprises, and the like).[46]

The relatively small numbers of colonists settled so far in planned communities, however, do not signify that total migration to Amazonia has also been negligible. Accurate estimates of interregional migration since the 1970 census are virtually nonexistent, although it is certain that the spontaneous flow of migrants to Amazonia since this data has far exceeded that recorded in official colonization projects. Thus, partially as a result of the problems enumerated above, an urgent concern of public agencies is now the effective absorption of this spontaneous contingent.

In the short run, at least, the existence of spontaneous immigration has given rise to serious social tensions stemming from questions of land tenure. Since the provision of legal titles has proceeded at a considerably slower rate than the influx of new migrant families, there have been many published accounts of squatters (posseiros) occupying (and frequently being expelled from) plots on private property, public lands, and Indian reservations. A rapid resolution of this situation has been impeded not only by the relative shortage of funds and staff available to INCRA but also by the existence of groups selling fraudulent titles to prospective settlers (grileiros).[47]

Economic Development

The strategies adopted primarily for furthering the integration-occupation goal in Amazonia are in many ways overlapping with those concerned with regional economic development. The expenditures from PIN and PROTERRA budgets on basic infrastructure (river and airport facilities, highways, electrification, and the like), and natural resource inventories (RADAM), for example, are obviously necessary (though not sufficient) in this sense. Likewise, the attraction of a labor force through planned colonization is also a potentially important ingredient in the development process. Adhering to the spirit of Operation Amazonia, however, the formation of new directly productive activities has been almost entirely entrusted to the private sector.

Through the array of fiscal advantages at its disposal, SUDAM has successfully attracted a significant amount of private capital to Amazonia (see Chapter 4). Mainly as a result of basic differences in the resource endowments of the Northeast and Amazonia, however, the investment patterns promoted by fiscal incentives in these two regions have been markedly divergent. Whereas in the former region investors have exhibited a preference for capital-intensive industrial projects, the preferred investment in the latter region has been land-intensive livestock projects.

In Amazonia, the economic advantages of investment in livestock (versus industry) are obvious: the existence of plentiful, inexpensive land subject to rapid capital gains, minimal personnel requirements, and a buoyant market for the product. In contrast, attempts to develop an import-substitution industrial base continue to be hampered by shortages of skilled labor, limited local markets, lack of sufficient credit, and competition from extraregional industry. By the late 1980s, production of the livestock projects approved by SUDAM may provide a major contribution to both the internal supply of beef and to the country's foreign exchange earnings; the projected annual production of 1 million head is equal to 70 percent of the 1970 production level of the combined North and central-western regions and about 10 percent of the national total in the same year.[48] However, several criticisms may be directed toward this particular mode of development.

First, the very nature of extensive livestock raising precludes any significant labor absorption except during the initial stages of clearing and preparing pastures. This aspect of development strategy thus appears to be in direct conflict with the major goals of regional policy that stress the human occupation of Amazonia.[49] A second criticism pertains to the equity aspects of this strategy. This criticism stems from the fact that the livestock projects are generally owned by extraregional corporations who, through the utilization of fiscal incentives, are able to purchase and develop their holdings at highly subsidized rates. Hence, one could hypothesize that most of the returns from these projects will ultimately flow from Amazonia to upper-income interests residing in other regions or abroad. Furthermore, the sheer physical immensity of the holdings has effectively preempted land that could have foreseeably been utilized for settling new migrants. Finally, the widespread clearing of virgin forest on SUDAM-approved projects (estimated at 5,000 square kilometers per year) has raised serious questions about the environmental impact of extensive cattle raising in Amazonia.

As discussed previously, a free-trade zone was established in Manaus in 1967 to counterbalance the spatial concentration of SUDAM fiscal incentives in eastern Amazonia. Although the priority given to livestock projects in Mato Grosso and Pará has perpetuated this intraregional imbalance of investment, the Zona Franca de Manaus (ZFM) has significantly improved the "investment climate" of western Amazonia (see Chapter 5). By the end of 1975, 140 industrial projects, with a total investment approaching Cr$ 4 billion, had been approved by SUFRAMA, the supervisory agency of the ZFM. In addition, the fiscal incentives of SUFRAMA have promoted a marked expansion of commercial activity based on sales of duty-free imported merchandise.

The initial impact of the ZFM has been to create a degree of prosperity in Manuas reminiscent of the "golden era" of the 1870-1912 rubber boom. Urban population has grown at an annual rate in excess of 5 percent while both income and employment levels have increased dramatically. The apparent success of the ZFM, however, is clouded by reservations as to its efficiency and future prospects as a policy tool for subregional economic development.

First, the economic benefits from the ZFM have been almost entirely confined to the vicinity of Manaus, with few effects evident beyond the municipal limits. Although the efficiency gains emanating from urban agglomerations are well documented in the regional development literature, the existence of Manaus as a "pole of attraction" runs counter to the economic and geopolitical objectives of populating the frontier areas of Amazonia. A second, and related, criticism concerns the pattern of investment encouraged by the fiscal incentives of SUFRAMA. In contrast to the experience of SUDAM, investors locating in Manaus have revealed an overwhelming preference for such industrial sectors as electronics and synthetic textiles. A serious drawback of these sectoral preferences, however, is that they are not based on the natural advantages of Amazonia and are dependent upon the indefinite continuation of fiscal subsidies. Finally, the rapid growth of imports stimulated by the ZFM legislation (in excess of 45 percent per year in real terms) has conflicted with attempts to improve the national balance of payments.

PRESENT DIRECTIONS: 1975-79

What the long-term holds for Amazonia is, of course, problematical at this point. Official documents, however, have already outlined the general directions of regional development policy for the second half of the 1970s. Before concluding, it is useful to briefly summarize their contents.

The Second National Development Plan

The overall objectives of regional policy for the 1975-79 period are contained in the Second National Development Plan (PND II).[50] Basically, this document continues to emphasize the national-integration philosophy of the PND I. The PND II recalls the socioeconomic complementarities of the Northeast, Amazonia, and the central West and recommends an expanded flow of productive factors and goods between them. The content and direction of these flows is left rather vague, although it is implied that Amazonia and the central West would function as markets for the industrial production of the Northeast. In what seems to be a contrast from the philosophy of its predecessor, the PND II suggests that the primary emphasis on agricultural colonization should be within the Northeast, and only on a limited basis in Amazonia and the central West. The role of the Center-South continues to reflect the center-periphery model implicit in the PND I, that is, the manufactured goods, capital, and technology of the more developed regions being exchanged for the raw materials of the less developed regions.

From the specific references to Amazonia in the PND II, one gets the impression that policy makers have finally decided that this region is really a "resource frontier" (hence, a great national asset) and not a typical depressed region (a national burden). Perhaps the most important new program reflecting this sentiment is the Programa de Pólos Agropecuários e Agrominerais da Amazônia (POLAMAZONIA). This program, originally established in 1974 (Decree 74,067 of September 29), provides for the creation of 15 "growth poles" selected on the basis of their perceived comparative advantages in various productive sectors. It is funded through the PIN and PROTERRA budgets (as well as other sources) at Cr$ 4 billion for the 1975-79 period.

In essence, POLAMAZONIA is a program of infrastructure development aimed at creating a more favorable "investment climate" for private enterprise. This general approach has been followed since the mid-1960s, although the investments of POLAMAZONIA are of a more comprehensive and integrated nature than those of previous programs. They are also entirely concentrated in areas other than major urban agglomerations. In what may very well be its most significant contribution, POLAMAZONIA will develop the basic infrastructure surrounding the huge iron ore reserves (estimated at 18 billion tons) of the Serra dos Carajás (Pará); actual production will be a joint venture of the Companhia Vale do Rio Doce and a foreign consortium.

The Second Amazon Development Plan

The future contribution of Amazonia to Brazil's international trade balance is also a major theme of the Second Amazon Development Plan (PDAM II).[51] In fact, this document even more clearly delineates the region's role as a "resource frontier" (although utilizing the term tropical frontier). This in itself is a great improvement over previous regional plans, which had mistakenly confused Amazonia with a depressed region like the Northeast (referred to as a "developing region" in the PDAM II). As a guide to its frontier strategy, the PDAM II employs what it calls an "unbalanced corrected" model. It is "unbalanced" in that it concentrates on certain key sectors (for example, mining, livestock, lumbering, modern agriculture, tourism) that have a high potential to either generate foreign exchange through exportation or conserve it through the substitution of imports. It is "corrected" in the sense that it calls for the establishment of mechanisms (for example, new federal investments and transfers, on-site processing of raw materials, and the obligatory reinvestment of corporate earnings) that would guarantee equitable levels of income retention within Amazonia.

Throughout the PDAM II, there is ample evidence that regional policy makers are aware of the serious problems still remaining in the areas of agrarian reform and colonization, industrialization policy, and environmental protection. In the first case (judging from the

budget of the PDAM II—see Table 1.2), it appears that planned colonization will proceed at a much slower rate during the remainder of
this decade. In this area, the major goals are to improve the functioning of existing colonies and to regulate the distribution of land titles in zones of spontaneous migration. Industrial development still
remains an important concern of the policy makers (see Table 1.2),
although the present desire is to base it more on the processing of
regional raw materials than on the model of regional import substitution. Finally, the concern for the natural environment of Amazonia is
evidenced in the plan's encouragement of scientific forest management and its suggestion that future livestock projects be located in regions of savanna vegetation (cerrado) rather than in heavily forested
areas.

SUMMARY

From the early 1900s to the end of World War II, public policies
for Amazonia were almost exclusively concerned with exploiting the
region's enormous reserves of natural rubber. These policies did,
for brief periods, bring some degree of prosperity. Their negative
impacts, however, were longer lasting. Through this limited con-
ception of development, policy makers of the era inadvertently perpetuated a mentality based on extractive agriculture, which persists, in
some degree, to the present day. This mentality has contributed to
the dispersion and nomadism of the Amazonian population and has also
retarded the introduction of modern agricultural techniques. In sum,
development planning before 1945 probably did more to restrict regional development than to further it.

During the two decades following World War II, attention turned
to the more traditional models of economic development. Perhaps
learning from the errors of their predecessors, policy makers of this
period sought to reduce the region's dependence on extractive agriculture and instead concentrated their efforts on the promotion of modern
agriculture, industry, and mining. They also stressed the need to
end the isolation of Amazonia through infrastructure development in
the areas of transportation and communications. Although this comprehensive approach was a step in the right direction, its ultimate
impact on the region was negligible. The basic problem was that the
objectives of SPVEA far exceeded the agency's financial and technical
capabilities. In addition, SPVEA committed the crucial error of
spreading its budget too thin in an effort to please all regional political
interests.

By the mid-1960s, the impotence of SPVEA had become so apparent that it was abolished and replaced by a new agency known as

SUDAM. This latter agency was molded along the lines of SUDENE, the analogous regional development agency for the Northeast. For its operational and philosophical guidelines, SUDAM was to follow the spirit of Operation Amazonia, a series of laws promulgated in 1966 and 1967. In its economic aspects, Operation Amazonia essentially called for a policy of import-substitution industrialization based on an array of fiscal and credit incentives to private enterprise. It also had an important geopolitical content that stressed the need to populate Amazonia through immigration and planned agricultural colonization. Operation Amazonia did manage to draw public attention to the region's problems, but by 1970 its concrete results were still difficult to discern. Industry was successfully attracted to Amazonia through the fiscal and credit incentives policy, but it started to become apparent that the model of industrialization for import substitution borrowed from the Northeast could not be easily transferred to a region with such markedly different characteristics. Furthermore, the pace of infrastructure development during this period was such that it threatened to constrain further efforts to accelerate the economic growth and occupation of Amazonia.

The 1970-75 period was characterized by a significantly increased role of the federal government in Amazonia. The theme that dominated these years was "national integration." This overall objective was to be achieved through an ambitious program of road building in conjunction with officially sponsored settlements along the major routes. Perhaps the most notable aspect of the national integration policies was the construction of the trans-Amazon highway, a 2,500-kilometer artery that, for the first time in history, would provide an overland link between the overpopulated Northeast and the sparsely populated North. By encouraging immigration via this highway, it was reasoned that population pressures in the Northeast could be relieved while simultaneously achieving the productive occupation of Amazonia. To this end, the federal government established a network of planned agricultural communities and actively recruited prospective settlers. The model of import-substitution industrialization was not completely abandoned during this period, although priorities turned more toward the development of livestock and mining activities. In this latter endeavor, development planners could now count on the logistical support provided by RADAM.

The interim results of the "national integration" era are mixed. On the positive side, recent infrastructure development has done much to end the historic isolation of Amazonia from the rest of Brazil and has opened previously inaccessible areas to productive use. Through the efforts of RADAM, moreover, many of the mysteries surrounding the region's stock of natural resources are now being dispelled. Furthermore, many viable alternatives to traditional extractive agriculture are revealing themselves. Included among these are the live-stock and mining projects of eastern Amazonia as well as the Manaus Free Trade Zone in the western subregion.

On the negative side, a series of fundamental errors have plagued the agricultural colonization programs, and only a fraction of the "excess" northeastern population has been effectively absorbed in Amazonia. Moreover, spontaneous migratory flows from the North-east and elsewhere have created grave social tensions due to unre-solved questions of land tenure. Finally, and perhaps most important in the long run, the policies of accelerated occupation, integration, and economic development have also accelerated the destruction of re-gional fauna and flora.

NOTES

1. According to one estimate, the per capita income of Ama-zonia grew at an average annual rate of 6.2 percent in the last half of the nineteenth century, almost four times faster than the national rate. See C. Furtado, The Economic Growth of Brazil (Berkeley: University of California Press, 1968), p. 163.

2. For greater details on this boom, see J. F. Melby, "Rub-ber River: An Account of the Rise and Collapse of the Amazon Boom," Hispanic American Historical Review 23 (1942): 452-69.

3. Asian rubber production jumped from 11,176 tons in 1910 to 54,356 tons in 1913. Brazilian production, on the other hand, fell from 38,547 tons to 36,232 tons during the same period. See C. Fonseca, A Economia da Borracha (Rio de Janeiro: Superintendência da Borracha, 1970), p. 16.

4. Ibid., p. 17.

5. A more detailed discussion of this period may be found in B. C. C. de Mello Petey, "Aspectos da Economia Amazônica à Época da Depressão (1920-1940)," Boletim Geográfico 21 (1972): 112-39.

6. According to the national censuses, the population of Ama-zonia rose from about 332,000 in 1872 to 1.4 million in 1920 on the basis of an estimated half a million (mainly northeastern) immigrants. The results of the 1940 census, in contrast, show almost no popula-tion growth during the following 20 years and estimates of emigration for this period are in excess of 190,000 persons. See D. H. Graham and S. B. de Hollanda Filho, Migration, Regional and Urban Growth and Development in Brazil: A Selective Analysis of the Historical Record, 1872-1970 (São Paulo: Instituto de Pesquisas Econômicas, 1971), pp. 98, 103; and Furtado, op. cit., pp. 142-43.

7. The Belterra-Fordlândia experiment is analyzed in H. Sioli, "Recent Human Activities in the Brazilian Amazon and Their Ecologi-

cal Effects," in Tropical Forest Ecosystems in Africa and South America, ed. B. J. Meggers, E. S. Ayensu, and W. D. Duckworth (Washington, D.C.: Smithsonian Institution Press, 1973), pp. 331-32.

8. The basic bibliographical source for this period is L. de M. Corrêa, A Borracha da Amazônia e a II Guerra Mundial (Manaus: Edições do Estado do Amazonas, 1967).

9. President Vargas's well-known "Discurso do Rio Amazonas" (Manaus, October 1940) is often cited as the philosophical basis of government efforts in Amazonia during the early 1940s. It is debatable, however, whether this rhetoric would have ever been acted upon had it not been for the outbreak of war between the United States and Japan in 1941. This speech is reproduced in Revista Brasileira de Geografia 4 (1942): 259-62.

10. A. de Andrade, Contribuição à História Administrativa do Brasil (Rio de Janeiro: Livraria Jose Olympio Editora, 1950), vol. 2, p. 48. Total migration to Amazonia during this period has been estimated at 150,000. See S. Benchimol, Amazonia (Manaus: Editora Umberto Calderao, 1977), pp. 249-51.

11. One dubious legacy of the wartime program was the maintenance of a government monopoly over the purchase and sale of natural rubber until 1966. For a strong critique of this policy, see Banco da Amazônia, S.A. (BASA), Desenvolvimento da Amazônia (Belém: Editora da Universidade Federal do Pará, 1967), pp. 205-26.

12. For a summary of these debates, see W. Bouhid, Amazônia e Desenvolvimento (Rio de Janeiro: SPVEA, Serviço de Documentação, 1961), pp. 20-23.

13. Superintendência do Plano de Valorização da Amazônia (SPVEA), Programa de Emergência (Belém, 1954).

14. Some steps to coordinate scientific research on Amazonia had been taken during the late 1940s and early 1950s. Most important were plans to establish an international institute (Instituto Internacional da Hiléia Amazônia) in Manaus under the auspices of UNESCO. Fearing negative geopolitical consequences, however, these plans were ultimately rejected by the Brazilian congress. See A. C. F. Reis, A Amazônia e a Cobiça Internacional, 4th ed. (Rio de Janeiro: Companhia Editora Americana, 1972), pp. 184-200.

15. Superintendência do Plano de Valorização da Amazônia (SPVEA), Primeiro Plano Qüinqüenal, 2 vols. (Belém, 1955).

16. See A. Mendes, "Amazônia: Primeira Grande Experiência Brasileira de Planejamento Regional," Revista do Conselho Nacional de Economia 14 (1965): 164.

17. See Superintendência do Plano de Valorização da Amazônia (SPVEA), Política de Desenvolvimento da Amazônia: SPVEA, 1954-1960, vol. 2, Nova Política de Desenvolvimento (Rio de Janeiro, 1961).

18. M. de B. Cavalcanti, Da SPVEA à SUDAM: 1964-1967 (Belém: SUDAM, 1967), p. 46.

19. H. de Castello Branco, Discursos—1965 (Secretaria da Imprensa), pp. 197–203.

20. A system of tax credits, previously utilized in the Northeast, was extended to Amazonia in 1963. As revised in 1965 by Constitutional Amendment 18, this legislation permitted registered corporations up to a 50 percent reduction in their income tax liabilities if the resulting savings were invested in industrial projects located within the legal Amazon and approved by SPVEA. The increasing role of the private sector in the economic development of Amazonia is clearly revealed by comparing the amount of funds accumulated through fiscal incentives to the budgetary resources of SPVEA. Whereas in 1964 total fiscal incentive funds were equivalent to less than 20 percent of the SPVEA budget, just two years later they amounted to more than double the resources of this agency (see Cavalcanti, op. cit., p. 86).

21. A convenient compendium of this legislation is Banco da Amazônia, S.A. (BASA), Amazônia: Legislação Desenvolvimentista (Belém: BASA—Departamento de Estudos Econômicos, 1969).

22. Several excellent surveys of development planning for the Brazilian Northeast are available. See, for example, D. E. Goodman and R. Cavalcanti de Albuquerque, Incentivos à Industrialização e Desenvolvimento do Nordeste, Coleção Relatorios de Pesquisa, no. 20 (Rio de Janeiro: IPEA/INPES, 1974), chap. 7; S. H. Robock, Brazil's Developing Northeast: A Study of Regional Planning and Foreign Aid (Washington, D.C.: Brookings Institution, 1963); A. O. Hirschman, Journeys toward Progress (New York: Twentieth Century Fund, 1963), pp. 18–86.

23. A well-researched survey of this general topic is L. A. Tambs, "Geopolitics of the Amazon," in Man in the Amazon, ed. C. Wagley (Gainesville: University Presses of Florida, 1974), pp. 47–87.

24. A typical example of the "pro-western Amazonia" argument may be found in Superintendência da Zona Franca de Manaus (SUFRAMA), SUFRAMA: Repercussões Sócio-econômicas de sua Atuação (Manaus: n.d.), pp. 13–15.

25. Superintendência do Desenvolvimento da Amazônia (SUDAM), Primeiro Plano Qüinqüenal de Desenvolvimento: 1967–1971 (Belém, 1967).

26. Superintendência do Desenvolvimento da Amazônia (SUDAM), Primeiro Plano Diretor; Triênio 1968/1970, 3 vols. (Belém, 1968).

27. According to the Plano Diretor, SUDAM's 1967 budget was only one-fourth as large as SPVEA's 1954 budget in real per capita terms. If this new fund had been enacted, SUDAM would have controlled almost 40 percent of the total investment fund devoted to the plan and appreciably strengthened its position in the administrative apparatus. Ibid. 1: 54–56; 3: 54.

28. This point is forcefully made in J. P. de A. Magalhães and N. Kuperman, "Estratégias Alternativas para o Desenvolvimento da Amazônia," mimeographed (Rio de Janeiro: Assessores Técnicos, Ltda., 1976).

29. Apparently, an east-west highway connecting the Northeast and Amazonia had been under consideration as early as 1967. It is not mentioned, however, in either the national development plan for 1968-70 (Programa Estratégico de Desenvolvimento) or SUDAM's First Five-Year Development Plan and Plano Diretor. For more detailed discussions of the background and official justifications for the PIN highway program, see D. C. Rebelo, Transamazônica: Integração em Marcha (Rio de Janeiro: Ministério dos Transportes, 1973), pp. 71-83; E. Rezende, "Estradas na Amazônia," in Problemática da Amazônia (Rio de Janeiro: Biblioteca do Exército Editora, 1971), pp. 383-405.

30. The most prolific writer on this topic has been Arthur Cezar Ferreira Reis, former governor of Amazonas and the first superintendent of SPVEA. His most well-known book is A Amazônia e a Cobiça Internacional, op. cit.

31. The standard reference on the "great lakes" controversy is Revista Brasileira de Política Internacional 10 (1968): 1-214.

32. See the final report of the Congressional Commission of Inquiry (Brazil), ibid., pp. 115-38; as well as O. D. Pereira, A Transamazônica: Prós e Contras, 2d ed. (Rio de Janeiro: Editora Civilização Brasileira, 1971), pp. 58-73.

33. Ibid., p. 273. The actual cost of the highway-construction program has never been officially divulged. Estimates as of 1975, however, are in the neighborhood of Cr$ 1.5 billion (in 1971 prices). The average exchange rate in 1971 was Cr$ 5.287 = U.S. $1.00.

34. See R. de O. Campos, "La Rage de Vouloir Conclure," in Transamazônica, ed. F. Morais et al. (São Paulo: Brasiliense, 1970, pp. 103-31.

35. The full text of this announcement is reproduced in O Globo, July 7, 1971.

36. See Jornal do Brasil, July 30, 1971.

37. República Federativa do Brasil, I Plano Nacional de Desenvolvimento (PND)—1972/74 (Rio de Janeiro: Fundação IBGE, Serviço Grafico, 1971), p. 29.

38. Superintendência do Desenvolvimento da Amazônia (SUDAM), Plano de Desenvolvimento da Amazônia: 1972-1974 (Belém, 1971), pp. 11-12.

39. Ibid., pp. 24-26.

40. See J. G. da Cunha Camargo, Urbanismo Rural (Brasília: Ministério da Agricultura—INCRA, 1973).

41. G. Müller et al., "Amazônia: Desenvolvimento Sócio-Econômico e Políticas de População," mimeographed (São Paulo: Centro Brasileiro de Análise de Planejamento, 1975), vol. 2, p. 93.

42. V. P. Tavares, C. M. Considera, and M. T. L. L. de Castro e Silva, Colonização Dirigida no Brasil: Suas Possibilidades na Região Amazônica, Coleção Relatórios de Pesquisa, no. 8 (Rio de Janeiro: IPEA/INPES, 1972), p. 121.

43. The difficulties currently being encountered in Amazonia are not without their historical precedents. Attempts to settle northeasterners in the Bragantina zone of Pará in the late 1800s and early 1900s were financial and ecological disasters. See E. F. Egler, "A Zona Bragantina no Estado do Pará," Revista Brasileira de Geografia 23 (1961): 75-103.

44. See I. C. Falesi, "Amazônia: A Terra é Pobre," Opinião 18 (1974).

45. During the past decade, a considerable amount of literature has been published on the ecological aspects of development in Amazonia. One of the most well researched and informative is R. J. A. Goodland and H. S. Irwin, Amazon Jungle: Green Hell to Red Desert? (Amsterdam: Elsevier, 1975).

46. See, for example, L. Pimentel, "A Transamazônica e o Problema da Integração Social," A Amazônia Brasileira em Foco 9 (1973-74): 24-60; B. K. Becker, "A Amazônia na Estrutura Espacial do Brasil," Revista Brasileira de Geografia 36 (1974); Müller et al., op. cit., 2: 33-50, 84-91.

47. Although problems of land tenure exist in all parts of Amazonia, they appear to be particularly acute in the territory of Rondônia. See, for example, O. Senna, "Operação Rondônia, Assalto à Mão Armada," A Amazônia Brasileira em Foco 10 (1974-75): 67-81; "Índios X Posseiros," Jornal do Brasil, vol. 12 (1976); N. Gall, "Letter from Rondonia," American Universities Field Staff Reports, nos. 9-13 (1978).

48. Data are from R. M. Paiva, S. Schattan, and C. F. T. de Freitas, Brazil's Agricultural Sector (Rio de Janeiro: Graphos, 1973), pp. 187-88.

49. On this theme, see R. D. de Garcia Paula, "A Ocupação da Amazônia: Pelo Homem ou pelo Boi?" A Amazônia Brasileira em Foco 9 (1973-74): 61-87.

50. República Federativa do Brasil, II Plano Nacional de Desenvolvimento—1975-1979 (Rio de Janeiro: Fundação IBGE, Serviço Gráfico, 1974), pp. 60-68.

51. Superintendência do Desenvolvimento da Amazônia (SUDAM), II Plano de Desenvolvimento da Amazônia; Detalhamento do II Plano Nacional de Desenvolvimento (1975-1979) (Belém, 1975).

2

Regional Population and Labor Force

The Brazilian Amazon has long been known as a dense tropical rainforest, practically devoid of human habitation. Indeed, it was this preoccupation that prompted the creation of government programs (PIN, PROTERRA, POLAMAZONIA) aimed at occupying the region and ending its isolation from the rest of the country. It is too early to judge the full demographic effects of the national-integration programs, but their future impact will no doubt be significant. The more modest purpose of the present chapter is to delineate the major characteristics of the Amazonian population and labor force in the period up to and including the 1970 Demographic Census (the "pre-national-integration" era). Since recent government policies to develop Amazonia are closely linked to those focused on the Northeast, the basic dissimilarities between these contiguous regions are emphasized.

TOTAL POPULATION AND AVERAGE DENSITY

The total population of the Brazilian Amazon, of course, varies with the geographical concept of "Amazonia" utilized in the computations (Table 2.1). In the broadest sense (the "legal Amazon" utilized for regional planning), the total population in 1975 was estimated to be 7.6 million, or about 7.1 percent of the national population. Since census data are presented at the state level, however, little else may be inferred about the composition of the population and labor force of the legal Amazon. Utilizing the more restricted definition adopted by IBGE (the North region or "classic Amazon"), one arrives at a population estimate for 1975 of 4.2 million, or about 3.9 percent of the national total. The underpopulation of the region, however, can only be appreciated by comparing the number of inhabitants to the available land area.

As Table 2.1 shows, the legal Amazon comprises almost 5 million square kilometers (about 58 percent of the national territory), giv-

TABLE 2.1

Amazonia: Total Population and Density, 1975

Administrative Unit	Total Population (thousands)	Percent of Total Population		Land Area (thousands of kilometers^2)	Percent of Total Land Area		Density (inhabitants per kilometer^2)
		North Region	Legal Amazon		North Region	Legal Amazon	
North region	4,214.7	100.0	55.8	3,551.3	100.0	72.9	1.19
Pará	2,544.3	60.4	33.7	1,227.5	34.5	25.2	1.99
Amazonas	1,089.7	25.9	14.4	1,559.0	43.8	32.0	0.70
Acre	249.1	5.9	3.3	152.6	4.3	3.1	1.63
Amapá	142.1	3.4	1.9	139.1	3.9	2.9	1.02
Rondônia	141.3	3.4	1.9	243.0	6.8	5.0	0.58
Roraima	48.2	1.1	0.6	230.1	6.5	4.7	0.21
Goiás (above thirteenth parallel)	543.9	—	7.2	285.8	—	5.9	1.90
Mato Grosso (above sixteenth parallel)	600.4	—	8.0	776.9	—	16.0	0.77
Maranhão (west of forty-fourth meridian)	2,192.7	—	29.0	257.5	—	5.3	8.52
Total (Legal Amazon)	7,551.7	—	100.0	4,871.5	—	100.0	1.55

Source: IBGE, Anuário Estatístico do Brasil, 1976.

ing an average population density of 1.55 inhabitants per square kilometer; this is significantly less than the national average of 12.59 and lower than any of the other major regions. This low average density is deceptive, though, and hides the fact that over 70 percent of the North is completely uninhabited. Major settlements occur in the state and territorial capitals, with medium to small agglomerations generally situated along the main course of the Amazon River and its many tributaries. Hence, population densities may vary from more than 800 inhabitants per square kilometer in Belém to less than 0.1 in some municípios of the interior.

GROWTH AND URBANIZATION

During the census periods of 1940-50, 1950-60, and 1960-70, the population growth rate of the North approximated or slightly exceeded the national rate. In all four census years, however, the regional population remained less than 4 percent of the total.[1] Between 1940 and 1970, the proportion of persons less than 15 years of age rose from 43.2 to 47.3 percent of the regional population. For Brazil as a whole, these percentages were 41.7 and 42.0 percent, respectively. Although these rapid rates of growth may be advantageous for the region in the long run (through the formation of a larger work force), at present they only serve to increase the young, nonproductive segment of the population and thus act as a drag on development efforts.

The regional population still remains predominantly rural but, following national trends, the urban rate of growth was more than double the rural rate during the 1940-70 period. Each administrative unit has progressively become more urbanized, although the present intraregional degree of urbanization varies considerably from the 45.1 percent regional average. In 1970, for example, the proportion of the population residing in urban areas ranged from a high of 53.6 percent in Amapá (ranked fifth nationally) to a low of 27.5 percent in Acre (twenty-fifth). The absolute number of urban inhabitants in these units is low, however, with almost 90 percent of the total regional urban population residing in Belém and Manaus.[2] In general, the rural population is highly dispersed because, in part, of the nature of extractive agriculture. This particular aspect of the regional settlement pattern tends to impede the introduction of basic social services (education, health, and the like) to this segment of the population and, as such, acts as a formidable barrier to effective regional planning.

INTERNAL MIGRATION

From the findings of studies on internal migration one can conclude that most of the recent population growth was internally generated since the North appears to have been the least affected by inter-regional migration of the country's macroregions.[3] Among the states and territories, only Rondônia and Amapá experienced significant population growth based on migratory influx. This phenomenon, however, did not appreciably affect regional growth rates due to the low absolute population of these units and because over 45 percent of the immigrants originated in other parts of the North.

The migration that did occur during the 1960s was mainly of an urban-to-urban nature rather than the more likely rural-to-urban flow.[4] Since those migrants with an urban destination showed a preference for cities of over 50,000 inhabitants, one could hypothesize that the incipient industrial development of Manaus and Belém played an important role in influencing these population movements. The motives behind population movements with a rural destination, however, are not so apparent. After an exhaustive analysis of census data and supplementary studies, M. de Mello Moreira and J. A. Magno de Carvalho conclude that, in spite of the inequitable distribution of landownership and generally poor employment possibilities, migrants still move to rural areas because they erroneously believe that land is readily accessible.[5]

Although supporting data are practically nonexistent, one would surmise that both intra- and interregional migratory flows are increasing in the 1970s as new access roads (trans-Amazon, Santarém-Cuiabá, Manaus-Porto Velho, and the like) increase the feasibility of migration, while new industrial and agricultural projects (encouraged by PROTERRA, POLAMAZONIA, and the fiscal incentives of SUDAM and SUFRAMA) increase the chances of locating gainful employment.[6] Since an essential part of these national-integration programs is the creation of "development poles," it seems likely that the rural-to-urban flow will be especially accelerated in future decades and that the urban population will grow at even faster rates than those experienced in the 1960s.

THE ECONOMICALLY ACTIVE POPULATION

Problems of comparing the economically active population (EAP) over various census periods basically arise from changes in the concept of the EAP from census to census. These methodological problems have been discussed elsewhere and need not be detailed here.[7] The Demographic Censuses of 1950, 1960, and 1970 are, with some exceptions, considered to be reasonably consistent. The only exception deemed important enough to call for an adjustment was the exclusion of the category, "persons seeking employment for the first time," from the EAP of 1970. The 1970 census was the first to include this category in the EAP and, hence, its inclusion in the time series would tend to overstate the size and rate of growth of the EAP in relation to the earlier census periods.

In dividing the EAP into its primary, secondary, and tertiary components, a further adjustment has been made here that diverges from the preference of most other writers on the topic. Instead of considering mining as part of the secondary (industrial) sector, it was included in the primary sector in all periods in order to differentiate between those economic activities that produce raw materials from those that produce intermediate or final goods. Since fewer than 10,000 persons in the total regional labor force are employed in mining (1970), the quantitative ramifications of this adjustment are slight.

General Aspects

Table 2.2 summarizes the data on the regional EAP for the census periods, 1950-60, 1960-70, and 1950-70, with computations for the North region and for the legal Amazon of SUDAM (approximated by adding the state of Maranhão to the North). In general, the regional labor force remains highly traditional (especially when Maranhão enters the calculations), but some slight modernizing tendencies can be noted over the 20-year period under consideration. By 1970, however, the region's agricultural labor force was still proportionately much larger, and its industrial and service labor forces proportionately much smaller, than the national averages.[8] In fact, the sectoral structure of the labor force in the area of SUDAM (the North plus Maranhão), appears to be even more traditional than that found under the jurisdiction of SUDENE.[9]

As implied by the spatial distribution of the total regional population presented in Table 2.1, significant variations also exist in the distribution of the work force. According to the 1970 Demographic Census, the states of Maranhão and Pará dominate in terms of absolute numbers of workers, with 80 percent of the regional EAP and 75 percent or more of the total work force in each of the three major productive sectors. In terms of the intersectoral distribution of the work force at the state and territorial levels, the greatest divergence from the regional norms occurs in Maranhão. In this state, one observes a highly traditional employment pattern with almost 80 percent of the labor force engaged in primary activities and less than 5 percent devoted to industrial pursuits. The pattern is only slightly less traditional in Acre where about 70 percent of the EAP is accounted for by the primary sector and only about 6 percent by industry. Because of the relatively high percentage of industrial workers, the labor force of Amapá appears to be the most modern. This observation is some-

TABLE 2.2

Amazonia: Aspects of the Economically Active Population (EAP)—1950, 1960, and 1970

Category/Year	Sector			Total	
	Primary[a]	Secondary	Tertiary		
EAP (thousands)					
1950	405.3 (811.4)	36.8 (53.8)	138.3 (204.5)	580.4	(1,069.7)
1960	518.0 (1,169.4)	48.1 (71.3)	219.7 (335.2)	785.8	(1,576.0)
1970[b]	593.6 (1,358.8)	109.7 (156.6)	319.1 (475.9)	1,022.4	(1,991.3)
Distribution (percent)					
1950	69.8 (75.9)	6.3 (5.0)	23.8 (19.1)	100.0	(100.0)
1960	65.9 (74.2)	6.1 (4.5)	28.0 (21.3)	100.0	(100.0)
1970	58.1 (68.2)	10.7 (7.9)	31.2 (23.9)	100.0	(100.0)
Annual growth rate (percent)					
1950–60	2.5 (3.7)	2.7 (2.9)	4.7 (5.1)	3.1	(4.0)
1960–70	1.4 (1.5)	8.6 (8.2)	3.8 (3.6)	2.7	(2.4)
1950–70	1.9 (2.6)	5.6 (5.5)	4.3 (4.3)	2.9	(3.2)

aIncludes extractive mining.
bExcludes persons seeking employment for the first time.

Note: Figures in parentheses represent the North and Maranhão (SUDAM).

Source: IBGE, Censo Demográfico, 1950, 1960, and 1970.

what misleading, however, because of the low absolute number of workers involved (3,860, or about 3 percent of the regional total) and their concentration in the traditional lumber industry.

Labor Absorption

Of the three major sectors, the primary sector was the only one to exhibit a persistent decline, in relative terms, throughout the 1950-70 period. This behavior should not be too surprising, since it conforms to national trends and has been generally observed among developing countries over time. A consideration of the sector's components, however, clearly reveals that a major change has taken place in the occupational structure.

Extractive activities, historically a mainstay of the regional economy, have continually declined as a source of employment for the rural population. Whereas in 1950 these activities accounted for over 40 percent of the employment generated by the primary sector, this proportion had fallen to 27.3 percent by 1970. Of particular interest in this respect is the rubber economy where employment in the North fell from 114,992 workers in 1960 to less than 90,000 workers in 1970. Since production did not appear to fall during this same period (regional rubber production has tended to vary between 25,000 and 35,000 metric tons per year since 1950), one must assume that the marginal product of these displaced workers was extremely low.

During the 1950-60 period, growth in the EAP was led by the tertiary (service) sector, which absorbed almost 40 percent of the total labor force. One must presume, however, that much of this increase represented additions to low-productivity ("informal") occupations.[10] The tertiary sector continued to be an important source of employment for the growing labor force in the 1960s, although at a rate considerably below that of the secondary (industrial) sector. The components of the North's tertiary sector generally followed national growth trends between 1950 and 1970, but by the end of the period such "modern" subsectors as financial services and the liberal professions were significantly underrepresented by national standards.[11]

The secondary sector is still the least important source of employment of the three sectors. It was particularly dynamic in the 1960s, however, achieving an average annual growth rate of 8.6 percent (8.2 percent in the area of SUDAM). Comparing the 1960 and 1970 censuses, one observes that the secondary sector absorbed more than 25 percent of the increment in the EAP (20 percent in the case of the legal Amazon). By subsectors, the most important source of employment was construction, which accounted for over 50 percent of the additions to the labor force. The rapid rates of urban growth that characterized this time period, as well as the regional road-building programs, are no doubt major factors explaining this behavior.

In terms of labor absorption, the manufacturing subsector provided employment at a rate only slightly less than that of construction, accounting for 46 percent of the total sectoral growth (38.7 percent in the area of SUDAM). Within the manufacturing subsector, employment gains were concentrated in relatively few, mainly traditional, lines of production. The wood-products industry, for example, generated 8,281 new jobs over the decade, or about 30 percent of the total in manufacturing. If we add to this total the new jobs created in textiles (4,164), furniture (2,917), nonmetallic minerals (2,616), and foods (2,395), we find that only five branches of industry accounted for over 70 percent of the employment growth in manufacturing.

LABOR PARTICIPATION RATES

Participation rates (or activity rates) are often utilized as a secondary indicator of labor conditions. In general terms, they measure the relationship between the potential labor force (in Brazil, all persons 10 years old or above) and the actual force. Since a variety of demographic, economic, and social factors may have an effect on these rates, however, one's interpretation is often subject to debate.

For Brazil as a whole, participation rates have generally declined in the three census periods from 1940 to 1970.[12] Since rural participation rates have risen slightly while urban rates have declined, it is commonly assumed that labor freed from agricultural pursuits has not been completely offset by labor demands in the secondary and tertiary sectors. The general trend by sex would indicate, moreover, a relatively more intensive use of female labor, especially in the service sector.

Calculations of participation rates for the North region are contained in Table 2.3. During the ten-year period considered, these rates fell in the urban and rural sectors and overall. In fact, by 1970 this region had the lowest participation rates in Brazil. This low rate of productive activity was especially acute in the case of females, with a rate of only about 75 percent of the national average.[13] It is interesting to note, however, that the urban feminine contingent was the only one to increase its participation rate between 1960 and 1970. Most of this growth in feminine activity, though, can be attributed to expanding employment in the traditional personal services. While only about 50 percent of the labor force in the personal services subsector was female in 1960, this proportion had risen to over 70 percent in 1970. The male-female ratios in industry and the other services did not change significantly.

TABLE 2.3

North Region: Labor Participation Rates by Sector and Sex, 1960-70

Sector/Sex	1960	1970
Urban	41.2	39.4
Male	67.6	60.8
Female	17.8	20.6
Rural	48.7	45.3
Male	80.2	78.2
Female	12.5	8.3
Total	45.8	42.6
Male	75.7	70.7
Female	14.7	14.4

Note: EAP as percentage of potential labor force.

Source: IBGE, Censo Demográfico, 1960 and 1970.

UNEMPLOYMENT AND UNDEREMPLOYMENT

Data on unemployment and underemployment in Amazonia are scanty and are confined to several tabulations on employment included in the 1970 census. [14] Of interest in this respect are the statistics on workers declaring themselves unemployed during the week preceding the census, number of months employed in the preceding year by the agricultural labor force, number of hours worked in the preceding week by the nonagricultural labor force, plus data on monthly incomes by productive sector.

In addition to difficulties in obtaining basic employment data, certain more or less arbitrary decisions had to be made concerning a working definition of the term "underemployment." For present purposes, "underemployment" refers to an agricultural laborer's being employed less than six months per year, or a nonagricultural laborer's employment for less than 15 hours per week. * An alternative

---

*Although this definition may be the only one possible, given the available data, one must question its compatibility with the theoretical concept of "underemployment." Since the census does not give the reasons why workers are employed on a part-time basis, we cannot know for certain whether their idleness is voluntary or involuntary. Also, some authors have contended that the term underemployed

measure of this concept is the worker who earns less than Cr$ 100 per month (about 75 percent of the regional minimum wage prevailing in 1970).

Calculations of the number of unemployed (including persons seeking employment for the first time) in the North region reveal extremely low rates by both international and Brazilian standards.[15] By sector, unemployment rates run from a low of 0.13 percent in agriculture to as high as 1.2 percent in industry.[16] Overall, the number of unemployed reached only 14,373 in a total labor force of over 1 million, or a rate of about 1.4 percent.[17] This latter rate compares with the national rate of 2.2 percent in the same year.

An unequivocal interpretation of those low unemployment rates is difficult although some authors have contended that they represent little more than "frictional" unemployment. This hypothesis stems from the belief that, in the absence of an official system of unemployment insurance, displaced urban workers are quickly forced to locate any source of income available (typically in the low-productivity "informal" sector). In the case of agriculture, it has been suggested that all subutilization of labor could be in the form of underemployment or disguised unemployment (workers employed at extremely low rates of income) and that seasonally unemployed workers do not consider themselves to be part of the labor force.[18] Therefore, although we cannot completely discount open unemployment as a serious labor problem in Amazonia, a far more relevant measure of regional labor conditions would seem to be underemployment.

The available information on underemployment in Amazonia is summarized in Tables 2.4, 2.5, and 2.6. Overall, it would appear that underemployment in this region is a more serious problem than is found in Brazil on the whole, although generally less serious than the situation in the Northeast. In agriculture, the proportion of the labor force employed less than six months during 1969-70 was 9.3 percent, slightly lower than the analagous figure for the Northeast (9.8 percent), but significantly higher than the national rate (6.5 percent).* The picture brightens, however, when monthly earnings are utilized as an indicator of underemployment. From this point of view, it would

---

should only be applied to those nonagricultural workers who are employed less than 40 hours per week. The "less than 15 hour" definition is adopted here since some occupations (for example, teaching and some public services), by their nature, require less than a 40-hour workweek.

*It is relevant to note that, in absolute terms, underemployed agricultural workers in the Northeast number almost one-half million, versus less than 50,000 in the North.

appear that the incidence of extreme rural poverty is much less preva-
lent in the North than in either the Northeast or in Brazil as a whole.
That is, while only 31.9 percent of the North's agricultural labor
force earned less than Cr$ 100 per month in 1970, this proportion
rose to 77.3 percent in the Northeast and 58.6 percent nationally (Table 2.5).[19]

In nonagricultural activities, the incidence of underemployment
in the North diverges from the national averages to a greater extent
and more closely approximates the situation in the Northeast. Of the
total nonagricultural labor force, 2.9 percent were employed less
than 15 hours per week in the North, versus 3.1 percent in the Northeast and 1.7 percent for Brazil as a whole (see Table 2.6). The incidence of underemployment was particularly high in industry, commerce,
transportation, and communications and "other," doubling, or even
tripling (in the case of transportation and communications), the average rates for Brazil. In fact, in some activities (for example, commerce, transportation, and communications) the rates of underemployment in the North were considerably higher than those experienced in
the Northeast.

Once again, though, the employment situation in the North appears more favorable when monthly earnings are considered. In this
respect, the proportion of the Amazonian nonagricultural labor force
earning under Cr$ 100 per month is less than that in the Northeast in
every branch of urban economic activity and less than the Brazilian
average in industry, commerce, social services, and public adminis-

TABLE 2.4

Number of Months per Year Worked by Agricultural Labor Force,
1969-70
(percent of total)

| Region | Number Months Employed | | | |
	Less than 3	3-6	6-9	9-12
North	0.7	8.6	25.4	65.3
Northeast	1.2	8.6	26.8	63.4
Brazil	1.1	5.4	18.7	74.7

Sources: IBGE, Censo Demográfico, 1970; D. E. Goodman and
R. Cavalcanti de Albuquerque, Incentivos à Industrialização e Desenvolvimento do Nordeste, Coleção Relatórios de Pesquisa, no. 20 (Rio
de Janeiro: IPEA/INPES, 1974), p. 66.

TABLE 2.5

Proportion of Total Labor Force Earning Less than Cr$ 100 per
Month, 1970
(percent of total)

Activity	Region		
	North[a]	Northeast	Brazil
Agriculture	31.9	77.3	58.6
Industry[b]	8.7	33.9	12.2
Commerce	10.8	28.8	15.4
Personal services	63.5	76.3	56.3
Transportation and communication	9.7	16.8	6.8
Social services	11.1	31.1	12.4
Public administration	3.5	12.5	7.5
Other	14.4	22.1	10.1
Total[c]	25.1	61.5	35.9
	(17.5)	(39.0)	(20.8)

[a]The regional minimum wage as of May 1, 1970, was Cr$ 134.40
per month.
[b]Includes mining.
[c]Figures in parentheses exclude agriculture.

Sources: IBGE, Censo Demográfico, 1970; D. E. Goodman and
R. Cavalcanti de Albuquerque, Incentivos à Industrialização e Desenvolvimento do Nordeste, Coleção Relatórios de Pesquisa, no. 20 (Rio
de Janeiro: IPEA/INPES, 1974), p. 67.

tration (see Table 2.5). The contrast between the North and Northeast
is especially striking in industry, with only 8.7 percent of this labor
contingent earning less than Cr$ 100 in the former region versus 33.9
percent in the latter.[20]

SUMMARY

The basic demographic characteristic of Amazonia is its low
average population density. Concentrated settlements occur in only
a few urban centers and the region's rural inhabitants are widely dispersed along the riverbanks. Aside from scattered Indian tribes, the
landlocked interior is mostly uninhabited. During the past 30 years,

TABLE 2.6

Proportion of Nonagricultural Labor Force Employed Less than 40 Hours per Week, 1970
(percent)

Activity	North		Northeast		Brazil	
	Less than 15 Hours	Less than 40 Hours	Less than 15 Hours	Less than 40 Hours	Less than 15 Hours	Less than 40 Hours
Industry*	2.7	8.2	2.8	14.0	1.1	6.0
Commerce	3.9	10.4	3.0	16.2	1.5	9.5
Personal services	2.5	19.2	3.3	22.5	2.4	16.6
Transportation, communication	3.8	11.2	2.0	12.2	1.1	8.5
Social services	2.8	35.2	5.4	47.4	3.4	44.8
Public administration	1.3	13.9	2.4	23.7	1.3	19.4
Other	2.9	13.2	2.7	21.5	1.5	16.1
Total	2.9	14.5	3.1	20.6	1.7	14.0

*Includes mining.

Sources: IBGE, Censo Demográfico, 1970; W. J. M. de Almeida, Serviços e Desenvolvimento Econômico no Brasil, Coleção Relatórios de Pesquisa, no. 23 (Rio de Janeiro: IPEA/INPES, 1973), p. 51.

total population growth has accompanied or slightly exceeded national rates; urban growth rates have been more than twice the rural rates. Because of the isolation of Amazonia, migratory flows from other regions have been unimportant in recent decades. The available data, however, indicate that immigration has greatly accelerated since 1970.

Census data show the regional labor force to be highly traditional and subject to significant underemployment. The primary sector, while still employing over two-thirds of the economically active population, has continued to decline in relative (but not absolute) terms. The stagnation of rural employment has been most evident in the extractive economy where over 25,000 rubber tappers were displaced during the 1960s. Urban employment has grown more rapidly, although at a slower pace than the overall urban population. The labor absorption that has taken place, moreover, has been generally confined to low-productivity pursuits such as wood products, textiles, construction, and personal services.

Future employment prospects in Amazonia are clouded at this point and depend to a great extent on government priorities. However, the emphasis on mining and extensive cattle raising in the regional development plans suggests low rates of labor absorption. An important conditioning factor will be the impact of the road-building programs on interregional migration. If the net effect is to promote a large inflow of poorly qualified workers, priorities must be shifted to more labor-intensive activities. In the absence of such activities, the projected migrations will not attenuate poverty, but only geographically disperse it.[21]

NOTES

1. Historically, the population of the North did rise to 4.7 percent of the national total in 1920. This relative growth was due to the net inflow of over 200,000 migrants (mainly from the Northeast) contracted to work in the extractive rubber economy. With the end of the rubber boom, however, many migrants returned to their states of origin and the net migratory balances for the North turned sharply negative. See A. V. Villela and W. Suzigan, Política do Governo e Crescimento da Economia Brasileira, 1889-1945, Série Monográfica, no. 10 (Rio de Janeiro: IPEA/INPES, 1973), pp. 276-86.

2. For details on population growth and urbanization by state and territory, see J. Saunders, "The Population of the Brazilian Amazon Today," in Man in the Amazon ed. C. Wagley (Gainesville: University Presses of Florida, 1974), pp. 160-80.

3. A detailed study of interregional migration in Brazil reveals small positive balances for the North in the 1950-70 period. See M.

da Mata et al., Migrações Internas no Brasil, Coleção Relatórios de Pesquisa, no. 19 (Rio de Janeiro: IPEA/INPES, 1973), pp. 57-90.

4. Of the total population movement, 40.9 percent was urban to urban; 30 percent, rural to rural; 14.6 percent, rural to urban; and 14.5 percent, urban to rural. See M. de Mello Moreira and J. A. Magno de Carvalho, Migrações Internas na Região Norte, vol. 2 (Belém: SUDAM, 1975), p. 14.

5. Ibid., p. 113.

6. Estimates by IBGE for 1975 already reveal high rates of population growth for towns along the trans-Amazon. In the 1970-75 period, for example, Marabá Pará (PA) grew by 27.0 percent, Itaituba (PA) by 25.8 percent, and Altamira (PA) by 21.1 percent (Jornal do Brasil, September 29, 1975, p. 7).

7. See, for example, D. E. Goodman and R. Cavalcanti de Albuquerque, Incentivos à Industrialização e Desenvolvimento do Nordeste, Coleção Relatórios de Pesquisa, no. 20 (Rio de Janeiro: IPEA/INPES, 1974), p. 50; and two papers by M. A. Costa: "Aspectos Demográficos da População Economicamente Ativa," mimeographed (IPEA/MINIPLAN, 1968), pp. 1-7; and "Aspectos Econômicos e Demográficos da Mão—de Obra no Brasil, 1940/64," mimeographed (IPEA/MINIPLAN, 1969), pp. 13-20.

8. The primary, secondary, and tertiary sectors comprised 44.6 percent, 18.0 percent, and 37.4 percent, respectively, of the total Brazilian labor force in 1970. See W. J. M. de Almeida and M. da Conceição Silva, Dinâmica do Setor Servicos no Brasil: Emprego e Produto, Coleção Relatórios de Pesquisa, no. 18 (Rio de Janeiro: IPEA/INPES, 1973), p. 176.

9. See Goodman and Cavalcanti de Albuquerque, op. cit., pp. 50-54.

10. In this respect, one author states that

only a small proportion of tertiary employment in the less developed labour surplus economies is a function of the income-elasticity of demand for services. The bulk is to be found in such traditional and unorganised services as shoeshining and petty retail trades bearing no observable relationship to effective labour demand. Here the supply of labour creates its own employment opportunities by sharing out a given amount of work.

From A. S. Bhalla, "The Role of Services in Employment Expansion," in Essays on Employment, ed. W. Galenson (Geneva: International Labour Office, 1971), p. 158.

11. See Almeida and Silva, op. cit., p. 180.

12. A general discussion and analysis of participation rates in Brazil is contained in Costa, op. cit., and Almeida and Silva, op. cit., pp. 154-59.

13. See W. J. Almeida, Serviços e Desenvolvimento Econômico no Brasil, Coleção Relatórios de Pesquisa, no. 23 (Rio de Janeiro: IPEA/INPES, 1974), p. 17.

14. Another useful source of employment information, the PNAD (Pesquisa Nacional por Amostragem de Domicílios), is unfortunately not available for the North region.

15. See, for example, D. Turnham, The Employment Problem in Less Developed Countries: A Review of Evidence (Paris: OECD, 1971); F. S. O'Brien and C. L. Salm, "Desemprego e Subemprego no Brasil," Revista Brasileira de Economia 24 (1970): 93-115; and C. Salm, "Evolução de Mercado do Trabalho, 1969/1972," Estudos CEBRAP 8 (1974): 105-19.

16. One author has calculated rates of "equivalent unemployment" for the North region. This concept is measured by dividing the total income received by the underemployed portion of the EAP (those earning less than the regional minimum wage) by the equivalent of a minimum wage and then subtracting this amount from the total number of underemployed persons. When this latter number is expressed as a percentage of the total EAP, we arrive at the rate of employment that would have prevailed if every worker was receiving the minimum wage or higher. For 1970, the overall rate or "equivalent unemployment" was about 16.4 percent. By sector, the rate varied from 18.8 percent in agriculture to 8.2 percent and 15.1 percent, respectively, in industry and services. See J. J. Oliveira e Silva, A Sociedade Amazônica e o Problema Social da Dosocupação e Subocupação (Belém: SUDAM, 1974), pp. 38-40.

17. It is significant to note that, of the total unemployed in the North region, almost 4,500 (31 percent) were new entrants to the labor force. This finding would suggest that unemployment rates among youths are considerably above the average. On the basis of PNAD data, other authors have found this to be generally true for other regions of Brazil. See Salm, op. cit., pp. 111-12; and D. E. Goodman, "O modelo Econômico Brasileiro e os Mercados de Trabalho: Uma Perspectiva Regional," Pesquisa e Planejamento Econômico 5 (1975): 89-116.

18. See O'Brien and Salm, op. cit., pp. 109-11; and H. C. Tolosa, "Dualismo no Mercado de Trabalho Urbano," Pesquisa e Planejamento Econômico 5 (1975): 27-28.

19. The 1970 average monthly income in the North's primary sector (Cr$ 159.83) was higher than the national average (Cr$ 138.00) and exceeded only by the averages attained in the states of the Center-South. See C. G. Langoni, Distribuição da Renda e Desenvolvimento Econômico do Brasil (Rio de Janeiro: Editora Expressão e Cultura, 1973), pp. 68, 165.

20. When average urban incomes are compared, the North (Cr\$ 329.52) falls below the national average (Cr\$ 388.00), but still remains higher than all other regions other than the Center-South. See ibid., pp. 70, 165.

21. Reports from Santarém Pará (PA) indicate that northeastern migrants entering the city via the Santarém-Cuiabá highway have already put severe strains on the urban economy. Local firms have been unable to absorb the new labor contingent, and estimates of overt unemployment run in the neighborhood of 20 percent. See Jornal do Brasil, October 10, 1975, p. 30.

3

The Regional Economy:
An Overview

As discussed in Chapter 1, the reduction of interregional income disparities has been an important goal of economic planning in postwar Brazil. To this end, special programs of infrastructure development, intergovernmental revenue transfers, fiscal incentives, and other policies have been directed toward improving the relative positions of the poorer regions. Despite almost three decades of such compensatory policies, however, the North and Northeast continue to lag far behind the more industrialized Center-South.

A number of published and unpublished studies have analyzed the regional disparities issue, but few have addressed themselves to the specific case of Amazonia. [1] This neglect appears to be related to the inconsequential presence of this region in the national economic indexes as well as to the unavailability of essential statistical data. Since this latter problem remains serious, the present chapter can offer only some tentative contributions to the debate as it applies to Amazonia. Moreover, a complete discussion of the disparities question would involve analyses not only of Amazonia but also of the other regional economies. Such an approach is beyond the scope of this study.

The major intent here is to provide an overview of the regional economy in the decade of the 1960s. In doing so, the aggregate economic performance of Amazonia will be examined in its interregional, intraregional, and international contexts. An attempt will be made to identify leading and lagging sectors, although detailed behavioral analyses are confined to the public sector and trade (see Chapter 4). To conclude, we will briefly consider land tenure conditions and the personal distribution of income.

AGGREGATE REGIONAL INCOME

Analyses of spatial inequalities in Brazil usually base their arguments on the historical behavior of regional income statistics. [2]

With the recent revisions of the national and regional social accounts,
however, the relative economic performance of the North may only
be assessed on the basis of data for 1949, 1959, and 1970.* The obvious drawback of this cross-section approach is that it reveals virtually nothing about trends within the interim periods. An additional
problem is encountered when one tries to convert the data to real
terms. Ideally, the proper "deflator" would reflect price behavior in
each region or state. Since such indexes are not generally available,
it was decided to adjust all data (unless otherwise specified) by the
Fundação Getúlio Vargas general price index (Conjuntura Econômica).

The Interregional Context

At approximately 2 percent, the North's share in the national income continues to be quite insignificant, especially considering that
the region comprises over 40 percent of the national territory. The
real average rates of growth achieved during the 1949-59 and 1959-70
periods, however, exceeded those attained at the national level and
were considerably higher than those of the Northeast.[3] Nevertheless,
the aggregate growth rate of the North fell below that of the Center-
South during the 1960s, and the overall income gap between these two
regions increased slightly.†
The meager contribution of Amazonia to the national income is
only partially explained by its low population density. This is made
clear by Table 3.1, which presents the regional income data in per
capita terms. Although the per capita income of this region has tended
to exceed that of the Northeast, its level continues to hover around
half the national average and one-third of the Center-South average.
Furthermore, the growing gap between the North and Center-South
noted during the 1960s is more accentuated on a per capita basis due
to the higher rate of population growth experienced by the former re-

---

*The concept of Amazonia utilized in social accounts conforms
to the IBGE "North region" or "classic Amazon" encompassing Rondônia, Acre, Amazonas, Roraima, Pará, and Amapá.
†It should be emphasized that the regional accounts measure income at its geographical origin, not necessarily at its destination.
Since a fundamental characteristic of the SUDAM and SUFRAMA incentive policies is the attraction of capital from other regions, one
must assume that a sizable portion of the income generated in the
North ultimately flows out of the region as profit remittances, divi-
dends, imports, and so on. This question is further discussed in
subsequent chapters.

gion.* Hence, we arrive at the preliminary conclusion that, although government policies of the 1960s may have positively affected the regional economic growth rate, they were incapable of preventing further increases in the gap between the developed center and the underdeveloped periphery.

TABLE 3.1

Per Capita Net Income at Factor Costs, 1949, 1959, and 1970
(constant 1975 prices)

	1949	1959	1970
North			
In cruzeiros	1,086	1,550	2,356
Annual growth (percent)		3.6	3.9
Percent of national average	48.1	54.0	52.2
Northeast			
In cruzeiros	917	1,270	1,821
Annual growth (percent)		3.3	3.3
Percent of national average	40.6	44.2	40.4
Center-South			
In cruzeiros	3,080	3,738	5,920
Annual growth (percent)		2.0	4.3
Percent of national average	136.3	130.0	131.2
Brazil			
In cruzeiros	2,260	2,872	4,513
Annual growth (percent)		2.4	4.2

Sources: Fundação Getúlio Vargas (IBRE), Sistema de Contas Nacionais: Metodologia e Quadros (Rio de Janeiro, 1974); population data from IBGE, Censo Demográfico, 1950, 1960, and 1970 (adjusted for 1949 and 1959).

The Intraregional Context

When viewed in an intraregional context, the economic activity of Amazonia is seen to be concentrated in a few geographical areas.

---

*As noted in Chapter 2, interregional migration explained little of the population growth of Amazonia during the past decade. In contrast to the Northeast and Center-South, therefore, this factor had a minor impact on the regional per capita income.

According to social accounts, 75 to 85 percent of the regional income in agriculture, industry, and services is generated in just two states: Amazonas and Pará.[4] Since these states contain about 80 percent of the region's land area and population, the observed degree of concentration should not be too surprising. When income data are assembled at the microregional level, however, it becomes apparent that most economic activity takes place in and around the state capitals of Manaus (Amazonas) and Belém (Pará). In 1970, for example, about 80 percent of the total income of Amazonas was accounted for by the microregion that roughly comprises the zone of influence of Manaus (Médio Amazonas). A similar situation may be noted in the state of Pará, where six relatively small microregions (Guajarina, Salgado, Bragantina, Belém, and Viseu), essentially the city of Belém and its suburbs, accounted for about 70 percent of the state's total income. Rates of spatial concentration are even more pronounced when agriculture is excluded, since this sector is more widely distributed within the region.

As implied in Chapter 1, regional development policies have generally accentuated the existing polarization of economic activity (especially industrial and commercial) around Manaus and Belém. In terms of efficiency, these strategies are probably justifiable, given the advanced state of infrastructure development in these cities as compared to the situation prevailing in their hinterlands. However, the economic advantages of Belém over Manaus (larger local market and labor pool, closer proximity to major national and international markets, more advanced infrastructure development, and the like) were quickly perceived by investors. By the late 1960s, investment patterns resulting from the SUDAM fiscal incentives clearly exhibited an intraregional bias. As a result, additional fiscal measures were extended to western Amazonia to compensate for this subregion's alleged disadvantages in attracting private capital.

Table 3.2 provides an indication of the two subregions' relative performances in the 1960–72 period. The apparent success of the compensatory fiscal legislation may be noted in the reversal of past trends of intraregional economic growth. During the period under consideration, the aggregate income of the western subregion grew by a real average annual rate of 6.5 percent as opposed to the the 5.3 percent rate achieved by the eastern subregion. Consequently, the western subregion's share of regional income rose from 41 percent in 1960 to 44.3 percent in 1972. When viewed in per capita terms, the relative gains of the West are even more impressive. Through a combination of a lower population growth rate and a higher economic growth rate, the per capita income of this subregion rose from 109 percent of the regional average in 1960 to 121 percent in 1972. The per capita income of the East, on the other hand, fell from 95 percent of the regional average to 88 percent during the same period.

TABLE 3.2

North Region: Net Income of Eastern and Western Subregions
at Factor Costs, 1960, 1969-72

	Eastern		Western	
	Index (1960 = 100)	Percent Regional Total	Index (1960 = 100)	Percent Regional Total
1960	100.0	59.0	100.0	41.0
1969	146.6	57.3	157.3	42.7
1970	158.7	54.3	191.9	45.7
1971	177.3	57.2	190.6	42.8
1972	186.0	55.7	212.9	44.3

Note: Eastern subregion includes Pará and Amapá; western subregion includes Rondônia, Acre, Amazonas, and Roraima.

Source: Fundação Getúlio Vargas (IBRE)/SUDAM, Agregados Econômicos Regionais, vol. 1: Produto Interno (October 1974).

By the nature of the special fiscal legislation for western Amazonia, however, most of the benefits have been confined to the vicinity of Manaus, thus encouraging (or at least not discouraging) a further concentration of economic activity within the subregion. The Zona Franca de Manaus, in particular, has no doubt been instrumental in equalizing development levels between Manaus and Belém, but few observable effects have spread to the rural areas of western Amazonia. Recognition of this problem (further discussed in Chapters 1 and 5) has resulted in legislation that provides additional infrastructure development and fiscal benefits to areas beyond the zone of influence of Manaus.

General Structural Aspects

Table 3.3 assembles the regional income data according to the major productive sectors. Viewed in this manner, services emerges as the largest and most rapidly growing sector. Between 1960 and 1972, income generated in this sector grew at a real average annual rate of 6.9 percent, thus increasing its share in the regional income from 56.1 to 63.2 percent.[5] During the same period, agriculture and industry grew at annual rates of 4.7 and 3.7 percent, respectively.

TABLE 3.3

North Region: Sectoral Distribution of Net Income at Factor Costs, 1960–72
(percent of total current prices)

	Agriculture	Industry	Services			
			Total	Commerce	Government	Other*
1960	23.0	20.9	56.1	24.6	9.0	22.5
1961	22.6	20.5	56.9	25.4	11.9	19.7
1962	20.1	21.5	58.3	23.8	10.4	24.1
1963	22.2	19.4	58.3	23.9	12.2	22.2
1964	23.8	18.6	57.6	23.6	13.3	20.7
1965	23.4	18.3	58.3	24.1	13.1	21.2
1966	21.1	19.0	59.9	23.4	13.3	23.2
1967	20.0	17.8	62.2	22.7	13.1	26.4
1968	19.4	18.4	62.6	23.7	10.9	27.6
1969	19.1	18.8	62.1	24.0	10.2	27.9
1970	21.5	18.0	60.5	22.3	13.3	24.9
1971	19.2	17.5	63.3	23.2	14.5	25.6
1972	20.3	16.5	63.2	23.8	24.2	25.3

*Includes financial intermediaries, transportation and communications, and rent.

Source: Fundação Getúlio Vargas (IBRE)/SUDAM, Agregados Econômicos Regionais, vol. 1: Produto Interno (October 1974).

In contrast to services, their shares in the regional income have tended to decline.

As may be expected in a region as large and diverse as the North, the general income structure presented in Table 3.3 obscures important intraregional variations. The intraregional heterogeneity in income structures is especially pronounced in the cases of Acre, Amapá, and Roraima. Acre, for example, is the most agricultural and least industrial among the administrative units. In contrast, Amapá is the least agricultural and most industrial. The territory of Roraima, while conforming to the regional average in agriculture, is characterized by the second lowest income share in industry and the highest share in the service sector.

In general, these marked differences from the regional norms are a reflection of the undiversified, export-oriented nature of these units' economies, that is, in which just one, or a very few, activities predominate. The fact that Acre is Brazil's largest producer of natural rubber, for example, highly influences its particular income structure. In the territory of Amapá, the mining of manganese accounts for 82.7 percent of the total income arising in its relatively large industrial sector. The industrial sector of Rondônia, which nearly approximates that of Amazonas and Pará in relative size, is also dominated by mining. In 1970, this activity accounted for 50.9 percent of the territory's total industrial income. Differing somewhat from Acre and Amapá, the territory of Roraima is still at the predevelopment stage. Although future possibilities appear promising in the areas of livestock, lumber, and mining, the single most important source of income as of 1970 was government wages and salaries.

It is only in Amazonas and Pará, with their larger urban populations, where we find anything approaching a modern, diversified economic structure. Even in these states, however, the agricultural, industrial, and service sectors are "modern" only in a relative, regional sense. Rudimentary agriculture is still predominant in both states (especially the former) and, with the exception of the new electronics firms in Manaus, industry tends to be concentrated in such traditional product lines as foods, wood products, and textiles.

THE IMPORTANCE OF THE PUBLIC SECTOR

On the basis of Table 3.3, it might be erroneously inferred that government has played only a minor role in the recent growth and development of Amazonia. That is, while this sector generally grew faster than the regional economy as a whole, its share in the regional income was still below 15 percent by 1972. For many reasons, though, the actual impact of the public sector, especially at the federal level, has been (and continued to be) much greater than these data would indicate.

First, the regional accounts measure government on the basis of wage and salary payments to public employees. As described in Chapter 1, however, infrastructure development (capital-intensive by definition) has been the main thrust of regional policies from the construction of the Belém-Brasilia highway in the late 1950s and early 1960s to the PIN and POLAMAZONIA projects of the 1970s. Hence, the exclusion of government fixed-capital formation, by itself, leads to a significant understatement of the public sector. Second, the public sector plays a number of more indirect roles that are not fully reflected in the regional accounts. An obvious example is the fiscal legislation that provides special benefits to firms located or locating in Amazonia—the fiscal incentives of SUDAM and SUFRAMA, and the "tax holidays" granted by the federal, state, and municipal governments; another is the regional redistributive system of federal tax sharing adopted in the mid-1960s. [6] As a result of the misleading treatment of government in regional accounts, the present section attempts to more precisely define its quantitative dimensions.

Tax Collections and Tax Burdens

In constant 1975 prices, total tax collections in the North increased from Cr\$ 515.2 million to Cr\$ 1.9 billion (370 percent) between 1960 and 1975. Among the three administrative levels, revenues of the federal government grew most rapidly (530 percent). Despite this impressive growth record, however, the contribution of Amazonia to the national treasury remains negligible in absolute and relative terms. In fact, during the period of reference the proportion of total federal taxes collected in the region actually declined slightly from 1.14 to 1.04 percent. Similar behavior was also recorded at the state and local levels.

Two obvious explanations of this situation are the region's low average income and sparse population. To the extent that income is an appropriate measure of the tax base, one would expect, in the first case, absolutely lower tax revenues to be collected in lower-income regions. This could be true even in nations like Brazil where the overall tax system is regressive. Tax collections in the North are low not only in absolute terms, however, but also in relation to current income. That is, the regional "formal" tax burden (1972) is only about 60 percent of the national average and approximates that of the Northeast. [7] In per capita terms, the tax burden of the North is still lower, at about 25 percent of the national average.

How does one reconcile the fact that a tax system that is regressive with respect to personal income is apparently progressive with respect to regional income? Certainly, many factors are involved in this question. One of these is that the North is characterized by a large subsistence population that essentially escapes taxation through its minimal contact with monetarized (that is, taxable) activities. Furthermore, even when activities performed by this segment of the population are taxable, their geographical dispersal greatly reduces the efficiency of tax administration. The small proportion of regional income generated by industry is also an important explanatory factor, since this sector normally constitutes the principal tax base of the federal and state governments. In addition, regional industry tends to be concentrated in those subsectors (for example, food, wood products) where tax rates tend to be lowest. Finally, tax collections in the North are lowered (at least in the short run) by the various tax exemptions granted to firms located in the region by the federal, state, and local governments.

It should be pointed out that the progressivity of the tax system on a regional basis is probably more apparent than real. In the specific case of the North, the chronic deficits experienced in interregional commerce and the nature of the major products traded (that is, raw material for manufactures) imply a high degree of tax importing from other regions (especially the Center-South). Therefore, the final burdens of taxation in this region are considerably higher (and those of the Center-South, considerably lower) than the formal burdens would indicate.

Tax Sharing

If we ignore the question of interregional tax shifting, net federal taxes collected in the North are still lower than those mentioned above. This is because these data do not take into consideration the systems of intergovernmental tax sharing that automatically return most (if not all) of these revenues to the region. In the case of certain federal taxes, net collections (gross collections less tax shares) are therefore zero or even negative. Although many federal taxes are currently shared with the state and local governments, the regional redistributive impact of tax sharing is clearest with respect to the Participation Fund (Fundo de Participação—FP) and the Special Fund (Fundo Especial—FE). [8]

In their original forms, the FP was to be constituted of 20 percent of the revenues from the most important and elastic federal taxes: the manufacturers sales (IPI) and income (IR) taxes. The amounts deposited were to be equally divided among a state participation fund (FPE) and two local participation funds (FPM); one for capital cities and the other for the remaining municípios. Individual shares of the

FPE and the FPM for capital cities were to be distributed according to criteria that incorporated land area, population, and per capita income. [9] Although the shares of the IPI and IR to be distributed fell to 10 percent in 1969, the FE, endowed with 2 percent of the IPI and IR, was created to compensate lower-income regions. For this purpose, at least 75 percent of the FE was to be distributed among states in the North and Northeast.

Since the mid-1960s, the FP and FE have constituted an important source of funds for state and local governments located in the North. Between 1967 and 1975, the amount of resources transferred through these mechanisms rose more than fourfold, from Cr$ 183.3 million to Cr$ 783.2 million in constant 1975 prices. In all but the first year, FP and FE distributions exceeded combined IPI and IR collections in the region. In fact, during three years (1968, 1971, and 1972), shares from these funds were greater than all federal tax collections; that is, the net federal tax burden was negative. Taking the 1967-75 period as a whole, transfers via the participation funds returned about 95 percent of all federal taxes collected in the North. [10]

The Net Inflow

In order to quantify the complete fiscal flow, one must account not only for transfers but also for government purchases. This is not an easy task, however, since most expenditures appearing in the national budget are not classified according to their regional destinations. Fortunately, recent estimates of the Fundação Getúlio Vargas do permit some calculations of net fiscal flow during the years 1970-73. These estimates include the expenditures of the federal government, semiautonomous institutes and funds linked to the federal government, federal enterprises, and the state and municipal governments. On the basis of these revised data, the public sector appears to be at least 50 percent larger than that indicated in regional social accounts.

Table 3.4 summarizes the various inflows and outflows of funds caused by federal government activity in Amazonia. In items 1, 2, and 4, expenditures and revenues are listed by category. The difference between total expenditures (3) and total current revenues (4) yields an item (5) referred to as "net inflow-A." This item closely corresponds to the concept of "net fiscal inflow" in the formal "balance-of-payments" sense. In all four years, this item was positive, indicating that the federal budget redistributed to the North income· that was originally generated in other regions. Moreover, since federal expenditures grew faster than federal revenues collected in the region, the redistributive impact increased during the period.

Although the fiscal incentives of SUDAM are not generally considered to be federal expenditures, they do present some of the characteristics of <u>tax expenditures</u>—a term denoting the opportunity costs of deductions and exemptions allowed by fiscal legislation. For this reason, they were added to net inflow-A to yield an alternative measure of the net fiscal inflow referred to as "net inflow-B." As Table 3.4 shows (6), the disbursements of SUDAM fiscal incentive funds constituted a relatively small and declining proportion of net inflow-A throughout the 1970–73 period. Nevertheless, the growth of net inflow-A offset this decline, and net inflow-B grew by an overall 20 percent in real terms.

TABLE 3.4

North Region: Net Inflow of Resources via the Federal Budget and
Fiscal Incentives, 1970–73
(Cr$ millions, 1975 prices)

Category	1970	1971	1972	1973
(1) Current expenditures	2,347.9	2,587.1	2,822.3	3,397.6
Consumption	1,001.0	1,147.8	1,237.5	1,338.7
Transfers	1,346.9	1,439.3	1,584.8	2,058.9
Intergovernmental	591.4	654.3	724.7	774.9
Other	755.5	785.0	860.1	1,284.0
(2) Capital expenditures	714.3	875.5	1,013.5	1,341.4
Fixed capital	685.7	855.7	994.9	1,318.2
Portfolio	28.6	19.8	18.6	23.2
(3) Total expenditures (1 plus 2)	3,062.2	3,462.6	3,835.8	4,739.0
(4) Current revenue	1,273.4	1,396.6	1,567.8	2,087.5
Taxes	974.4	1,043.3	1,156.3	1,564.0
Other	299.0	353.3	411.5	523.5
(5) Net inflow-A (3 minus 4)	1,788.8	2,066.0	2,268.0	2,651.5
(6) Fiscal incentives*	879.0	726.4	610.6	560.6
(7) Net inflow-B (5 plus 6)	2,667.8	2,792.4	2,878.6	3,212.0

*Amounts effectively distributed during year.

Note: Federal budget includes federal government and semiautonomous institutes and funds operating at federal level (SUDAM, SUFRAMA, IBGE, INPS, PIS, FGTS, and the like).

Sources: Fundação Getúlio Vargas (IBRE)/SUDAM, <u>Agregados Econômicos Regionais</u>, vol. 3: <u>Setor Público</u> (April 1976); and data provided by SUDAM.

It is evident from the data that the growth of the net fiscal inflow resulted largely from the doubling of federal expenditures on fixed-capital formation. By 1973, in fact, fixed-capital expenditures in the North were approximately equal to consumption expenditures, as opposed to a national consumption-to-capital ratio of 3:1. This observation is not unexpected, however, since the 1970-73 period coincides with the massive PIN-financed infrastructure development. This aspect is clearly revealed by the functional distribution of federal fixed-capital formation. During the 1970-73 period, about 75 percent of these expenditures were on transportation and communications.

Although the data do not permit precise calculations, it seems reasonable to assume that the public sector (all levels of government, including public enterprises) was responsible for upward of 50 percent of all fixed-capital formation in the region during these years.* It also seems reasonable to assume that these percentages are considerably higher than those that prevailed during the 1960s.

THE ROLE OF FOREIGN AND DOMESTIC TRADE

In its role as a producer of primary goods, Amazonia has traditionally maintained strong economic relationships with extraregional interests. Moreover, these commercial linkages have generally conformed to the so-called center-periphery or dependency model in which income earned through exporting raw materials is utilized for financing imports of capital and consumer goods. As the historical record has shown, this system brought prosperity to Amazonia when the region's major exports were highly sought after, but collapse and stagnation when they were not. In the past, therefore, trade functioned more as an economic destabilizer than as an agent of sustained regional growth and development.

The present section characterizes and assesses the major trade flows of Amazonia from the late 1950s to the early 1970s. One objective of this exercise is to reveal to what extent this region still conforms to its historical dependent role in relation to international and domestic markets. A second objective is to measure the degree to which exports have contributed to (or retarded) the recent pace of regional economic growth. A final objective is to analyze the effects of selected government policies on the foreign and domestic trade of Amazonia.

---

*Of the total fixed-capital formation of the public sector, approximately 70 percent was accounted for by the federal government (including semiautonomous institutes and funds and federal enterprises).

A Note on Data Sources and Limitations

In attempting to analyze trade flows on a regional basis, the re-
searcher is immediately confronted with formidable statistical barriers. Although these problems are most serious when dealing with
interregional trade, they also arise in the foreign sector. In general,
the data on foreign trade are more reliable and complete than those on
interregional trade. Data on total foreign exports and imports by port
are published annually in the IBGE's Anuário Estatístico, a basic
source of information for the present discussion. Since the published
totals are in values registered at the final embarkation or disembarka-
tion of a product, however, statistical distortions may arise. These
distortions occur in cases where goods originating in other regions
are shipped from ports in Amazonia or where imports arriving in extraregional ports are subsequently transferred to Amazonia. The net
result of these two cases tends to be an overstatement of exports and
an understatement of imports.

A more serious problem arises when one seeks to measure export and import content, since regional foreign trade data have not
been published on a product-by-product basis since the late 1950s.
This difficulty was partially surmounted by choosing two benchmark
years (1958 and 1974) for temporal comparisons. The data for the
latter year were gathered from unpublished accounts of the Banco do
Brasil—CACEX (for exports) and Ministério da Fazenda—CIEF (for
imports). This approach makes an analysis of major structural
changes possible, although it reveals little about the year-to-year aspects of these changes. A final statistical problem arises from the
changes in the method of product classification that occurred during
the period under study. Since these changes rendered temporal comparisons of regional trade structure impracticable, it was decided to
convert the 1958 data to the classification method utilized in 1974—
the Nomenclatura Brasileira de Mercadorias (new NBM). Although
this reclassification process was to some extent arbitrary, the resulting product groupings are reasonably consistent.

The statistical problems encountered when dealing with interregional trade are far more serious than those noted above. The basic
source of these problems is the fact that goods crossing state or regional borders are subject to fewer fiscal and statistical controls than
goods exchanged between nations. This difficulty is compounded in
Amazonia where state and territorial borders may still be rather
vaguely defined. Hence, a significant amount of merchandise entering or leaving the region is probably never officially recorded. Of
the data available on interregional trade, those pertaining to goods
shipped overland (air, rail, highway) are generally the most unreliable and incomplete. Since overland routes (except for air transport)

have only recently become an important means of transportation in Amazonia, their exclusion in the 1958-61 segment of the time series is not a significant drawback. Overland commerce is included in the 1967-70 series, although the absence of data for particular states in some years necessitated the use of estimates to complete the interregional trade matrix. Thus, while providing a general picture of the major interregional trade flows during the 1960s, data for individual years should be interpreted with a great deal of caution.

Overall Trends

The basic statistical series on regional exports and imports for the 1958-74 period is contained in Table 3.5. Although one may note a number of sharp annual oscillations, certain trends are evident. First, one is struck by the region's poor export performance in the 1960s. During this decade, total exports (E) practically stagnated at about Cr$ 1.7 billion per year. Through disaggregation, one may observe that the export growth that did occur was entirely confined to the foreign sector (e_1). This growth, however, was barely sufficient to offset the average annual decline in interregional exports (i_2) of 1.6 percent.

The performance of foreign exports apparently improved in the early 1970s, although the 11.3 percent annual growth rate of this period is largely attributable to the 32 percent increase experienced in 1974. Unfortunately, complete data on interregional trade are not available after 1970. Based on the recent sales of Zona Franca de Manaus industries, however, it is probable that interregional exports have achieved some degree of dynamism since this date (see Chapter 5). At any rate, it does seem evident that exports were not an important source of growth during the 1960s. Indeed, one could argue that their lackluster performance exerted a drag on the regional economy. This conclusion is further supported by the calculations in Table 3.6, which show the export share in regional income falling from 33.8 to 19.8 percent between 1960 and 1970.

The behavior of imports, on the other hand, has been markedly different. In contrast to the sluggish pace of exports observed during the 1960s, total regional imports (I) grew, from Cr$ 1.6 billion to Cr$ 3.6 billion, at an annual rate of 9 percent. By dividing total imports into their foreign (i_1) and interregional (i_2) components, one may note that the former expanded at an annual rate over three times greater than that of the latter (18.8 versus 5.4 percent). Not surprisingly, total imports as a percentage of regional income increased significantly during the 1960-70 period, from 31.7 to 41.4 percent (Table 3.6). Although domestic purchases still remain the most im-

TABLE 3.5

North Region: Foreign and Interregional Trade in Selected Years, 1958–74

(Cr$ millions, 1975 prices)

	Exports (f.o.b.)			Imports (CIF)			Surplus (+) or Deficit (−)		
	Foreign (e_1)	Inter-regional[a] (e_2)	Total (E)	Foreign (i_1)	Inter-regional[a,b] (i_2)	Total (I)	$e_1 - i_1$	$e_2 - i_2$	$E - I$
1958	511.7	837.7	1,349.4	218.2	1,298.5	1,516.7	+293.5	−460.8	−167.3
1959	560.6	780.5	1,341.1	245.5	1,389.8	1,635.3	+315.1	−609.3	−294.2
1960	826.0	918.0	1,744.0	230.8	1,404.7	1,635.5	+595.2	−486.7	+108.5
1961	1,019.3	988.6	2,007.0	259.5	1,389.1	1,648.6	+758.8	−400.5	+358.4
1967	612.1	750.5	1,362.5	310.4	2,140.7	2,451.1	+301.7	−1,390.2	−1,088.6
1968	879.2	820.4	1,699.6	895.9	2,241.4	3,137.3	−16.7	−1,421.0	−1,437.7
1969	850.5	852.4	1,702.9	568.3	2,290.3	2,858.6	+282.2	−1,437.9	−1,155.7
1970	982.3	766.0	1,748.3	1,291.2	2,365.7	3,656.9	−308.9	−1,599.7	−1,908.6
1971	1,102.7	—[c]	—	1,242.5	—	—	−139.8	—	—
1972	1,049.6	—	—	1,627.6	—	—	−578.0	—	—
1973	1,158.5	—	—	2,140.3	—	—	−981.8	—	—
1974	1,529.9	—	—	2,898.3	—	—	−1,368.4	—	—

[a]Coastal shipping and overland (1967–70); coastal shipping only (1958–61).
[b]In f.o.b. values.
[c]Not available.

Sources: IBGE, Anuário Estatístico do Brasil (various years); Ministério da Fazenda (SEEF), Comércio de Cabotagem do Brasil (various years); and special tabulations of IPEA/INPES.

TABLE 3.6

North Region: Share of Foreign and Interregional Trade in Regional Income, Selected Years, 1960–72
(percent)

	Exports (f.o.b.)			Imports (CIF)			Degree of Openness		
	Foreign (e_1)	Inter-regional (e_2)	Total (E)	Foreign (i_1)	Inter-regional[a] (i_2)	Total (I)	$\frac{e_1+i_1}{2}$	$\frac{e_2+i_2}{2}$	$\frac{E+I}{2}$
1960	16.0	17.8	33.8	4.5	27.2	31.7	10.3	22.5	32.8
1961	16.8	16.3	33.2	4.3	22.9	27.2	10.6	19.6	30.2
1967	10.1	12.4	22.6	5.1	35.4	40.6	7.6	23.9	31.2
1968	12.1	11.3	23.5	12.4	31.0	43.3	12.3	21.1	33.4
1969	11.0	11.0	22.0	7.3	29.6	36.9	9.2	20.3	29.5
1970	11.1	8.7	19.8	14.6	26.8	41.4	12.9	17.7	30.6
1971	11.8	—[b]	—	13.3	—	—	12.5	—	—
1972	10.4	—	—	16.1	—	—	13.3	—	—

[a]In f.o.b. values.
[b]Not available.

Note: Net income at factor costs.

Sources: IBGE, Anuário Estatístico do Brasil (various years); Ministério da Fazenda (SEEF), Comércio de Cabotagem do Brasil (various years); Fundação Getúlio Vargas (IBRE)/SUDAM, Agregados Econômicos Regionais, vol. 1: Produto Interno (October 1974); and special tabulations of IPEA/INPES.

portant in absolute and relative terms, the overall increase of the import share has been entirely due to purchases in foreign markets.

The combined effect of the divergent rates of growth of exports and imports has been a widening of the regional trade deficit. During the pre-1968 period, the foreign trade balance of Amazonia was in a surplus position while its interregional balance was in deficit (see Table 3.5). In fact, during two years (1960 and 1961), the region's foreign exchange earnings were large enough to completely cover the deficit incurred in the interregional account. After 1967, both the foreign (except 1969) and interregional trade balances showed deficits. Since earnings from foreign trade no longer function to offset the deficits experienced in interregional trade, one must assume that the increased volume of imports has been financed through the net inflows of public and private funds. This would imply, however, that the multiplier effects of public and private expenditures in the region are greatly diminished by import leakages.

Foreign Trade

In comparison with national totals, the foreign trade of Amazonia is quite insignificant. Whereas the combined Southeast and South regions dominate the Brazilian trade balance with 80 and 90 percent, respectively, of total exports and imports, the North accounts for less than 4 percent of the total in both cases. This observation is not unexpected, given the latter region's sparse population and low level of development. When coefficients of "openness" are taken into consideration, however, it becomes apparent that the North is more dependent on the foreign sector than any of the other macroregions.* It is thus important to more closely consider the reasons behind the slow growth of exports and the rapid growth of imports observed in the 1960s and 1970s.[11] This will be accomplished through a brief discussion of the structural aspects of regional foreign trade.

Exports

When regional foreign exports are disaggregated to the product level, much diversification is observed between 1958 and 1974. In the first years, just two products (manganese ore and Brazil nuts) accounted for almost 90 percent of the region's foreign exchange earn-

---

*Coefficients of "openness" to foreign trade $(e_1 + i_1/2Y)$ for the IBGE macroregions (1970) are: North, 13.38; Northeast, 8.59; Southeast, 6.92; South, 9.41; and central West, 0.50. Y signifies the regional net income at factor costs.

ings. During the subsequent 16 years, however, adverse demand and supply conditions caused the exports of these products to stagnate. The volume of manganese exports, for example, increased by 152 percent (from 585,711 to 1.5 million tons) between 1958 and 1974, while its per-ton price fell by 27 percent (from 45.61 to U.S. $33.45 in current prices). Thus, by 1974 they were comprising a considerably smaller, though still significant, 40 percent of the total. Many other products of the extractive sector (for example, animal skins, natural rubber, vegetable gums) shared the same fate for similar reasons.

Although total exports of the extractive sector fell from 97 to 63 percent of regional exports between 1958 and 1974, this relative decline was entirely due to the stagnation of mineral exports. Extractive vegetable products, on the other hand, actually increased their share slightly in the export balance, from 34.1 to 34.8 percent. The explanation of this paradox is that the poor performances of natural rubber, Brazil nuts, and other forest products were more than offset by the spectacular growth of exports linked to the timber industry (lumber, wood products, rosewood oil). Rudimentary and predatory techniques also prevail in these product lines, but stagnation and decline have been so far avoided by a strong international market and the vast reserves of the Amazon forest. Exports of cultivated crops were also strong during the 1958-74 period, increasing their share in total regional exports from 1 to almost 16 percent. It should be evident, however, that black pepper was virtually the only such export crop. Nevertheless, the experience of black pepper suggests that other export possibilities may exist in the agricultural sector if proper organizational and technological methods are applied.

Industrial exports, although amounting to less than one-third of extractive exports in 1974, were much more dynamic than the latter during this period. Exports of "traditional" industries (based on the simple processing of regional primary products) totaled about U.S. $20 million in 1974 and continued to predominate in absolute terms. The most rapid rates of growth, however, were encountered in the exports of "modern" industry (for example, refined mineral fuels, chemicals, machinery, synthetic textiles, plastics). From a value of only U.S. $57,000 in 1958 (1974 prices), this group of exports rose to almost U.S. $15 million in 1974. In spite of this impressive growth record, however, "modern" industry still only contributed about 8 percent to total regional exchange earnings.

Imports

A disaggregation of regional imports reveals that the high overall rates of import growth were not confined to just a few product categories. Considering the relative weights of each category in the regional total, however, one may observe that over half of the growth was associated with imports of capital goods and consumer durables such as machinery and electrical equipment, audio and optical equipment, and watches. In contrast, the previously important category of minerals and fossil fuels (comprising over 50 percent of the regional total in 1958) grew at a much slower rate than the regional average and explained less than 20 percent of the weighted annual growth.

On the basis of the general time pattern of foreign imports (see Table 3.5), one would expect the behavior of regional imports to be closely related to the establishment of the ZFM in 1967. Although a lack of data on imports organized by category and port of entry precludes a direct verification of this hypothesis, other data tend to confirm it. First, almost 97 percent of the total import growth observed in the 1958-74 period occurred after 1966. Second, over 80 percent of this post-1966 growth was accounted for by the port of Manaus. Finally, imports entering Manaus explained about 90 percent of the growth in the machinery and electrical equipment category and virtually all of the growth in the audio and optical equipment and watches categories between 1958 and 1974 (see Chapter 5).

The import requirements of commerce and industry located in Manaus have radically altered previously existing foreign trade patterns within Amazonia, that is, the imports of western Amazonia have risen from one-third of the regional total in 1958 to over 80 percent in 1974. In the meantime, exports of this subregion have remained a relatively stable 15-20 percent of the regional total. Thus, while eastern Amazonia continues to show a surplus in its international trade balance, the western subregion has experienced ever-increasing deficits since 1967. These deficits wholly explain the present situation of the North.[12]

Domestic Trade

As previously discussed, analyses of inter- and intraregional trade are severely limited by the quantity and quality of the data. For Amazonia, only partial data exist for the 1960s; practically no data are available after 1970. This latter shortcoming is especially lamentable, since it prevents any assessment of the undoubtedly significant trade effects generated by the new highway systems. Because of these limitations, the present section confines itself to some brief comments on conditions prevailing during the 1960s.

Structure and Performance

The interregional and foreign trade patterns of Amazonia were quite similar between 1960 and 1970. First, the structure of both continued to reflect the region's peripheral, dependent role vis-à-vis extraregional markets. For example, in 1969 (the only year for which reasonably accurate data exist), almost 50 percent of total interregional exports took the form of raw materials. Exports of such products as chemicals and pharmaceuticals, machinery and vehicles, and "modern" manufactures, amounted to less than 25 percent of the total. In contrast, these latter products accounted for about 50 percent of total interregional imports. In absolute terms, imports of these products were 30 percent greater than total interregional exports (1969 data). The dependence of Amazonia on foodstuffs produced in other regions is also shown by the data; in 1969, total expenditures on foods and beverages (Cr$ 483 million in 1975 prices) absorbed almost 60 percent of the region's interregional "exchange" earnings.

A second similarity between the interregional and foreign trade of Amazonia concerns the aggregate behavior of exports and imports. Both foreign and interregional exports performed poorly, while imports increased rapidly (see Table 3.5). By 1970, total interregional exports were lower, and imports 70 percent higher, than their 1960 levels in real terms. The stagnation of interregional exports is best explained by the adverse internal market situations for two of Amazonia's traditional products: natural rubber and jute. In both cases, high-cost production methods reduced the demand from extraregional industrial interests and promoted the utilization of substitutes (synthetic and nonsynthetic) and foreign imports. [13]

The disproportionate growth of imports, on the other hand, is principally related to the increased inflow of private and public funds to the region during the last half of the 1960s. These resources provided the additional purchasing power that was subsequently transformed into capital and consumer goods acquired in other regions. Since public policies of this era stressed industrialization, it must be presumed that a large portion of interregional imports represented inputs for the new industry. This point is most clearly illustrated by the ZFM experience (see Chapter 5). Although not readily quantifiable, it is likely that increased extraregional purchases were also associated with the improved communications and transportation systems implanted during this period. This correlation is not unexpected since such systems normally cause a standardization of national consumption patterns (via the "demonstration effect") and also change the relative prices of regionally and extraregionally produced goods.*

---

*Before the existence of shorter, overland routes, the isolation of Amazonia tended to protect local industry from outside competition. By the same token, this isolation also raised the CIF (cost, insurance, and freight) prices of regional exports. The fact that imports grew much faster than exports upon the opening of overland routes confirms

Integration

Although the major road-building programs did not occur until the 1970s, the federal highway system of Amazonia did increase (in terms of kilometers in use) by 260 percent during the 1960s. In fact, two highways completed in this period (Belém-Brasilia and Cuiabá-Acre) established the region's first overland links with the South. A reasonable hypothesis, therefore, is that the integration of Amazonia had begun even before the advent of PIN. If this hypothesis is valid, one would expect to observe rising coefficients of openness to interregional trade. This expectation is not confirmed, however, by the calculations in Table 3.6; that is, the 1970 coefficient (17.7 percent) is approximately 5 percent lower than that of 1960. Does this finding indicate that Amazonia actually became more isolated during the 1960s? Additional evidence casts doubt on this latter conclusion.

To further test our hypothesis, a partial (imports only) regional trade matrix was calculated for the years 1960 and 1970 (Table 3.7). An important point emerges from these data: For most states and territories within Amazonia (with the exceptions of Roraima and Amapá), one notes a significant decline in intraregional purchases as a proportion of total domestic purchases.* Moreover, the relative decline of intraregional commercial ties is almost totally explained by an increase of such ties with the Center-South. The data also suggest that this process was most detrimental to Pará, since (with the exception of Amapá) this state became a relatively less important source of supply to each of the other administrative units.†

In sum, the data in Table 3.7 suggest that, notwithstanding declining coefficients of openness, Amazonia became more integrated with the national economy during the 1960s. Unfortunately, the data do not permit a more precise quantification of this phenomenon. One would suppose, however, that the integration of Amazonia was closely linked to the growing economic power of the Center-South (especially

———————————

the general notion that the demand for manufactures is more price-elastic than the demand for raw materials.

*The territories of Roraima and Amapá are only now being integrated with the rest of Amazonia, hence their divergence from the general trend.

†Since the data provide no information on the importance of re-exports, we cannot ascertain whether the major loss has fallen on the industry or the commerce of Pará. It would appear, however, that the intermediary (entrepot) function of Belém has been diminishing (especially with respect to western Amazonia). It would also appear that (as of 1970) the new industry of Belém had not appreciably substituted imports.

TABLE 3.7

North Region: Domestic Purchases (Imports) by Region and Selected States, 1960 and 1970
(percent)

	Destination											
	Rondônia		Acre		Amazonas		Roraima		Pará		Amapá	
Origin	1960[a]	1970[b]	1960	1970	1960	1970	1960	1970	1960	1970	1960	1970
North	63.7	34.6	68.8	57.5	30.6	22.0	58.7	59.5	15.7	10.7	38.2	55.7
Rondônia	—	—	0.0	0.3	2.9	3.7	0.0	0.7	0.7	0.2	0.0	0.0
Acre	0.0	0.4	—	—	8.0	1.1	0.0	0.0	7.1	2.9	0.0	0.0
Amazonas	27.7	23.6	21.3	42.8	—	—	51.4	53.2	6.2	7.0	0.6	9.9
Roraima	0.0	0.0	0.0	0.0	1.4	0.8	—	—	0.0	0.0	0.0	0.0
Pará	36.0	10.6	47.4	14.4	18.3	16.4	6.4	5.6	1.7	0.6	37.6	45.8
Amapá	0.0	0.0	0.1	0.0	0.0	0.0	0.9	0.0	—	—	—	—
Northeast	9.5	4.3	7.9	2.8	15.6	12.9	13.4	5.3	20.0	20.2	2.6	6.0
Center–South	26.8	61.1	23.3	39.7	53.8	65.1	27.9	35.2	64.3	69.1	59.2	38.3
São Paulo	7.2	38.4	13.3	20.2	28.5	40.8	15.8	21.2	27.1	37.6	5.2	19.3
Guanabara	19.3	9.1	9.5	9.5	21.1	14.6	11.9	10.1	30.0	15.9	53.5	27.0
Total	100.0	100.0	100.0	100.0	100.0	100.0	100.0	100.0	100.0	100.0	100.0	100.0

[a]1960 figures include purchases via coastal shipping only.
[b]1970 figures include purchases via coastal shipping and overland.

Sources: Ministério da Fazenda (SEEF), Comércio de Cabotagem do Brasil, 1960/61 (Rio de Janeiro, 1962); IBGE, Anuário Estatístico do Brasil—1971; partially estimated.

São Paulo), and this latter region's quest for new internal markets. Moreover, this market penetration was facilitated by the improved communication systems and highways of the period; the former increasing the efficiency and range of marketing campaigns and the latter reducing the CIF prices of many goods. The impact of the highway is most readily observable in the data for Rondônia and Acre, which show the relative importance of the Center-South increasing drastically between 1960 and 1970. Since Rondônia and Acre were the units most directly affected by the Cuiabá-Acre highway, one must assume that more direct access to southern markets was the most relevant explanatory variable.

LAND DISTRIBUTION AND USE

The current pattern of land distribution and use undoubtedly constitutes a major barrier to the development of rural Amazonia—particularly in terms of its social ramifications. The origins of this "land problem" are not difficult to perceive. First, Amazonia is a region that is only now being extensively mapped and surveyed. Therefore, boundary lines and rights of possession still tend to be ill-defined and arbitrary. This aspect was less important in the past when most areas of the region were inaccessible by overland means and thus virtually uninhabited. In such an environment, a superimposition of property rights could exist with a minimum of conflict.[14] The new access roads and improved knowledge of the region's natural resource potentials, however, have irrevocably altered the status quo. With both migrants and large corporate interests entering Amazonia in increasing numbers, greater precision is now being demanded in the delineation of both property boundaries and ownership rights.

A second source of the problem is the pattern of land distribution and use inherited from the past. For the most part, the distribution of land that characterizes Amazonia today is a reflection of a rural economy historically based on extractive activities and extensive cattle raising. This aspect has necessarily given rise to a "minifundia-latifundia complex" where extremely large landholdings exist side by side with small subsistence plots utilized for the cultivation of manioc, rice, corn, beans, and so forth. Moreover, since land is the region's most abundant productive factor, there has been little incentive to intensify its use and hence raise its productivity. Thus, the most common manner in which to increase agricultural production has been to cultivate new land as the soils of previously cultivated lands become impoverished.[15]

Some data on land distribution and use are available in the IBGE Agricultural Censuses and INCRA cadastral surveys.* The most recent information is from the 1972 INCRA survey. Table 3.8 presents data from this source for the North, Northeast, Center-South, and Brazil as a whole according to categories established by the Estatuto da Terra (Law 4504 of November 30, 1964).† It can be observed that the minifundia-latifundia complex is generalized in Brazil. In the case of the North, however, almost 90 percent of the land area falls in the two latifundia categories, as opposed to the 75-80 percent range in the other macroregions and for Brazil as a whole. On the other hand, only about 5 percent of the surveyed land is accounted for by minifundia, a proportion considerably lower than that observed in the rest of the country.‡ The North and Northeast present similar low percentages in the theoretically efficient and equitable "rural enterprise" category, less than 2 percent of the total "rural properties" and about 5 percent of their land areas. In sum, the data tend to confirm that land is not only unequally distributed in the North but also inefficiently utilized. Furthermore, it would appear that inefficient land use in this region is associated more with the underemployment of large landholdings than with excessive fragmentation.

---

*These primary data sources are not strictly comparable since the working definition of "landholding" is different in each case. In the census estimates, the unit surveyed is the "establishment" (estabelecimento), defined as a continuous landholding devoted to agricultural pursuits and under a common administration. INCRA, on the other hand, utilizes the "rural property" (imóvel rural) as its basic unit. This latter concept considers landholdings according to their common ownership rather than administration. Hence, one INCRA "rural property" may encompass many census-defined "establishments."

†Article 40 of this law categorizes "rural properties" by a method incorporating both efficiency and equity considerations. In this scheme, the minifundio and latifundio-B fail on both counts; the former being too small to permit efficiency and the latter being subutilized in relation to its possibilities. The latifundio-A may be efficiently organized, although it is too large (larger than 600 times the "rural model" established by INCRA) to meet the equity criterion. Of the four categories, only the "rural enterprise" is considered to be both equitable and efficient.

‡It should not be inferred from this data that the average minifundio of the North is smaller than that of the Northeast and Center-South. On the contrary, the average minifundio of the North (about 40 hectares) occupies over twice the area of those situated in the other macroregions.

TABLE 3.8

Landholdings by Category, 1972
(percent of total)

	North		Northeast		Center–South		Brazil	
	Number	Area	Number	Area	Number	Area	Number	Area
Minifundio	69.8	5.3	79.5	20.0	68.8	11.0	71.9	12.5
Rural enterprise	1.8	5.2	1.4	5.2	6.3	12.0	4.8	9.7
Latifundio (A)	28.4	78.2	19.1	71.0	24.9	72.8	23.3	72.9
Latifundio (B)	0.0	11.3	0.0	3.8	0.0	4.2	0.0	4.9
Total (percent)	100.0	100.0	100.0	100.0	100.0	100.0	100.0	100.0
Total (absolute)*	72,596	39,427.6	998,948	86,030.3	2,315,629	244,817.4	3,387,173	370,275.3

*Area in thousands of hectares.

Source: Instituto de Colonização e Reforma Agrária (INCRA), Estatísticas Cadastrais/1 (Brasilia, 1974), pp. 311–12.

TABLE 3.9

Size Distribution of North Region Landholdings, 1960-72
(percent of total)

	Size Groupings (hectares)					
	Less than 10	10-100	100-1,000	1,000-10,000	Over 10,000	Absolute Total*
IBGE (1960)						
Number	48.8	41.6	6.0	1.1	2.5	138,241
	(48.8)	(90.4)	(96.4)	(97.5)	(100.0)	
Area	1.1	6.9	9.6	19.7	62.7	23,453.1
	(1.1)	(8.0)	(17.6)	(37.3)	(100.0)	
IBGE (1970)						
Number	41.1	41.0	15.1	0.9	1.9	261,145
	(41.1)	(82.1)	(97.2)	(98.1)	(100.0)	
Area	1.7	15.1	35.2	24.7	23.3	23,182.1
	(1.7)	(16.8)	(52.0)	(76.7)	(100.0)	
INCRA (1967)						
Number	17.5	54.9	19.9	7.2	0.5	77,837
	(17.5)	(72.4)	(92.3)	(99.5)	(100.0)	
Area	0.2	4.6	15.2	44.3	35.7	38,731.8
	(0.2)	(4.8)	(20.0)	(64.3)	(100.0)	
INCRA (1972)						
Number	11.9	54.9	24.6	7.9	0.7	72,596
	(11.9)	(66.8)	(91.4)	(99.3)	(100.0)	
Area	1.1	3.7	12.6	42.1	40.5	39,427.6
	(1.1)	(4.8)	(17.4)	(59.5)	(100.0)	

*Area in thousands of hectares.

Note: Cumulative percentages in parentheses.

Sources: IBGE, Censos Agropecuários (1960 and 1970); IBGE, Anuário Estatístico do Brasil (1969); INCRA, Estatísticas Cadastrais/1 (Brasilia, 1974), pp. 311-12.

Table 3.9 provides further information on the equity aspects of land tenure in the North. Here the data are arranged according to their purely dimensional characteristics. Four observations spanning the 1960-72 period are utilized: the Agricultural Censuses of 1960 and 1970, and the INCRA cadastral surveys of 1967 and 1972. While each of these four estimates is generally consistent with the type of land tenure implied in Table 3.8, one notices some apparent inconsistencies between the IBGE and INCRA data.[16] Most important, the census data show a clear trend of decentralization between 1960 and 1970 that is not reflected in the INCRA data. Of special interest are the sharp decline in the area occupied by establishments of over 10,000 hectares and the sharp rise in the area of those under 1,000 hectares. Since the total land area surveyed by the censuses changed only slightly during this period, one is led to believe that a redistribution of land occurred in the 1960s through either the fragmentation of large estates or a marked intensification of agricultural activity. Neither hypothesis, however, is supported by the INCRA surveys or other available data. A more plausible explanation would seem to be statistical discrepancies caused by readjustments of property boundaries, or rights of possession, or both.[17]

Further details on land use in the North are contained in Table 3.10, from which the underutilization of the land surveyed is immediately apparent. Of the 39.4 million hectares encompassed by "rural properties," only 13.5 million (about one-third) are actually in productive use. Of the 26 million hectares of land not in productive use, about 16 million are classified as "unusable" or in legal forest reserves. This still, however, leaves about 10 million hectares of usable, though idle, land. Thus, there seems to be considerable room for agricultural expansion, if only on the basis of increasing the land input, and this contention is further strengthened by the fact that almost 90 percent (316 million hectares) of the North is still in the public domain.

The relative importance of the various agricultural systems and products is also indicated in Table 3.10. These data suggest that the region's historical dependence on extractive activities and extensive cattle raising remains essentially intact. These two activities account for over 90 percent of the land use, with extractive activities alone accounting for almost two-thirds of the total area. Moreover, in Amazonas, Acre, and Rondônia, the area devoted to extractive activities rises to over 80 percent of their respective land areas in use. In contrast, the relative area in crops does not account for more than 10 percent in any of the territories or states comprising the North region.

A final, though extremely important, characteristic of land tenure in Amazonia is the high proportion of "rural properties" held with no definitive legal title. In this respect, the 1972 INCRA survey indi-

TABLE 3.10

North Region: Landholdings by Use, 1972
(thousands)

State/Territory	Total Area (hectares)	Area in Use (AIU)							
		Total		Crops		Livestock		Extractive	
		Hectares	Percent Total	Hectares	Percent AIU	Hectares	Percent AIU	Hectares	Percent AIU
Rondônia	2,137.0	917.9	43.0	22.3	2.4	56.9	6.2	838.6	91.4
Acre	5,537.9	3,174.5	57.3	93.8	3.0	117.5	3.7	2,963.2	93.3
Amazonas	7,863.4	3,045.1	38.7	224.9	7.4	333.3	10.9	2,486.9	81.7
Roraima	1,737.3	799.2	46.0	19.3	2.4	727.6	91.0	52.4	6.7
Pará	20,909.7	5,141.3	24.6	489.7	9.5	2,303.1	44.8	2,348.5	45.7
Amapá	1,242.3	392.7	31.6	27.7	7.1	211.9	54.0	153.2	39.0
Total	39,427.6	13,470.7	34.2	877.7	6.5	3,750.3	27.8	8,842.8	65.6

Source: INCRA, Estatísticas Cadastrais/7 (Brasilia, 1974), pp. 4–5, 10–15.

79

cates that 71 percent of the total landholdings (occupying almost 40 percent of the total area) fall into this category. (For Brazil as a whole, excluding the North, only about 22 percent of the total "rural properties," occupying 11 percent of the total area, do not possess definitive land titles.) This problem is particularly acute in Rondônia, Acre, and Roraima, where the number of small landholdings (under 500 hectares) without definitive legal titles runs to well over 90 percent of the total in this size range. One can probably attribute this situation to recent migration to these frontier areas. With corporate interests simultaneously entering the region, however, this undefined agrarian structure has created conditions for violent social conflict. Under Brazilian law, certain rights are accorded to individuals occupying land, even when this land is privately owned. In order to establish these rights (posse), the individual (posseiro) must have occupied a given plot for at least one year and have cultivated and improved the land (for example, through clearing, fencing, construction of corrals, and the like). Conflicts typically arise when the legal (and frequently absentee) owners try to evict families claiming posse rights. While owners are required to indemnify evicted posseiros, this law is commonly violated in practice.

DISTRIBUTION OF PERSONAL INCOME

Calculations based on the 1970 Demographic Census reveal that the North had the lowest index of income concentration among the major regions. Whereas the top 10 percent and lowest 50 percent of income earners in the Northeast received 47.1 and 16.3 percent—and in Brazil as a whole, 47.3 and 15.0 percent—the comparable figures for the North were 39.9 and 21.6 percent (Table 3.11). Furthermore, even though the average incomes prevailing in the North and Northeast were only a fraction of the national average, the incidence of extreme poverty by regional standards was much greater in the latter region. This point is made clear by the significantly higher proportion of workers earning less than the regional minimum wage in the Northeast as compared with the North. That is, as of May 1970, the minimum wage prevailing in the North was Cr$ 134.40 versus Cr$ 124.80 for most of the Northeast.

Problems of comparability between the 1960 and 1970 censuses prevent a direct assessment of changes in the personal distribution of income in the North. Data for the combined North and central West (Mato Grosso, Goiás, and the Federal District) suggest that some increase in income concentration did occur, but to a lesser degree than at the national level. During this same period, however, real per capita income grew by only 10 percent in the North and cen-

TABLE 3.11

Indicators of Personal Income Distribution, 1970

Indicator	North	Northeast	Brazil
Percentile[a]			
Top 10 percent	39.85	47.11	47.30
Lowest 50 percent	21.63	16.28	15.04
Gini coefficient	.46	.56	.57
EAP < RMW (percent)[b]	40	60–70[c]	40

[a]Data expressed in percentage of total regional income received.
[b]Proportion of economically active population earning less than the regional minimum wage.
[c]Not available for entire region; figure varies within these limits according to subregion.

Source: C. G. Langoni, Distribuição da Renda e Desenvolvimento Econômico do Brasil (Rio de Janeiro: Editora Expressão e Cultura, 1973), chaps. 1 and 7.

tral West versus the 36.9 percent rate attained by Brazil as a whole.[18] From this set of facts, one could hypothesize that, due to a generally lower rate of economic activity, these regions did not experience the labor shortages (and, hence, increasing wage differentials) to the extent experienced in the more economically dynamic regions.

Table 3.12, which disaggregates the regional income distribution into its primary and urban components, demonstrates that the low regional index of concentration is completely attributable to the highly even distribution of income among the rural population. This holds true for all of Brazil's regions, with the degree of rural income concentration appearing to be positively associated with the level of modernization in the agricultural sector. According to one interpretation, this tendency is due to the extensive nature of agriculture in poorer regions and the relative homogeneity of the labor input.[19] This explanation would seem to be especially applicable to Amazonia where (with the exception of black pepper cultivation) agricultural techniques remain primitive and gains in production are achieved mainly through the utilization of new land.[20] Differentiation among the agricultural labor force also seems to be negligible, with almost 62 percent of the rural population classified as illiterate. For these reasons, it is possible to partially reconcile the relatively even distribution of rural income in poorer regions with the relatively inequitable distribution of land that characterizes these same areas.

TABLE 3.12

North Region: Indicators of Personal Income Distribution in Primary
and Urban Sectors, 1970

Indicator	Primary Sector	Urban Sector
Percentile[a]		
Top 10 percent	29.91	44.11
Lowest 50 percent	24.00	17.35
Gini coefficient	.30	.53
Average income (Cr$ per month)	159.83	329.52
EAP < RMW (percent)[b]	40	30

[a]Data expressed in percentage of total sectoral income received.
[b]Proportion of economically active population earning less than
the regional minimum wage.

Source: C. G. Langoni, Distribuição da Renda e Desenvolvimento Econômico do Brasil (Rio de Janeiro: Editora Expressão e Cultura, 1973), chaps. 1 and 7.

The distribution of income among the urban population is considerably more concentrated than among the rural population. The explanation would seem to lie in the greater diversity of the urban occupational structure. This heterogeneity is perhaps most evident in the region's relatively large service sector where occupations (and concomitant remuneration) vary widely.[21] In addition, it is probable that the supply of trained urban workers is highly inelastic and that increases in demand are almost entirely reflected in wages and salaries.

SUMMARY

Considering its size, Amazonia accounts for an insignificant portion of national production and income. Aggregate economic growth has slightly exceeded national rates in the postwar years, but per capita income levels remain at half the Brazilian average. Within the region, income and economic activities are concentrated in a few geographical areas, namely, Belém and Manaus. Furthermore, it appears that government policies have encouraged even greater polarization. The Zona Franca de Manaus, however, while contributing to greater income concentration within the state of Amazonas, has apparently narrowed average economic differentials between eastern and western Amazonia.

The structure of the regional economy is traditional with a small and relatively declining industrial sector. Agriculture, which also stagnated during the 1960s, is of the most rudimentary type. As of 1970, it employed about 70 percent of the regional labor force, but generated only 20 percent of the regional income. Services comprise the largest and most dynamic of the productive sectors. The dynamism of this sector is attributed not only to the high urban growth rates of the 1960s but also to the expanding developmental role of the public sector. From data for the early 1970s, it was shown that the federal government channels significant net flows of resources to the region each year.

Trade continues to be an important aspect of the regional economy, although a general stagnation of exports (both foreign and interregional) has reduced potential economic growth rates. Imports, on the other hand, have been characterized by unusually high rates of growth. This latter phenomenon has been primarily caused by public policies; that is, government transfers and tax credit funds have provided the necessary purchasing power, while industrialization and "integration" programs have stimulated demand. As a result, the trade balance of Amazonia has turned sharply negative on both interregional and international accounts. Although the trade structure modernized somewhat during the period of study, it continues to reflect a "center-periphery" relationship with extraregional markets.

The agrarian structure of Amazonia is characterized by concentrated ownership and extensive use of the land. Since most of the region is newly opened frontier, however, boundary lines and possession rights still tend to be ill-defined and arbitrary. With new migrants and corporate interests simultaneously entering Amazonia, this latter aspect of the land tenure situation has created conditions for violent social conflict that will not be easily resolved in the near future.

Somewhat surprisingly, the income distribution prevailing in Amazonia is the most equitable among Brazil's macroregions. Moreover, it was shown that the distribution is considerably more equal in rural areas than in the cities. The positive aspects of well-distributed rural incomes, however, are almost completely mitigated by the very low average incomes characteristic of rural occupations.

NOTES

1. For general studies of this nature (with emphasis on the Northeast), see R. Cavalcanti de Albuquerque and C. de V. Cavalcan-

ti, Desenvolvimento Regional no Brasil, Série Estudos para o Planejamento, no. 16 (Brasilia: IPEA/IPLAN, 1976); O. E. Rebouças, "Interregional Effects of Economic Policies: Multi-Sectoral General Equilibrium Estimates for Brazil" (Ph.D. diss., Harvard University, 1974); P. Haddad and T. A. Andrade, "Política Fiscal e Desequilíbrios Regionais," Estudos Econômicos 4 (1974): 9-54; H. Gauthier and R. Semple, "Tendências nas Desigualdades Regionais na Economia Brasileira, 1947-1966," Dados 9 (1972): 103-13; D. H. Graham, "Divergent and Convergent Regional Economic Growth and Internal Migration in Brazil, 1940-1960," Economic Development and Cultural Change 18 (1970): 362-82; and W. Baer, "Regional Inequality and Economic Growth in Brazil," Economic Development and Cultural Change 12 (1964): 268-85.

2. A critique of this approach may be found in J. Redwood, III, "The Recent Evolution of Regional Income Disparities in Brazil," Texto para Discussão, no. 39, mimeographed (Recife: Universidade Federal de Pernambuco/PIMES), 1976.

3. Using 1970 as a benchmark year introduces a distortion when comparing income behavior in the Northeast with that of other regions. Due to a severe drought in this year, the gross income of the Northeast achieved an unusually low growth rate of 2.1 percent. Unfortunately, the regional accounts for the Northeast are not completely consistent with those of the North and, thus, another year could not be utilized for comparison. See Superintendência do Desenvolvimento do Nordeste (SUDENE), Estimativas do Produto e da Formação Bruta de Capital do Nordeste no Período 1965-1972 (Recife, 1974), p. 12.

4. Most of the data for the following discussion are adapted from Fundação Getúlio Vargas (IBRE)/SUDAM, Agregados Econômicos Regionais, vol. 1: Produto Interno (October 1974), and are expressed in 1975 constant prices. The average exchange rate in 1975 was Cr$ 8.126 = U.S. $1.

5. The dynamism of the service sector is undoubtedly related to the accelerated rate of urbanization observed in the North during the 1960s. However, the hypertrophy of the Commerce subsector (almost 25 percent of total regional income) is often attributed to the aviamento system of rural credit. This system, a form of debt peonage in its worst manifestations, is usually associated with the extractive economy. Its workings are discussed at length in R. Santos, "O Equilíbrio da Firma Aviadora e a Significação Econômica," Pará Desenvolvimento 3 (1968): 7-30; N. Miyazaki and M. Ono, "O Aviamento na Amazônia," Sociologia, vol. 20 (1958); and C. Wagley, Amazon Town: A Study of Man in the Tropics (New York: Macmillan, 1953).

6. These examples, of course, are by no means exhaustive. In the very broadest sense, every public activity (for example, for-

eign exchange and tariff policies, price and wage controls, money and credit, and the like) will have some impact on every region in an open economy. For further research on this topic, see Rebouças, op. cit.; J. Redwood, III, "Algumas Notas sobre Exportações e Desenvolvimento Regional," Pesquisa e Planejamento Econômico 6 (1976): 431-59. With specific reference to Amazonia, also see A. D. Mendes, "Uma Nova Política de Valorização da Amazônia," Revista de Ciências Jurídicas, Econômicas e Sociais 1 (1963): 163-87; and J. Hebette et al., A Amazônia no Processo de Integração Nacional (Belém: Universidade Federal do Pará, NAEA/FIPAM, 1974).

7. Calvacanti de Albuquerque and Cavalcanti, op. cit., p. 123.

8. Other federal taxes shared with the state and local governments are the "sole taxes" (impostos únicos) on petroleum products, electric energy, and minerals and the "education tax" (salário educação). For each of these taxes, the sharing formulas have also tended to favor the North. This point is quantitatively verified in A. B. de Araujo, M. H. T. T. Horta, and C. M. Considera, Transferências de Impostos aos Estados e Municípios, Relatório de Pesquisa, no. 16 (Rio de Janeiro: IPEA/INPES, 1973), pp. 79-87.

9. Municípios other than capital cities were to receive their shares on the basis of population only. The distribution criteria are explained in more detail in ibid., pp. 52-58.

10. Although intergovernmental transfers have greatly augmented the funds available to states and municípios, they also have reduced the fiscal autonomy of these governments in poorer regions. In the North, transfers from the federal government account for 60 percent of local revenues and 48 percent of state revenues (1975 data). Budgetary independence is further reduced by the stipulation that tax shares be earmarked by specific economic and functional categories. For more details, see ibid.

11. Although they are not directly analyzed here, it is doubtful whether the export-incentive policies adopted in the late 1960s and early 1970s did much to stimulate exports of the North. On the contrary, most of the benefits of these policies have been confined to the Center-South. It must be remembered, however, that Amazonia did gain an incentive to import capital and technology through the creation of the Zona Franca de Manaus. For a more detailed treatment of these questions, see Chapter 5 and Redwood, op. cit., pp. 431-59.

12. It has been argued that this situation has created a system of intraregional dependency where "eastern Amazonia earns foreign exchange, which appears in the statistics for Amazonia as a whole, while the western subregion spends it for its own benefit." This thesis, however, seems to be stretching the concept of "dependency" as the two subregions added together account for less than 4 percent of

total Brazilian imports and exports. See A. Mendes, A Invenção da Amazônia (Belém: Universidade Federal do Pará, 1974), pp. 116, 187.

13. Domestic production of synthetic rubber had already surpassed that of natural rubber by 1963. Ten years later, it was five times as large (data from Conjuntura Econômica 30 [1976]: 87). Jute (used mainly for coffee sacks) has also been gradually replaced by plastic sacks and by containerized shipments. However, a large, unsatisfied internal demand persists. In 1974, for example, Brazil imported 30,000 tons of jute, an amount equal to 50 percent of Amazonia's annual production.

14. A major exception to this rule occurred during the 1870-1912 boom when control over prime rubber-producing areas was commonly achieved through violent means. A fascinating account of these episodes is R. Collier, The River That God Forgot: The Story of the Amazon Rubber Boom (London: Collins, Ltd., 1968).

15. This technique is, of course, "rational" only in a situation of low population density. When practiced on a large-scale basis, it can be extremely harmful to the natural environment. See B. J. Meggers, "Environment and Culture in Amazonia," in Man in the Amazon, ed. C. Wagley (Gainesville: University Presses of Florida, 1974), pp. 91-110.

16. Coefficients of concentration (Gini) based on the 1970 Agricultural Census are as follows: Brazil, .84; Northeast and central West, .85; North, .83; Southeast, .75; and South, .72. According to the 1960 census, the coefficient for the North was .94. See R. Hoffman and J. F. Graziano da Silva, "A Estrutura Agrária Brasileira," in Tecnologia e Desenvolvimento Agrícola, ed. C. R. Contador, Série Monográfica, no. 17 (Rio de Janeiro: IPEA/INPES, 1975), pp. 246-51.

17. Further discussion of this question may be found in G. Müller et al., "Amazônia: Desenvolvimento Sócio-Econômico e Políticas de População," mimeographed (São Paulo: Centro Brasileiro de Análise e Planejamento, 1975), 1: 48-49.

18. C. G. Langoni, Distribuição da Renda e Desenvolvimento Econômico do Brasil (Rio de Janeiro: Editora Expressão e Cultura, 1973), p. 172.

19. Ibid., p. 167.

20. According to calculations made by George Patrick, 97 percent of the growth in the North's production of crops in the 1948-69 period was due to increases in the land input. See G. Patrick, "Fontes de Crescimento na Agricultura Brasileira: O Setor de Culturas," in Tecnologia e Desenvolvimento Agrícola, ed. C. R. Contador, Série Monográfica, no. 17 (Rio de Janeiro: IPEA/INPES, 1975), p. 96.

21. A recent study of nine metropolitan areas of Brazil shows
that the highest average urban incomes are earned in the technical
and scientific occupations and the lowest in the personal services.
For the total sample, average incomes received in the former occupations exceeded those received in the latter by a ratio of 8.3:1. In
the case of Belém, the only Amazonian city in the sample, this ratio
rose to 9.3:1. Indeed, the findings of this study indicate that the rate
of income dispersion among all urban occupations tends to be higher
in the North and Northeast than in the South and Southeast. See
C. A. Lodder, Distribuição de Renda nas Áreas Metropolitanas,
Coleção Relatórios de Pesquisa, no. 31 (Rio de Janeiro: IPEA/INPES,
1976), pp. 29–39.

4

Fiscal Incentives of Sudam

Since the early 1960s, regional policies in Brazil have clearly been a joint venture of the public and private sectors. In general, the role of the public sector has been to improve the preinvestment conditions of the poorer regions through infrastructure development, colonization, research, and other programs. The private sector, on the other hand, has been entrusted with the establishment of directly productive activities in industry, agriculture, and the services. In this latter endeavor, government has further enhanced the "investment climate" through an impressive array of fiscal incentives.[1]

The use of the fiscal mechanism for inducing desired modes of economic behavior is by no means novel; it has been employed in a number of countries (both developed and underdeveloped) with varying degrees of success.[2] Nowhere, however, has this policy tool been used more extensively for promoting regional development than in Brazil.[3] In this latter case, fiscal incentives have been designed to artificially lower the relative price of capital in the capital-scarce Northeast and Amazon. In conjunction with complementary public expenditures, they have thus raised the profitability of private investment in these regions and induced economic activities that presumably would not have existed otherwise. Although serious questions may be raised about the allocative efficiency of such a strategy (in national terms), policy makers evidently consider this factor to be a short-run trade-off unavoidably linked to the goal of more balanced regional growth.[4]

The purpose of this and the following chapters is to critically evaluate the fiscal incentive as a policy tool for the economic development of Amazonia. More specifically, we quantify and analyze the volume and pattern of investment induced by this mechanism and, in turn, assess the appropriateness of this investment to the region's socioeconomic and natural environments. Since the fiscal legislation pertaining to Amazonia is both comprehensive and complex, the present chapter concentrates on the system of investment tax credits jointly administered by SUDAM and BASA. Other types of fiscal incentives operating in Amazonia, for example, "tax holidays" and exemptions from customs duties, are described in Chapter 1. The additional fiscal incentives at the disposal of SUFRAMA are the principal subjects of Chapter 5.

THE TAX-CREDIT MECHANISM

The system of investment tax credits currently applying to Amazonia traces its origins to 1961 (Law 3995 of December 14) when such a mechanism was set up to attract industrial capital to the Northeast.[5] Identical legislation was extended to Amazonia in 1963 (Law 4216 of May 6) and, in a modified form, still remains as the core of the system. However, since it applied during the greatest number of years (1966-74), the relevant legislation for present purposes is Law 5174 (October 27, 1966).

The basic element of Law 5174 was that registered Brazilian corporations (pessoas jurídicas could take up to a 50 percent credit against their federal income tax liability if the resulting savings were invested in projects located within the "legal Amazon," and approved by SUDAM. Since the early 1970s, 50 percent of these deposits have been earmarked for PIN and PROTERRA. This obligatory deduction applies not only to SUDAM deposits but also to those of SUDENE and the sectoral development agencies: IBDF (forestry), EMBRATUR (tourism), and SUDEPE (fishing). Investment projects could be new enterprises or simply represent the expansion or modernization of existing enterprises. Moreover, they could be in the areas of agriculture, livestock, industry, and basic services.

Once a firm opted for the tax credit, its funds were deposited in a blocked account with BASA and could only be utilized upon their commitment to a specified approved project. The legislation further stipulated that deposits not committed within two years automatically reverted to BASA. Such funds could then be employed by BASA for the financing of private investment deemed essential to the economic development of Amazonia (through the Fundo para Investimentos Privados no Desenvolvimento da Amazônia—FIDAM).

As previously indicated, firms with a project located (or desiring to locate) in Amazonia had to first obtain approval from SUDAM before they were permitted to absorb tax-credit deposits. This stage was crucial since it determined the proportion of "fresh money" (recursos próprios) that the beneficiary firm would be required to con-

tribute to its own investment project.* In order to determine priority levels, SUDAM relied upon a ranking system according to which
any given project would be assigned to one of four categories. De-
pending on the priority assigned to a project, tax-credit funds could
constitute up to 75 percent of total investment. Although selection
and ranking criteria have changed several times over the years, rank-
ings have tended to be positively related to use of regional inputs,
employment generation, level of technology, contribution to the national balance of payments, and location in priority areas. The most
recent ranking system is outlined in SUDAM's Resolution 2525 (April
12, 1976).

Under Law 5174, firms seeking investment of their tax-credit
deposits could choose a project of their own (if approved by SUDAM)
or select among a list of other approved projects. To effect the transfer of funds in the latter type of transaction, the interested parties
commonly employed private brokerage houses specifically established
for this purpose. Upon completion of the transaction, the depositor
most often received shares of preferred, nonvoting stock in the beneficiary firm that could not be negotiated for a period of five years.
Under special circumstances, tax-credit funds could take the form of
loan capital, but with the proviso that no more than 20 percent of the
loan could be amortized in any one year, at an interest rate not exceeding 12 percent.

With the most recent modification of the tax-credit legislation
(Decree-Law 1376 of December 12, 1974), the intermediary function
has been absorbed by a mutual fund (Fundo de Investimentos da Amazônia—FINAM) under the supervision of SUDAM and BASA. Similar
funds have been set up for investing the tax-credit deposits of SUDENE
and the sectoral development agencies. The investment function is
performed by these mutual funds at a nominal 3 percent fee. Under
Decree-Law 1376, depositors initially receive shares in FINAM.
The fund, in turn, acquires shares of stock in firms carrying out
projects approved by SUDAM. The depositors may hold or sell their
shares in the fund or trade them for corporate stock held by FINAM.
Depositors with their own projects may directly acquire shares of
their own stock. However, all corporate stock acquired from the
FINAM portfolio is nonnegotiable for a period of four years.

---

*It also determined a given project's eligibility for supplemen-
tary financing by BASA. Since this financing was generally extended
at below-market interest rates, it, in itself, constituted an important
incentive. The most favorable terms were extended to the highest
priority projects as determined by SUDAM.

THE FLOW OF FUNDS:
SUPPLY AND DEMAND FACTORS

The problem of equilibrating the supply of, and demand for, tax-credit funds has been an ongoing concern of the agencies entrusted with their administration. When supply exceeds demand, for example, regional and/or sectoral development plans are constrained by low rates of private capital formation. In the opposite case, development is impeded by the inability to finance new, deserving projects and by the difficulty in providing funds, on schedule, to projects already in the initial stages of implementation.

In general, the total supply of tax-credit funds is a function of corporate profits, which are, in turn, contingent upon national economic conditions. The factors governing the flow of funds to any one option, however, are not so obvious. One would expect that a depositor's choice of option would be principally determined by the prospects of profit in a given region or sector, as well as by the intrinsic merits of the available projects. The degree of profitability, however, is determined by a host of factors including infrastructure development, the existence of a market, the size and quality of the local labor force, the expected tax burden, and the availability of necessary inputs. To this list of factors one must also add the influence of regionalism, which may affect the depositors' knowledge of economic conditions in regions or sectors other than their own and their ability to properly supervise the implementation and subsequent operation of their investments.

The factors governing the demand for tax-credit funds would seem to be closely associated with those influencing their supply. (In fact, when depositors have their own investment projects, supply creates its own demand.) Like the supply side, the demand for tax-credit funds is related to expected profits, even when the beneficiary firm is not using its own deposits; this is because deposits are not really "free" in the economic sense and because the beneficiary firm must always provide some "fresh money" to its investment project. That is, if a beneficiary firm uses its own tax-credit deposits, it must consider the opportunity costs of forgoing alternative investment projects; if it uses the deposits of others, it must pay a nominal return on the preferred stock or loan capital, plus any brokerage fees. Another factor affecting the demand for funds is the nature of the selection process, since demand cannot be effective until an investment project has been approved. In this respect, a faster and more perfunctory selection process will produce a much greater effective demand for tax-credit funds than one characterized by careful, prolonged analyses. Of course, the latter method may very well be the most effective in the long run.

Table 4.1 illustrates the supply of investment tax credits, by option, during the period from 1962 to 1975. As may be noted, SUDAM and SUDENE were virtually the only competitors for these funds during the early part of the 1960s. Until 1966, SUDENE clearly dominated, accounting for around 90 percent of total available funds. For the rest of the decade, however, SUDAM rapidly gained on SUDENE in relative terms, despite competition from the new sectoral development agencies. Although many factors may be suggested to explain the favorable reaction to investment opportunities in Amazonia, perhaps the most important were the completion and paving of the Belém-Brasilia highway, the increased national awareness of the region produced by Operation Amazonia, and the liberalization of the basic tax-credit mechanism.*

In real terms, the amount of tax-credit funds available for regional development reached its peak in 1970. During 1971 and 1972, both SUDAM and SUDENE experienced sharp absolute and relative declines in their supply of funds. Although a slight recovery is evident in the 1973-75 period, total tax credits at their disposal in the latter year were still less than the 1970 level in real terms. A major explanation of this unfavorable trend was the creation of PIN and PROTERRA in 1970 and 1971, respectively. As has been previously mentioned, the financing of these programs effectively reduced the absolute supply of tax-credit funds by 50 percent. The relative declines of SUDAM and SUDENE, however, are more closely linked to further modifications of the fiscal legislation, which greatly increased the attractiveness of the IBDF (forestry) option and also created new options not subject to PIN-PROTERRA earmarking.[6] Together these factors created serious problems for SUDAM (and SUDENE) in terms of meeting its obligations to approved projects as well as in its capacity to approve new projects.

Another aspect of supply with important implications for the economic development of Amazonia is the regional origin of tax-credit deposits. From Table 4.2, one may observe that, in the 1968-75 period, over 95 percent of all tax-credit options were owned by extraregional interests. Corporations registered in São Paulo, by

---

*Article 27 of Constitutional Amendment 18 (December 1, 1965) made firms with foreign capital eligible for tax-credit funds (previously, beneficiary firms had to be 100 percent national). Law 5174 expanded the choice of investment opportunities by permitting the use of tax credits in agricultural, livestock, and service projects (previously, the choice was confined to industry) and by raising the ceiling on the proportion of total investment costs financed by tax-credit funds from 50 to 75 percent.

TABLE 4.1

Corporate Investment Tax Credits by Option, 1962–75

(1975 prices)

	SUDAM		SUDENE		IBDF (forestry)		EMBRATUR (tourism)		SUDEPE (fishing)		Other[a]		Total	
	Cr$ Millions	Per-cent	Cr$ Millions	Per-cent	Cr$ Millions	Per-cent	Cr$ Millions	Per-cent	Cr$ Millions	Per-cent	Cr$ Millions	Per-cent	Cr$ Millions	Per-cent
1962	—	—	253.3	100.0	—[b]	—	—	—	—	—	—	—	253.3	100.0
1963	27.4	12.3	195.4	87.7	—	—	—	—	—	—	—	—	222.8	100.0
1964	44.1	8.2	496.0	91.8	—	—	—	—	—	—	—	—	540.1	100.0
1965	110.7	8.0	1,268.0	92.0	—	—	—	—	—	—	—	—	1,378.7	100.0
1966	287.5	17.1	1,391.9	82.9	—	—	—	—	—	—	—	—	1,679.4	100.0
1967	487.8	22.5	1,681.5	77.5	—	—	—	—	—	—	—	—	2,169.3	100.0
1968	636.0	22.8	1,796.6	64.5	43.2	1.6	138.9	5.0	170.4	6.1	—	—	2,785.1	100.0
1969	830.9	23.4	2,000.5	56.4	131.9	3.7	142.4	4.0	442.9	12.5	—	—	3,548.6	100.0
1970	1,022.8	22.0	2,503.5	53.7	306.1	6.6	181.3	3.9	622.6	13.4	24.3	0.5	4,660.6	100.0
1971	736.2	17.6	1,649.2	39.3	921.8	22.0	207.0	4.9	530.4	12.7	149.6	3.6	4,194.2	100.0
1972	563.2	16.8	1,502.6	44.8	748.5	22.3	145.3	4.3	205.5	6.1	191.2	5.7	3,356.3	100.0
1973	625.6	15.8	1,820.4	46.0	917.2	23.2	195.4	4.9	170.8	4.3	231.7	5.9	3,961.1	100.0
1974	848.1	17.7	2,167.6	45.2	1,154.9	24.1	201.1	4.2	114.4	2.4	308.1	6.4	4,793.9	100.0
1975	812.8	16.7	2,565.2	52.8	937.5	19.3	121.6	2.5	100.9	2.1	317.6	6.5	4,855.6	100.0

[a]Empresa Brasileiro de Aeronautica (EMBRAER), (aircraft industry), Espírito Santo (state development), Movimento Brasileiro de Alfabetizacao (MOBRAL), (literacy campaign).

[b]Not applicable; option not in existence.

Note: Excludes allocations to PIN and PROTERRA (1970–75 period); prices adjusted by Fundação Getúlio Vargas general price index (Conjuntura Econômica, column 2).

Sources: IBGE, Anuário Estatístico do Brasil (various years); Banco Central do Brasil.

TABLE 4.2

SUDAM Corporate Investment Tax Credits by Geographical Origin, 1968–75

	North		Northeast		Southeast		South		Central West	
	Percent of Total	RP[a]	Percent of Total	RP	Percent of Total	RP	Percent of Total	RP	Percent of Total	RP
1968	3.1	3.52	0.4	0.06	77.2	1.01	14.2	1.01	5.1	2.22
1969	4.2	4.77	0.4	0.06	74.6	0.86	14.6	1.12	6.2	2.66
1970	3.7	4.93	0.5	0.09	77.1	1.01	13.9	0.98	4.8	1.55
1971	4.0	4.35	1.6	0.30	77.5	1.00	10.9	0.81	6.0	2.25
1972	4.6	5.35	0.4	0.08	75.4	0.97	13.9	1.04	5.7	1.85
1973	3.5	4.07	0.4	0.90	76.9	0.99	12.7	0.91	6.5	1.74
1974	4.3	5.38	0.3	0.70	76.3	1.01	12.9	0.87	6.2	1.56
1975[b]	3.7	5.30	0.3	0.03	73.2	0.98	14.9	1.00	7.9	1.83

[a]Regional preference = $\dfrac{\text{SUDAM options in region}}{\text{Total SUDAM options}} \Big/ \dfrac{\text{Corporate income tax collections in region}}{\text{Total corporate income tax collections}}$

[b]FIDAM option.

Note: IBGE macroregions.

Source: IBGE, Anuário Estatístico do Brasil (1969–75).

themselves, accounted for about 60 percent of the total. Of course, the regional concentration of tax-credit ownership is highly related to the concentration of taxable activities in São Paulo, and in the Center-South generally. With this fact in mind, a measure of "regional preference" was calculated that compares a given macroregion's percentage participation in total federal corporate income tax collections to its percentage ownership of SUDAM tax-credit deposits.

On the basis of these calculations, one may observe that a certain amount of regionalism is involved in the choice of tax-credit options. This point is illustrated by the relatively high "regional-preference" coefficients (a coefficient of 1.00 is considered "neutral") of corporations registered in the North and central West (the latter macroregion is partially included in "legal Amazonia") and the extremely low coefficients of corporations registered in the Northeast. Obviously, corporations located in areas eligible for regional development options prefer to use tax credits for their own benefit or for the benefit of local entrepreneurial groups. In contrast, corporations located in the industrialized Southeast and South are essentially "neutral" about the SUDAM option; that is, their percentage participation in total SUDAM options approximates their relative contribution to total corporate income tax receipts.

Even though Center-South corporations are neutral in their choice of the SUDAM option, the fact remains that they own or control a significant proportion of recent private investment in Amazonia. Although this phenomenon is probably inevitable, given the present regional distribution of corporate savings, its impact on development efforts in Amazonia is not necessarily neutral.

Perhaps the greatest risk involved is the heightened possibility that earnings from functioning investment projects will flow back to the Center-South (in the form of profit remittances or by the importation of inputs) rather than being retained in the region, thus greatly reducing intraregional production linkages. Another possibility increased by the regionally concentrated ownership of tax-credit funds is that depositors will take only a minimal interest in the actual operation of their investment project, delegating this function instead to administrators who may or may not be qualified for the task. The severity of this latter problem would seem to be directly related to the project's geographical distance from the investing corporation's main headquarters. It would also seem to be related to the extent the product line of the investment project differs from that of the investing corporation.

Table 4.3 summarizes the supply and demand aspects of SUDAM tax-credit funds during the 1963-75 period. Immediately apparent from these data is the changing relationship between tax-credit deposits and their commitment to approved projects. Until 1971, the annual

TABLE 4.3

Flows of SUDAM Tax-Credit Fund, 1963-75
(Cr$ millions)

Year	Deposits (1)	Deposits (2)	Commitments (1)	Commitments (2)	Disbursements (1)	Disbursements (2)
1963	1.1	27.4	—	—	—	—
1964	3.3	44.1	0.35	4.7	—	—
1965	13.0	110.7	0.75	6.4	1.1	9.3
1966	46.8	287.5	17.8	109.3	9.4	57.7
1967	101.9	487.8	28.7	137.5	30.4	145.6
1968	164.9	636.0	75.7	291.9	80.5	310.5
1969	260.2	830.9	131.6	420.2	149.8	478.3
1970	383.7	1,022.8	313.9	836.6	329.8	879.0
1971	332.6	736.2	442.0	978.1	328.2	726.4
1972	297.7	563.2	520.5	984.9	322.7	610.6
1973	380.6	625.6	696.2	1,144.3	341.0	560.5
1974	664.1	848.1	859.5	1,097.7	453.3	578.9
1975	812.8	812.8	1,239.3	1,239.3	986.8	986.8
Total	3,462.7	7,033.1	4,326.3	7,250.9	3,032.8	5,343.6

Note: Columns (1) and (2) are in current and 1975 prices, respectively.

Sources: Anuário Estatístico do Brasil (various years); unpublished data provided by Banco Central do Brasil; and SUDAM.

supply of funds (deposits) was always greater than the demand (commitments) for them. This tendency obviously gave rise to a wide margin of uncommitted resources (accumulated deposits less accumulated commitments), which, by 1970, was equivalent to about 50 percent of the accumulated deposits as of that year (in real terms).

After 1970, the former situation completely inverted, as annual commitments persistently exceeded annual deposits. This new state of affairs was essentially caused by SUDAM's failure to reduce project approvals at a rate commensurate with declining trends on the supply side. As an inevitable consequence, the margin of uncommitted funds fell rapidly during the early 1970s and completely disappeared by 1975. Also inevitable was the intensified competition for tax-credit funds among firms with approved projects. In this competition, the equilibrating factor was the brokerage fee charged for "capturing" deposits. Although these fees were limited by law to 5 percent of the transaction, in reality they rose to 30 percent or higher for smaller, lesser-known firms. As a result, otherwise viable projects were forced to delay their implementation while they sought additional funding from SUDAM (via project "reformulations") and/or from the banking system (private or official). This extremely undesirable aspect of the supply and demand disequilibrium was perhaps the most important factor leading to the establishment of FINAM in late 1974.

A relatively slow rate of project implementation is reflected in the data on disbursements. As illustrated in Table 4.3, the rate of absorption rose rapidly during the 1960s and then dropped off during the 1970s. Though the growth of tax-credit deposits also slowed during this latter period, net accumulated deposits (accumulated deposits less accumulated disbursements) were higher in 1975 than in 1970 (Cr$ 1.7 billion versus Cr$ 1.6 billion, in real terms). For the entire 1963-75 period, about 76 percent of total deposits were actually spent. The high cost of intermediation is an important factor explaining the slow rate of project implementation (and resource absorption), but by no means the only one.

Another important factor was the delay generally encountered by firms submitting projects to SUDAM for analysis. These bureaucratic delays often lasted for two years during which time original project specifications became increasingly unreal as a result of the effects of inflation.[7] Therefore, even projects receiving the full amount of requested funds expressed in nominal terms found themselves highly underfinanced in real terms. Quite obviously, the actual implementation of such projects was contingent upon locating a source of supplemental funds on reasonable terms. This unexpected requirement, at best, delayed implementation and at times caused the entire project to be abandoned.

With the recent modification of the tax-credit mechanism and the creation of FINAM, many of the factors causing supply and demand disequilibriums should be eradicated. Certainly, the disappearance of exorbitant brokerage fees will greatly improve the system's efficiency on the supply side. In efficiently organizing the demand side, it would seem that the major burden rests on the project-selection apparatus of SUDAM. Since the tax-credit mechanism is presently in a deficit situation (accumulated commitments exceed accumulated deposits), the rate of new-project approval is constrained by the current inflow of tax-credit funds; that is, SUDAM must earmark a sizable portion of current inflows for honoring past commitments. One would hope that this situation is promoting greater precision and efficiency in the project-analysis stage.

In a very real sense, the new tax-credit mechanism has reduced the autonomy of SUDAM and the private sector vis-à-vis the central government. As contrasted to the previous system, SUDAM must now submit its projected fund commitments for approval by the Economic Development Council (Conselho de Desenvolvimento Econômico). The council, in turn, may accept the proposed budget or shift the available tax-credit funds among the various regional and sectoral alternatives in accordance with national priorities.* Although these innovations will not necessarily work to the detriment of Amazonia, they do interfere with the individual depositor's freedom to choose among regions and sectors. It is too soon, however, to tell whether they will promote a more (or less) rational allocation of resources.

GENERAL INVESTMENT PATTERNS

To further characterize and evaluate the tax-credit mechanism, data were gathered on 541 firms located, or locating, within "legal Amazonia." Each of these firms was approved by SUDAM and, to some extent, financed through tax-credit deposits. The present section considers the general characteristics of these enterprises, while the following discuss more specific aspects on a sectoral basis. The primary data employed in the analyses were drawn from original project specifications (pareceres) submitted to SUDAM as a required part of the selection-and-approval process; for this reason, the findings may be regarded only as approximations of reality. (See the Appendix for a more detailed discussion of the methodology utilized in processing these data.) In partial compensation, the analyses are supplemented by secondary sources dealing with the actual operation of these projects.

Temporal and Sectoral Trends

Between 1964 and mid-1976, SUDAM approved over 800 projects for tax-credit funds: 329 industrial, 462 livestock, and 27 in the "basic services." Of this total, 472 were new to the region (implantações), 106 were expansions or modernizations (ampliações/modernizações) of existing enterprises, and 242 were "reformulations" (reformulações) of projects previously approved by SUDAM. As a first approximation, the efficiency of the tax-credit mechanism

*Adjustments in the supply of tax credits are effectuated through transfers among the SUDAM, SUDENE, and sectoral mutual funds, that is, one mutual fund purchases shares of another. Legislation also permits the central government to purchase shares of the mutual funds, although these shares may not be traded for corporate stock.

(especially its administrative dimensions) is indicated by the time pattern and category of these approvals.

In terms of both numbers and projected investment, the peak period was 1967-72. During these six years, SUDAM approved 368 new projects (78 percent of this category) and 65 expansions or modernizations (61 percent). These firms represented projected investments of Cr$ 19.3 billion (in 1975 prices), or over 80 percent of the total approved through mid-1976. In contrast, the highest frequency of "reformulations" (169, or 70 percent of this category) is observed after 1971.

These data suggest that in recent years, SUDAM has been primarily engaged in recuperating projects approved during the 1960s and early 1970s, rather than innovating with new types of projects. Of course, a major explanation of this situation has been the declining supply of investment funds caused by the PIN-PROTERRA earmarking provisions and the high intermediation costs characterizing the pre-1975 system, factors that have necessarily put a ceiling on new project approvals. To a certain extent, however, the high incidence of "reformulations" since 1971 reflects a bureaucratic process that, in the past, has given approval to projects of dubious economic viability.

The time series on project approvals also illustrates the sectoral priorities of both SUDAM and the owners of tax-credit deposits. From these data, it may be observed that the most important period for industry occurred between 1966 and 1970, an era roughly coinciding with Operation Amazonia and its emphasis on import-substitution industrialization (see Chapter 1). Excluding "reformulations," 131 industrial projects were approved during these years, accounting for over 60 percent of total approvals and expected investment in this sector. The relative attractiveness of the livestock sector becomes apparent, however, as early as 1967 when 46 such projects were approved (as opposed to 26 in industry). In all years since 1967, moreover, approvals in the livestock sector have equaled or exceeded, usually by a wide margin, those in the industrial sector. Approvals in the basic services sector, in contrast, have remained numerically small with no obvious temporal pattern.

The incentive given to livestock development is further confirmed by the relatively high ratios of tax credits to total investment observed in this sector. Averaging all projects approved through mid-1976, this percentage rises to over 70 percent, indicating that livestock projects have generally been placed in the highest-priority category during the selection-and-approval process. For industrial and basic services projects, the relative importance of tax credits is considerably less, accounting for 47 and 30 percent, respectively, of their total equity capital. Although BASA financing has been most gen-

erously applied in the industrial sector, future credit allocations indicate an increasing preference for the livestock sector. During the
1975–79 period, for example, livestock is expected to receive 86 percent of this bank's agricultural loans, and almost 50 percent of the
grand total.

Despite the numerical superiority and higher priority of livestock, the industrial sector leads in total approved projected investment. Through mid-1976, over Cr$ 10 billion of industrial invest-
ment had been approved by SUDAM, as opposed to Cr$ 8.8 billion in
livestock and Cr$ 4.3 billion in the basic services (1975 prices). As
depicted in Table 4.4, estimates of investment realized between 1965
and 1975 also show industry in the lead. Because of the higher tax-
credit-to-total investment ratios encountered in livestock, however,
projects in this sector have absorbed the greatest amount of tax-
credit deposits: Cr$ 2.6 billion, versus Cr$ 2.4 billion by industry
and Cr$ 361 million by basic services. Of the Cr$ 9.7 billion total
investment (U.S. $1.2 billion) realized by SUDAM-approved enter-
prises, Cr$ 4.9 billion (U.S. $600 million) is accounted for by industry, Cr$ 3.6 billion (U.S. $443 million) by livestock, and Cr$ 1.2
billion (U.S. $146 million) by the "basic services." A comparison
of realized investment with projected investment further confirms
our earlier observations concerning the slow rate of project implementation. Through 1975, only 35 percent of total projected investment had actually been carried out.

Locational Aspects

When the data are tabulated according to states and territories,
one observes that investment has not been evenly distributed within
legal Amazonia. Almost 90 percent of the total has been (or will be)
realized in just three states, Pará, Mato Grosso, and Amazonas
(Table 4.5). A possible explanation of this pattern is the extreme
variation in population among the various administrative units. In
reality, however, per capita investment varies to an even greater
degree than the total, with the average in Mato Grosso being over
twice that of Pará and Amazonas, and over 30 times larger than that
of Maranhão. For a clearer understanding of locational factors one
must thus consider the data in more disaggregated terms. It should
be pointed out, however, that the state of Maranhão is also eligible
for SUDENE-administered tax-credit funds. Hence, its total benefit
from this mechanism has been considerably greater than these data
would imply.

Data at the sectoral level suggest that the main thrust of industrialization has been in the states of Pará and Amazonas; here, one

TABLE 4.4

SUDAM: Estimated Realized Investment, by Sector, 1965–75
(1975 prices)

	Industry		Livestock		Services		Total	
	Cr$ Millions	Per-cent	Cr$ Millions	Per-cent	Cr$ Millions	Per-cent	Cr$ Millions	Per-cent
1965	19.2	100.0	—*	—	—	—	19.2	100.0
1966	104.6	91.3	10.0	8.7	—	—	114.6	100.0
1967	195.3	73.4	69.9	26.3	0.8	0.3	266.0	100.0
1968	297.1	47.7	160.6	25.8	165.4	26.5	623.1	100.0
1969	457.8	53.3	335.2	39.0	66.5	7.7	859.5	100.0
1970	674.9	41.7	626.3	38.4	329.1	20.2	1,630.3	100.0
1971	609.3	45.7	504.0	37.8	221.2	16.6	1,334.5	100.0
1972	449.5	41.1	471.8	43.1	172.7	15.8	1,094.1	100.0
1973	520.9	52.7	397.2	40.2	70.7	7.2	988.8	100.0
1974	535.8	53.0	417.7	41.3	58.3	5.8	1,011.9	100.0
1975	1,031.2	58.5	631.3	35.8	101.8	5.8	1,764.3	100.0
Total	4,895.1	50.4	3,624.1	33.6	1,186.7	12.2	9,705.9	100.0

*Not applicable.

Source: IPEA/SUDAM/NAEA (unpublished survey).

TABLE 4.5

SUDAM: Spatial Distribution of Projected Investment
(1975 prices)

State/Territory	Industry		Livestock		Services		Total	
	Cr$ Millions	Per-cent	Cr$ Millions	Per-cent	Cr$ Millions	Per-cent	Cr$ Millions	Per-cent
Rondônia	82.3	0.8	35.7	0.4	6.8	0.2	124.8	0.5
Acre	26.8	0.3	214.7	2.4	34.9	0.8	276.4	1.2
Amazonas	2,425.9	23.9	313.5	3.6	1,945.8	45.4	4,685.2	20.2
Roraima	—	—	—	—	—	—	—	—
Pará	5,481.0	54.1	2,338.2	26.5	1,352.6	31.5	9,171.8	39.5
Amapá	236.7	2.3	—	—	651.1	15.2	887.8	3.8
Maranhão	794.6	7.8	132.7	1.5	78.1	1.8	1,005.4	4.3
Mato Grosso	804.1	7.9	5,397.2	61.2	217.0	5.1	6,418.3	27.6
Goiás	280.5	2.8	386.1	4.4	2.1	0.1	668.7	2.9
Amazonia	10,131.9	100.0	8,818.1	100.0	4,288.4	100.0	23,238.4	100.0

Note: Includes projects approved through mid-1976. Dashes indicate there were no approved projects.

Source: IPEA/SUDAM/NAEA (unpublished survey).

finds over three-fourths of total projected investment in both industry and the basic services. This pattern is not surprising, given that Belém and Manaus are the two most important urban centers of the region. Indeed, the data arranged by microregions indicate virtually all of the projected investment in Amazonas taking place in the Greater Manaus area (médio-Amazonas microregion). The rate of concentration within Pará is considerably less, with Greater Belém (Belém, Bragantina, and Viseu microregions) accounting for about 70 percent of the projected investment in industry and the basic services. However, if we exclude one large mining project (Mineração Rio do Norte) located in the northeast of Pará from the state total, the rate of concentration in the Belém area rises to almost 90 percent. From these findings one must conclude that, despite the stated desires of SUDAM, investors have found the hinterland of Amazonia an unattractive place to locate. Furthermore, as long as the interior continues to lack population and infrastructure, industrial investment will probably continue to concentrate in capital cities, except in instances where occurrences of natural resources fully compensate for the other locational disadvantages.

Livestock development has also concentrated within the region, although obviously over a much wider geographical area. As shown in Table 4.5, about 90 percent of the total projected investment in this sector is accounted for by the states of Mato Grosso and Pará, the former state alone accounting for over 60 percent. Aside from the existence of abundant, inexpensive land (which exists throughout Amazonia), the locational preferences of livestock project owners have been primarily influenced by the new interregional highway systems. Hence, we find the Pará projects concentrated in the eastern and southeastern part of the state in microregions (principally Araguaia Paraense, Guajarina, Xingú, and Marabá) that are adjacent to the Belém-Brasilia and trans-Amazon highways. The influence of the former highway system is also observed in the spatial distribution of projects in Goiás and Maranhão. The projects of Mato Grosso, on the other hand, are mainly grouped around the recently inaugurated Santarém-Cuiabá highway, which provides access to markets in both cities, as well as to those of Brasilia and the Center-South.

Employment and Capital Intensity

As emphasized in Chapter 1, one of the most important goals of public policies for Amazonia has been its human occupation. Clearly implicit in this goal is the generation of gainful employment, not only for the new settlers but for the native population as well. That the tax-credit mechanism was adopted to further this end, however, is somewhat paradoxical. Through the fiscal incentives and subsidized credit lines at their disposal, SUDAM-sponsored investors are actually encouraged to substitute capital (or land) for labor in their respective production functions. Although the implications of this will be more fully discussed later in this chapter, a few indicators serve to illustrate the point.

According to project specifications, SUDAM-approved enterprises will directly create about 58,000 new jobs when they reach their full implementation stages: 34,672 in industry, 15,468 in livestock, and 6,661 in the basic services (see Table 4.12). While the employment provided by industrial projects is equivalent to about one-fourth of the region's total industrial labor force, the figures for livestock and basic service projects are insignificant when compared with existing employment levels in the region's primary and tertiary sectors (see Table 2.2). Moreover, the data on the labor-absorption potential of industry are probably exaggerated because of the statistical treatment of projects in the expansion-modernization category. Data on employment in these cases are in gross (total employment generated by the firm), rather than in net, terms (employment gains generated by the expansion or modernization itself). Therefore, the real employment gains emanating from such projects (especially the modernization type) may approach zero. By excluding these projects from the total, the number of new jobs created in the industrial sector falls to less than 25,000, and the grand total to less than 50,000.

It seems likely that the strong subsidy to the capital (or land) input inherent in the tax-credit mechanism has been responsible for these low rates of labor absorption. For a greater (though still preliminary) perspective on this question, average capital-to-labor ratios were calculated for SUDAM projects and compared with those of alternative programs in Amazonia and the Northeast. The results of this procedure are presented in Table 4.6. It is apparent from these data that SUDAM projects have been extremely capital- or land-intensive, both in absolute terms and in relation to the SUDENE experience in the Northeast. In terms of average financial costs per workplace, SUDAM projects range from a low of U.S. $31,622 in industry to an astronomical U.S. $70,158 in the livestock sector. SUDENE projects (both industrial and agricultural), in contrast, have absorbed labor at an average financial cost of around U.S. $25,000. Equally striking is the huge difference in costs involved in employing rural workers on a cattle ranch as opposed to settling them in an agricultural colony.

INDUSTRIAL PROJECTS

Broad-based industrialization is usually considered to be the major avenue of escape from the problems associated with underde-

TABLE 4.6

Amazonia and Northeast: Capital-to-Labor Ratios
(U.S. dollars)

Colonization	
Amazonia (V. Tavares, IPEA)[a]	2,000
Altamira, Pará (FAO/IBRD)	1,944
Agriculture, livestock	
SUDAM	70,158
SUDENE (G. Patrick, IPEA)	25,156
Industry	
SUDAM[b]	31,622
SUFRAMA	17,948
SUDENE (D. Goodman, IPEA)[b]	23,652
Services	
SUDAM[b]	55,346

[a]Greatest frequency among various projects; refers to average cost per family.

[b]New projects (implantações) only.

Note: Converted at average 1975 rate, Cr$ 8.126 = U.S. $1.

Sources: S. S. Panagides and V. L. Magalhães, "Amazon Policy and Prospects," in Man in the Amazon, ed. C. Wagley (Gainesville: University Presses of Florida, 1974), p. 257; IPEA/SUDAM/NAEA (unpublished survey).

velopment. This point of view was obviously held by government officials who established the basic tax-credit mechanism in the early 1960s. Within Amazonia, industrialization was initially viewed as a means of freeing the regional economy from outside influences—both foreign and domestic. In the first instance, the desire was to avoid the destabilizing impact of the international markets for primary products (principally rubber). In the second, there was the feeling that the regional economy could not be self-sustaining until it reduced its dependence upon industrial interests located in the Center-South. In addition, it was felt that a policy of industrialization could provide gainful employment for the rapidly growing urban population as well as for rural families displaced by the decline of extractive agriculture. The purpose of the present section is to inquire whether the industry attracted by SUDAM tax incentives is likely to fulfill these expectations.

Industrial Structure and Production

As it was pointed out in Chapters 2 and 3, the industrial sector
of Amazonia has never been an important source of income and employment. In fact, during the 1960-72 period, the rate of growth of
value added in this sector lagged considerably behind that of agriculture and the services. Labor absorption in the industrial sector did
average a high 8.2 percent during the 1960s, but over 50 percent of
this employment was accounted for by construction. With many of
the regional public works projects (for example, highways, airports,
dams, and the like) now completed or nearing completion, it is doubtful whether construction can continue to absorb new additions to the
labor force at its former rate. In the future, therefore, a greater
burden will fall on mining and manufacturing. Industry must also be
expected to share with the service sector the responsibility of employing increasing numbers of rural-to-urban migrants.

Intrasectoral Investment Patterns

As discussed previously, SUDAM approved 178 industrial projects between 1964 and mid-1976. These projects represent a total
investment exceeding Cr$ 10 billion. Of this total, about 70 percent
is accounted for by new industry. Although the industrial censuses do
not include data on the stock of capital, it would appear that the new
industry attracted by fiscal incentives has significantly increased the
productive capacity of Amazonia. Assuming an average capital-to-
output ratio of 2:1, the Cr$ 7 billion invested by these new firms is
more than triple the industrial stock of capital estimated for 1964.

Of course, the future impact of SUDAM industrial projects will
not be determined solely by total investment; its intrasectoral distribution is also of prime importance. As illustrated by Table 4.7,
approved projects have been spread among 20 industrial subsectors.
Investment, however, has not been evenly distributed among them.
Two-thirds has been concentrated in just five subsectors: foods,
20.7 percent; mining, 15.3 percent; wood products, 12.9 percent;
chemicals, 10.4 percent; and nonmetallic minerals, 6.9 percent.
The investment pattern with respect to new industry, which will presumably trace the intermediate and long-term course of regional industrialization, is much the same. It is slightly more concentrated
in the five leading subsectors (70.7 percent), however, and mining
moves into first place ahead of foods.

Few data are available on industrial input-output relationships,
but the overall investment pattern exhibits little evidence of vertical
integration. Particularly conspicuous by their absence are major new
investments related to the lumber industry. That is, while 17 new
projects were approved in the wood-products subsector (accounting

TABLE 4.7

SUDAM-Approved Industrial Investment by Subsectors
(1975 prices)

	New		Modernization/Expansion		Total	
	Cr$ Millions	Number	Cr$ Millions	Number	Cr$ Millions	Number
Mining	1,369.4	6	187.9	2	1,549.5	8
Manufacturing	5,589.2	112	2,985.7	58	8,574.9	170
Nonmetallic minerals	525.1	5	177.8	2	702.9	7
Metallurgy	504.0	6	49.5	2	553.5	8
Electronics	443.7	7	88.4	2	532.1	9
Transport equipment	50.6	2	349.6	3	400.2	5
Wood products	972.7	17	337.0	6	1,309.7	23
Furniture	4.9	1	—	—	4.9	1
Paper	1.6	1	15.6	1	17.2	2
Rubber	68.4	2	100.7	3	169.1	5
Leather	62.7	2	22.5	1	85.2	3
Chemicals	824.8	17	231.6	11	1,056.4	28
Pharmaceuticals	72.0	1	—	—	72.0	1
Perfumery	34.8	2	49.5	1	84.3	3
Plastics	46.2	2	25.6	1	71.8	3
Textiles	371.7	10	245.8	5	617.5	15
Apparel	63.9	1	50.4	2	114.3	3
Foods	1,222.1	26	879.1	11	2,100.2	37
Beverages	210.4	5	123.1	3	333.5	8
Tobacco	2.5	1	—	—	2.5	1
Miscellaneous	107.8	4	239.5	4	347.3	8
Total	6,959.3	118	3,173.6	60	10,131.9	178

Note: Projects approved through mid-1976.

Source: IPEA/SUDAM/NAEA (unpublished survey).

for a total investment of Cr\$ 973 million), only two projects were approved in the furniture and paper subsectors. These latter two projects accounted for a total investment of only Cr\$ 6.5 million. The implication here is that the lumber industry has articulated practically no forward linkages within the region beyond sawmills and plants manufacturing plywood.*

So far, the same observation holds true for the important mining and livestock sectors. In the first case, it is relevant to point out that over 90 percent of the approved investment in mining (and about 15 percent of all industrial investment) is accounted for by one firm—Mineração Rio do Norte. This project, owned by the Companhia Vale do Rio Doce (a government enterprise) and ALCAN, is primarily engaged in the extraction and direct exportation of bauxite. Though there are plans to link this project with aluminum manufacture within the region, it remains to be seen whether this will actually occur. The major project approved in the metallurgical subsector (SIDERA-MA), is based entirely on regional raw materials; unfortunately, it has been inoperative for a number of years because of financial and technical problems. Aside from a few meat-packing plants, livestock projects have also had a minimal impact on regional industry. This point is evidenced by the relative unimportance of project approvals in the leather and apparel subsectors. As greater numbers of livestock projects reach their full operational stages, however, such forward linkages could be established.

A lack of integration is also observed between the textiles and apparel subsectors. While ten new projects have been approved in the former subsector (representing a total investment of Cr\$ 372 million), only one project has been approved in the latter (an investment of Cr\$ 64 million). Here, however, the similarity with lumber mining and livestock industries is more apparent than real. A more disaggregated view of the textiles subsector reveals that the majority of firms receiving tax-credit funds are engaged in the processing of jute, a fiber not commonly employed in the manufacture of clothing.

Intrasectoral Production Patterns

Due to intrasectoral differences in capital-to-output ratios, the general investment pattern briefly sketched above does not necessarily reflect the various subsectors' potential contribution to industrial production. It also provides little insight into whether or not SUDAM projects have diversified the region's industrial park. In order to

---

*An important incentive to the wood-products industry is legislation that prohibits the direct exportation of unprocessed logs.

consider these two aspects in greater detail, data on value added by new projects were tabulated according to subsectors. For comparative purposes, similar data were gathered from the 1960 and 1970 Industrial Censuses.

According to Table 4.8, new industrial projects approved by SUDAM should generate Cr$ 4 billion in value added when they reach their full operational stages (assuming full-capacity utilization). Although this production is unlikely to affect the national growth rate to any great extent, it does represent a doubling of the value added by industry in Amazonia during 1964. Considered by subsector, the data on value added reaffirm the importance of foods, mining, chemicals, wood products, and nonmetallic minerals. A major change, however, is the electronics subsector's ascent from seventh place in terms of investment to first place in terms of value added. This phenomenon is explained by the fact that most electronics firms are of the assembly type. Moreover, they are concentrated in Manaus to take advantage of the zona franca legislation that allows the tax-free importation of components from abroad and other parts of Brazil. In contrast to electronics, the contribution of mining to industrial value added is relatively low compared to the amount of investment approved in this subsector. This relationship is not unexpected, however, given the capital-intensive bias of mining.

The data indicate that SUDAM projects have done (or will do) much to diversify regional industry. The most obvious example is the creation of an electronics subsector, something that did not previously exist in Amazonia. Wood products and nonmetallic minerals, while having some importance before the advent of the tax-credit mechanism, seem sure to have a much more important role in the future. Moreover, both subsectors have important locational advantages due to the proximity of raw materials. Considerable diversification has also been encouraged in the chemicals subsector, though this fact is hidden by the level of aggregation utilized in our tabulations. From the data presented in Table 4.8, it would appear that Amazonia had a relatively well-developed chemical industry as early as 1959. In fact, almost all of the value added attributed to this subsector in the 1960 Industrial Census was generated by a petroleum refinery (COPAM) established in Manaus during the late 1950s. SUDAM-approved projects, on the other hand, are much more varied and include plants manufacturing paints, detergents, matches, and miscellaneous industrial chemicals.

In contrast to the subsectors mentioned above, the data suggest that textiles, rubber, and mining will play a progressively diminishing role in the future of Amazonia. With respect to the first two subsectors, this prediction is based on their declining shares of industrial value added observed during the intercensus period as well as their

TABLE 4.8

SUDAM: Industrial Value Added by New Projects
(1975 prices)

Sector	Census (percent)		SUDAM	
	1959	1970	Cr$ Millions	Per-cent
Mining	17.1	19.9	408.6	10.0
Manufacturing	82.9	80.1	3,690.9	90.0
Nonmetallic minerals	3.6	5.2	290.4	7.1
Metallurgy	2.4	2.1	99.0	2.4
Machinery	0.0	1.2	—	—
Electronics	—	0.3	737.6	18.0
Transport equipment	0.7	1.1	35.7	0.9
Wood products	5.2	10.1	586.1	14.3
Furniture	1.1	1.4	1.6	0.0
Paper	0.2	0.3	0.6	0.0
Rubber	4.5	3.9	33.4	0.8
Leather	1.8	1.2	39.4	1.0
Chemicals	16.9	12.7	614.0	15.0
Pharmaceuticals	0.2	(x)	33.8	0.8
Perfumery	3.1	2.1	1.8	0.0
Plastics	—	(x)	22.3	0.5
Textiles	14.1	9.2	186.9	4.6
Apparel	1.2	0.8	44.8	1.1
Foods	16.9	16.3	697.2	17.0
Beverages	5.1	3.8	85.4	2.1
Tobacco	3.6	2.7	112.2	2.7
Publishing	2.2	2.9	—	—
Miscellaneous	0.2	2.3	68.7	1.2
Total	100.0	100.0	4,099.5	100.0

Note: Projects approved through mid-1976. Census data refer to all industrial firms in existence in 1959 and 1970. Dashes indicate zero or no industrial projects. (x) indicates that data were not disclosed in the source, even though they do exist.

Sources: IBGE, Censo Industrial, 1960 and 1970; IPEA/ SUDAM/NAEA (unpublished survey).

relatively small contributions to the total value added by new SUDAM projects. As implied in earlier chapters, both jute and rubber have been beset by problems on the demand side that stem from rudimentary, high-cost production methods and competition from synthetic substitutes. Unless demand conditions improve considerably, the stagnation of these subsectors is likely to continue.

Despite the impression given by Table 4.8, the same fate does not seem to be in store for mining. On the contrary, mining may very well be the leading industrial subsector of Amazonia over the next few decades.* Although mining accounts for only 10 percent of the total value added by new projects (versus the 17.1 and 19.9 percent shares of value added by total industry observed in 1969 and 1970, respectively), other projects are contemplated that are not financed through tax-credit deposits. The most important of these new ventures is the Carajás project of southeastern Pará. Although it is currently stalled because of financial difficulties, total investment may eventually exceed U.S. $1 billion. When full capacity is reached, annual exports of high-grade iron ore are estimated at 44 million tons. Another venture of this magnitude is the Jari project of northeastern Pará.† The Jari project is totally financed by the Brazilian subsidiary of National Bulk Carriers and encompasses not only mining but also agriculture, livestock, and wood products (cellulose). The mining component alone, however, which has already begun operations, calls for the exportation of 440,000 tons of kaolin annually by the 1980s.

The Implications for Labor Absorption

It was noted earlier in this chapter that SUDAM industrial projects have generated relatively little direct employment. The data on

---

*It is worth pointing out that almost all of the value added by mining in the 1960 and 1970 censuses was generated by the ICOMI manganese project (a joint venture of local capital and Bethlehem Steel) located in Amapá. In fact, until the 1960s, ICOMI and the COPAM petroleum refinery were the only sizable industrial enterprises in the entire region.

†This project, which started in the mid-1960s, is by far the largest private undertaking in Amazonia. Moreover, with an area in excess of 1 million hectares, it is probably the largest single landholding in private hands. Estimates of total investment to date are in the neighborhood of U.S. $500 million although it is possible that this sum will rise to U.S. $1 billion by the time the entire project is completed.

employment contained in project specifications are admittedly frag-
mentary, but it appears that the job opportunities created by these
enterprises are equivalent to no more than 2-3 percent of the total
regional labor force existing in 1970. This finding should not be surprising, however, since the most common types of fiscal incentives
(that is, tax allowances and grants, exemptions from import duties,
accelerated depreciation, and the like) tend to have capital-intensive
biases. Research on the Brazilian Northeast, and other countries
where such measures have been adopted, have verified the limited
efficacy of the fiscal incentive as an employment-generating instrument. [8]

The data contained in Table 4.9 further confirm the capital-
intensive bias of the tax-credit mechanism administered by SUDAM.
They also suggest that employment creation was not the major variable considered during the project selection-and-approval process.
Except for wood products, all of the major subsectors (in terms of
total investment) are characterized by capital-to-labor ratios that
are significantly higher than the average for all new projects. The
highest such ratio is observed in mining where the financial cost per
workplace reaches Cr$ 1.8 million (or approximately U.S. $220,000).
This observation is extremely relevant in view of the important role
this subsector is likely to play in the future development of Amazonia.
That is, the new mining projects will have a much greater effect on
regional production than on regional employment.

The fact that industry attracted to Amazonia by the tax-credit
mechanism is generally more capital-intensive than that attracted to
the Northeast was established earlier in the present chapter. The
data in Table 4.9, however, indicate that this phenomenon is generalized among most of the industrial subsectors. The average for all
SUDAM industry is obviously influenced by the relatively greater
weight of mining, but even among the manufacturing subsectors only
wood products, paper, leather, chemicals, and textiles are less capital-intensive in Amazonia than in the Northeast.

What are the implications of these comparisons? First, it may
be argued that the creation of new employment opportunities is much
more urgent in the Northeast and that comparisons of capital-to-labor
ratios observed in this region to those of Amazonia are irrelevant.
Second, it may be argued that the ability of the latter region to support
human habitation is intrinsically limited, and that its comparative advantages lie in exploiting natural resources in a capital- or land-intensive manner. Both arguments have considerable merit, especially
when one accepts that Amazonia is a resource frontier and not a classic depressed region like the Northeast. The fact remains, however,
that Amazonia is currently characterized by both high urban growth
rates and substantial immigration via the new highway systems.

TABLE 4.9

SUDAM and SUDENE: Industrial Capital-to-Labor Ratios of New
Projects
(1975 prices)

Sector	SUDAM (Cr$ thousands)	SUDENE (Cr$ thousands)	SUDAM/ SUDENE
Mining	1,802.0	149.3	12.07
Manufacturing			
Nonmetallic minerals	471.4	188.4	2.50
Metallurgy	488.4	330.4	1.48
Electronics	130.7	108.2	1.21
Transport equipment	160.0	99.4	1.61
Wood products	133.4	154.6	0.86
Furniture	153.1	63.4	2.41
Paper	160.0	186.9	0.86
Rubber	1,076.0	233.3	4.61
Leather	117.0	166.3	0.70
Chemicals	297.5	491.2	0.61
Pharmaceuticals	328.8	201.9	1.63
Perfumery	348.0	183.6	1.90
Plastics	375.6	156.6	2.40
Textiles	75.1	194.7	0.39
Apparel	237.5	42.2	5.63
Foods	322.6	111.9	2.88
Beverages	217.8	201.9	1.08
Tobacco	9.6	31.9	0.30
Miscellaneous	164.7	91.5	1.80
Subtotal	207.3	193.0	1.07
Total	260.3	192.2	1.35

Note: Projects approved through mid-1976.

Sources: D. E. Goodman and R. Cavalcanti de Albuquerque,
Incentivos à Industrialação e Desenvolvimento do Nordeste, Coleção
Relatórios de Pesquisa, no. 20 (Rio de Janeiro: IPEA/INPES, 1974),
pp. 249-50; IPEA/SUDAM/NAEA survey.

Therefore, any policy that promotes the human occupation of the region must also include provisions for occupying its new residents.[9] As in the Northeast, the tax-credit mechanism appears to be an unnecessarily expensive method of achieving this goal.

The Three Models of Industrialization:
Pros and Cons

Since the era of SPVEA, public policies for Amazonia have always stressed the need for industrialization. There has been considerable vacillation, however, as to the appropriate model to be followed. In general, the choice has centered on three approaches: regional import substitution, "enclave import," and "enclave export." The purpose of the present section is to compare and contrast these approaches and to assess their appropriateness to the environment of Amazonia.

Regional Import Substitution

Official interest in the regional import substitution industrialization (RISI) model reached its peak in the mid-to-late 1960s. In essence, it was an attempt to transfer the SUDENE model, which was at that time considered successful, to Amazonia. The rationale of such an approach is well known: by substituting imports, a peripheral region (that is, a net exporter of primary products) may reduce its dependence upon industry in the dynamic centers. By doing so, the import-substituting region hopes to change the interregional terms of trade in its favor and increase income retention through a reduction of import leakages. The RISI model has the additional noneconomic attraction of raising regional self-esteem.

Despite its apparent attractiveness, RISI has probably been the least successful of the three approaches. In the first place, it is based on a false analogy with the national import-substitution model, which assumes the existence of tariff or nontariff trade barriers. When these barriers do not exist (as is the usual case within nations), industry in peripheral regions has no way of protecting itself from the more established (and presumably more efficient) industry of the dynamic centers. In the specific case of Amazonia, the RISI model had some validity before the 1960s when the region's physical isolation acted as a de facto trade barrier. Upon the completion of the Belém-Brasilia highway, however, this isolation was irrevocably broken. Since most import-substituting industries (foods, beverages, tobacco, apparel, chemicals, and the like) were concentrated in Greater Belém, this highway was the death knell for inefficient firms and those demonstrating no real comparative advantage. This point is indirectly demonstrated by the changes in intra- and interregional trade flows observed between 1960 and 1970 (see Table 3.7).

Although the internal inconsistency of the RISI model was its greatest flaw, other conditions prevailing in Amazonia contributed to its lack of success. Perhaps the most important of these was the small size of the regional market (in terms of numbers of potential consumers and their average incomes) and its extreme geographical dispersion. This aspect obviously retarded the development of industries (for example, metallurgy, machinery, petroleum refineries) in which economies of scale are reached only at relatively high levels of production. The problem of market size was further compounded by the establishment of the Zona Franca of Manaus in 1967. That is, through the additional fiscal incentives provided to firms approved by SUFRAMA, Belém-based industry was put at a severe competitive disadvantage vis-à-vis regional and extraregional markets. Moreover, since residents of Manaus were permitted to purchase imported goods at "duty-free" prices, there was little incentive for them to patronize Belém-based manufacturers.

Credit shortages and a general lack of managerial skills also plagued the RISI model. Both problems were closely related to the fact that the ownership of import-substituting industries was mostly local. Although local ownership is ostensibly a positive factor, entrepreneurs in Belém were denied access to the internal financing a larger parent corporation could have supplied in times of need. This was an especially crucial factor during the late 1960s and early 1970s when the demand for SUDAM and BASA financing greatly outstripped its supply.[10] Furthermore, because of Amazonia's traditional dependence on extractive activities, few local entrepreneurs had a knowledge of modern industrial management techniques.[11] Obviously, this factor worsened their competitive positions still further.

Enclave Import

The enclave import model came into vogue with the establishment of the Zona Franca de Manaus. Its underlying premise is that underdeveloped countries have much to gain from starting with "last" industries rather than building upward from the processing of primary products. Problems created by unreliable domestic producers are thus avoided, and outlets are provided for relatively small amounts of capital. As markets are created for the products of enclave import industries, so, it is argued, backward linkages are articulated within the country and domestic components are gradually substituted for those formerly imported.[12]

While the argument presented above may hold true for nations, it is not necessarily valid at the regional level. This has been demon-

strated by the experience of the Zona Franca de Manaus where enclave import industries (for example, electronics, synthetic textiles)
have created practically no backward linkages with the regional economy. Although the intermediate goods utilized by these "last" industries are becoming increasingly domestic, the benefits of this transition are accruing to industrial interests in the Center-South rather
than to regional manufacturers.

For all its faults, however, the enclave-import model has
probably been more successful than RISI. This is because firms established in Manaus suffer few of the disadvantages encountered by
import-substituting firms located elsewhere in Amazonia. First, enclave import industries produce for a wide national market rather
than a limited regional one. Second, their fiscal advantages are so
great that competition from extraregional industry is not a serious
threat. (In fact, the opposite case is more apt to be true.) Third,
such industries are usually branch plants of established domestic
corporations or multinationals. Hence, problems with internal financing, management, and trademark recognition are greatly diminished.

Enclave Export

At present, the enclave export model seems to be the favored
approach of regional planners. That the RISI model is not appropriate
for Amazonia was officially recognized in the first and second Amazon Development Plans (PDAM I and PDAM II). In fact, the latter
plan stresses Amazonia's role as an expanding market for goods manufactured in the Center-South and Northeast (see Chapter 1). The enclave import model has also fallen from grace among regional planners. This change in attitude is traceable, however, more to its
conflict with national balance-of-payments considerations than to any
internal inconsistencies the model may possess (see Chapter 5).

The enclave export model, of course, is based on the exportation of primary products.* In the industrial sector, this would include
projects in mining, wood products, rubber, and textiles (jute). The
SUDAM livestock projects should also be added to this list. Together,
these lines of production represent an investment of Cr$ 14 billion
(U.S. $1.7 billion), or over 75 percent of the total approved by SUDAM
(excluding expansion and modernization projects). Moreover, when

---

*An "export" is defined here as any sale in an extraregional mar-
ket, be it foreign or domestic. "Primary products" are considered
to be any products sold in their natural states (for example, mineral
ores) or with only minimal processing (for example, lumber, jute
sacks).

one considers other major projects not directly receiving tax-credit funds (for example, Carajás and Jari), the future importance of the enclave export model becomes even clearer.*

Of the three approaches to industrialization, the enclave export model is probably the most appropriate for a "resource frontier" such as Amazonia. That is, leaving the region's natural resources untapped would involve enormous opportunity costs in terms of forgone foreign exchange earnings. It would also deprive national industries of essential raw materials. One must question, however, the long-term impact of such a model on the regional economy. First, since enclave export industries deal with primary products, they are practically devoid of backward linkages. Second, their export orientation greatly reduces the possibility that forward linkages will be developed.[13] Third, they are usually capital-intensive (especially mining enterprises) and thus provide relatively little employment for the regional labor force. Finally, the most important enclave export industries are controlled by large domestic (though not local) corporations or multinationals (as in the cases of Mineração Rio do Norte, ICOMI, Carajás, Jari, and most lumber and livestock projects).

All of the factors mentioned above suggest that enclave export industries are not likely to retain much income within Amazonia. Moreover, any income that does remain will accrue to a relatively small elite of highly trained technicians. The Brazilian federal government does assess royalties on mineral production that could be utilized for promoting regional income retention. The rates, however, are so low (7 percent on iron ore and 4 percent on most other nonferrous minerals) that relatively little revenue is generated. (In 1975, for example, this tax generated only Cr$ 37 million (U.S. $4.6 million) in revenues in the entire Amazon region.) Furthermore, the shares of these royalties transferred back to the states and municípios (90 percent of the total) on an origin basis are completely earmarked for programs that directly or indirectly benefit the mining industry. For this reason, the real tax burden on mining enterprises (at least with respect to production royalties) is insignificant.

In sum, the enclave export model, while based on the comparative advantages of Amazonia, does not fulfill the expectations of the early proponents of regional industrialization. It does not end the region's dependence upon international markets for primary products nor does it reduce the influence of outside economic interests. In

----

*POLAMAZONIA should also be viewed as a variant of the enclave export model. Although "development poles" are distributed throughout the region, enclave export industries have tended to locate in eastern Amazonia.

fact, both of these problems are exacerbated by the model. Moreover, enclave export industries cannot be expected to generate significant employment. The enclave export model is a promising solution to some of Amazonia's problems (that is, the productive use of its natural resources), but it can never resolve all of them.

LIVESTOCK PROJECTS

As it was pointed out earlier, cattle ranches have been the preferred investment of the majority of tax-credit depositors. Judging from the high tax credit-to-total equity ratios of approved projects, development of the livestock sector has also been a high-priority goal of SUDAM. In the present section we examine these projects in greater detail so as to evaluate their contribution to the development of Amazonia. It should be made clear at the outset, however, that such an evaluation can only be of a preliminary nature, since no more than 20-25 percent of the approved projects have actually reached their full operational stages. Thus, many of our observations are based on the expectations of project designers, rather than on actual results.

Livestock in Amazonia: A Brief Characterization

Overall, the livestock sector of legal Amazonia is among the most rudimentary of Brazil.[14] While approximately 60 million hectares of the region are suitable for cattle, the total herd (as of 1970) amounts to less than 6 million head. The cattle that form this herd, moreover, are generally of the most inferior quality. The lack of progress in this sector is attributable not only to unfavorable ecological conditions but to inefficient production methods as well. Theoretically, the approach followed by the majority of SUDAM-approved projects represents a major step forward. It is useful, however, to compare and contrast this approach to the traditional production models observed in other parts of Amazonia.

Before the arrival of SUDAM projects, two such models predominated in the region: traditional superextensive and traditional extensive.[15] The first is most commonly encountered in Amapá, Roraima, Amazonas, and northeastern Pará. It is practiced in areas ecologically unfavorable for livestock, but has survived because of the demand for animal products in the nearby markets of Belém and Manaus. Cattle in these regions graze natural pastures during part of the year and are moved to upland areas (terra firme) in the flood season. During this stage, the cattle are poorly nourished and subject

to significant weight loss, and average annual productivity is only
around 3 kilos of beef per hectare.

The traditional extensive model, as practiced in Acre, Rondônia,
north-central Pará, and parts of northeastern Mato Grosso and Goiás,
is only slightly more advanced than the system described above. In
contrast to the superextensive model, however, pastures are partially
enclosed and the cattle are of a somewhat higher quality. Also observed is a greater receptibility to improved technology such as the
formation of artificial pastures in ecologically favorable zones. Modern veterinary practices, though, are practically nonexistent. As a
result, average productivity levels are still a low 16.1 kilos of beef
per hectare annually.

Most of the SUDAM projects fall into a third category, the modernizing extensive model. Ranches adopting this production method
are generally found in eastern and southeastern Pará, northern Mato
Grosso and Goiás, and western Maranhão (Imperatriz microregion).
These ranches are located in areas essentially favorable for livestock
and tend to specialize in beef production. The types of cattle employed
are much superior to those observed in the other two models, with
Indian breeds such as Gyr and Nellore predominating. Pastures are
mainly artificial, though advanced methods of management and soil
conservation are infrequently utilized. Veterinary practices also
tend to be underdeveloped. Nevertheless, the productivity of ranches
employing the modernizing extensive model is considerably higher
than that observed in other parts of Amazonia, averaging about 41.5
kilos of beef per hectare per year.

Output Considerations

According to data presented in project specifications, SUDAM
cattle ranches should make a significant contribution to the regional
supply of beef and foreign exchange earnings. By the middle to late
1980s, the total herd should reach 5.3 million head, with an annual
production exceeding 1 million head. As shown in Table 4.10, this
output would double the 1970 level achieved in microregions where
SUDAM livestock projects are located. Furthermore, it would equal
10 percent of the national beef production observed in the early 1970s.
If all this production were exported, annual foreign exchange earnings
(at 1975 prices) would amount to approximately U.S. $350 million, or
175 percent of total regional exports in 1975.

Intraregional Variations

Table 4.10 also illustrates the spatial distribution of production.
As implied from the earlier discussion of investment patterns, about

TABLE 4.10

SUDAM: Livestock, Projected Herd and Annual Production by States and Territories
(thousand head)

State/Territory	Herd			Production		
	1970 Census*	SUDAM	Variation (percent)	1970 Census*	SUDAM	Variation (percent)
Rondônia	10.9	24.3	222.9	1.4	4.6	328.6
Acre	15.5	95.3	614.8	4.7	18.3	389.4
Amazonas	177.1	136.6	77.1	36.2	27.6	76.2
Pará	812.9	1,221.7	150.3	101.4	257.5	253.9
(049)	30.7	652.6	2,125.7	3.0	133.6	4,453.3
(051)	53.6	352.7	658.0	14.8	86.3	583.1
Other	728.6	216.4	29.7	83.6	37.6	45.0
Maranhão	270.8	76.7	28.3	38.2	15.7	41.1
Mato Grosso	1,247.4	3,438.8	275.7	147.8	664.7	449.7
(901)	229.3	2,847.3	1,241.7	25.3	547.9	2,165.6
Other	1,018.1	591.5	58.1	122.5	116.8	95.4
Goiás	1,096.2	261.2	23.8	234.7	52.1	22.2
Total	3,630.8	5,254.6	144.7	526.2	1,040.5	197.7

*State totals include only microregions containing SUDAM-approved projects; microregions in parentheses.

Note: Projects approved through mid-1976.

Sources: IBGE, Censo Agropecuário, 1970; IPEA/NAEA/SUDAM (unpublished survey).

two-thirds of the projected herd and production are accounted for by
the state of Mato Grosso. Within this state, moreover, over 80 percent of the cattle are located in microregion 901 (Norte Matogrossense). Ecologically, the Norte Matogrossense is a region of transition between the wet equatorial climate to the north and the drier
climate of the central plateau to the south; it is mostly forested, however, especially in low-lying areas. It is also a region of sparse
settlement with an average population density of only 0.1 inhabitants
per square kilometer. Although cattle ranches had been previously
established in this microregion, SUDAM projects are likely to dominate its future development. This is made clear by Table 4.10,
which predicts the eventual production of these projects at over 20
times greater than that registered in the 1970 Agricultural Census.

The other major areas of concentration occur in eastern and
southeastern Pará, especially microregions 049 (Araguaia Paraense)
and 051 (Guajarina). The first of these microregions is similar to
the Norte Matogrossense in its ecological aspects and forms part of
Brazil's newest agricultural frontier; its average population density,
however, is slightly higher at 0.8 inhabitants per square kilometer.
Livestock projects are far less numerous in the Araguaia Paraense
than in the Norte Matogrossense (51 versus 162), but their socioeconomic impact on the former microregion may be relatively greater.
As of mid-1976, SUDAM cattle ranches owned almost 20 percent of
the total land area of the Araguaia Paraense, as opposed to about 7
percent of the Norte Matogrossense. When they reach their full operational stages, moreover, the beef production of these enterprises
should represent a 4,500 percent increase over the 1970 level. In
contrast to the other two microregions, Guajarina lies entirely within
the wet equatorial ecosystem, its predominant natural vegetation being dense tropical forest. It is also more populated, averaging 2.3
inhabitants per square kilometer, having been an early focal point of
settlement along the Belém-Brasilia highway. An additional feature
is its closer proximity to the market and port facilities of Belém, an
important locational advantage in terms of minimizing transportation
costs.

With the possible exceptions of Rondônia and Acre, other SUDAM
projects have located in areas of Amazonia where substantial livestock
development had already been established. This is especially true in
the cases of Goiás, Amazonas, northeastern Pará, and central Mato
Grosso. In the latter three areas, ranches have tended to cluster
around capital cities (Manaus, Belém, and Cuiabá, respectively) with
the intent of meeting growing urban demands for beef.

Productivity

Because of the scarcity of field data on functioning cattle ranches
in Amazonia, it is difficult to measure the productivity of the SUDAM

livestock projects with a high degree of precision. Some tentative estimations, however, may be made on the basis of interviews and available published sources. First, the data in Table 4.10 would suggest that, on the average, SUDAM ranch projects are more productive than other ranches in the region. This point is illustrated by comparing the slaughtering rates of ranches included in the 1970 census—it is assumed that few SUDAM livestock projects were actually operating at the time of the census—with those financed by tax credits. In the first case, the rate averages 14.5 percent; in the second, almost 20 percent.[16] It is doubtful, however, that the slaughtering rates utilized by project designers are accurate. In livestock-producing areas of the Center-South (São Paulo and Rio Grande do Sul), for example, slaughtering rates on the most efficient ranches seldom rise above 18 percent.[17] Furthermore, estimates based on a small sample of operating SUDAM ranches are close to the average for Amazonia observed in the 1970 census (14.6 percent).[18] If one applies this latter rate to the projected herd, annual production falls from 1 million to 770,000 head.

In addition to the slaughtering rate, the projected size of the total herd may be questioned. As a rule, herd size is determined by the number of hectares of available pasture and the support capacity of that pasture. The latter, in turn, is determined by a host of factors including soil fertility, type of forage, intensity of grazing, breed of cattle, and so on. According to project specifications, the support capacity of pastures on SUDAM projects ranges from 0.87 head per hectare in Goiás to 1.77 in Maranhão. On the basis of published reports and personal interviews, however, these ratios seem excessive. A more accurate estimate would be in the neighborhood of 0.5 head per hectare on artificial pastures and considerably less on natural savannas (cerrados).[19] Multiplying this ratio times the total number of hectares in pasture on SUDAM projects (4.3 million) gives a maximum feasible herd of only slightly more than 2 million head, or 40 percent of that predicted by project designers. Furthermore, if we multiply this herd by the more realistic slaughtering rate of 14.6 percent, annual production falls to 311,000 head, or less than one-third of the total depicted in Table 4.10. Moreover, assuming a carcass weight of 225 kilos (the national average in 1975), this level of production implies an average annual return of only 16 kilos of beef per hectare of pasture, the return on ranches utilizing the traditional extensive model.

Obviously, a more accurate assessment of the livestock potential of Amazonia must await detailed on-site research. The rough estimates presented above should be considered as the lower limits of this potential. Recent studies suggest that the productivity of livestock can be significantly increased (at least in the southern extremities of legal Amazonia) through intensified research and its dissemination among ranch managers.[20] If this step is not taken, however, the future gains in beef production and foreign exchange emanating from SUDAM livestock projects may not be nearly as great as originally imagined.

Profitability

To the entrepreneur, the question of whether livestock development is a viable alternative for Amazonia is viewed in terms of private costs and revenues, that is, profitability. Unfortunately, the data contained in project specifications do not permit a detailed analysis of this topic. Although data are presented on expected profits, these were estimated before the implementation of the project. Moreover, they were calculated on the basis of productivity indexes that appear to be overly optimistic.

The limited field research that is available indicates that many cattle ranches in Amazonia are only marginally profitable. A survey commissioned by SUDAM in the early 1970s is illustrative of this point. For this study, information was gathered on 12 ranches: one in north-central Pará (Jari project), six in eastern Pará, three in southeastern Pará, and two in northern Mato Grosso. All were located on forested terra firme that had been cleared and planted in pastures. Calculations of annual private costs and revenues showed annual net profits on most of these ranches to be approximately U.S. $3 per hectare after 10 years, and less than U.S. $6 after 20 years.[21] These margins were so low that efficiency of management frequently determined whether the ranch as a whole operated at a profit or a loss.

Data limitations prevent us from ascertaining whether these low profit margins are generalized among SUDAM livestock projects. It appears, however, that cattle raising is not a particularly lucrative business even in regions of Brazil where it has been long established and, presumably, where technology is more advanced. An FAO study, for example, estimated that rates of return on livestock projects in Rio Grande do Sul average between 4 and 6 percent, with a 7-10 percent return possible on exceptionally efficient ranches.[22] Judging from the available evidence, it is probable that SUDAM projects are grouped at the lower end of this spectrum.

If the profitability of livestock projects is really as low as it appears, one must wonder why cattle ranches have been such a popular choice of investors. This preference is particularly curious when it is remembered that the parent corporations are usually industrial or financial entities with little or no past experience in the livestock sector. One obvious answer is that these investments are subsidized by the tax-credit mechanism and preferential credit lines. This can only be a partial explanation, however, since corporations with income tax liabilities are free to choose among a number of alternative investment opportunities—industry in Amazonia or the Northeast, forestry, fishing, tourism—that may be closer to their principal lines of business. A more plausible hypothesis is that investments in land provide a good hedge against inflation. That is, corporations may consider rural property as store of value rather than as a factor of production. If rural property is, in fact, inflation proof, the aversion of many investors to the riskier industrial sector is completely understandable.

To test the latter hypothesis, data were gathered on the average sale prices of pastureland during the period from 1966 to 1975. Time series were constructed for Brazil as a whole, Mato Grosso, and that part of Mato Grosso that falls within legal Amazonia.* These series, in turn, were compared with the national wholesale price index covering the same period (Table 4.11).

The overwhelming impression one gets from these calculations is that rural property has been an excellent hedge against inflation, especially since 1970. For Brazil as a whole, the real value of pastureland increased at an annual rate of approximately 9 percent between 1966 and 1975; during the 1970-75 period, this rate increased to around 25 percent. Rates of growth observed in Mato Grosso are even higher. For the state as a whole, real prices increased at an annual rate of 17.8 percent over the entire ten-year period, accelerating to 28 percent during the last five years. Although generally lagging behind the rate of inflation during 1966-70, the prices received for pastureland in northern Mato Grosso have skyrocketed during the years since. Between 1970 and 1975, rural land in this area increased at a nominal rate averaging 65-70 percent per year, or about 38 percent annually in real terms.

The reasons behind these price increases are not completely evident, although they are probably associated with the availability of easy rural credit and the opening of new overland means of access. The implications of these data, however, are much clearer. They would suggest that many owners of SUDAM livestock projects have made (or stand to make) huge unearned, and untaxed, capital gains on their investments. Although land values undoubtedly vary within

---

*The average sale prices do not include all the municípios of northern Mato Grosso. However, they do include some municípios (for example, Barra do Garças and Porto dos Gaúchos) with heavy concentrations of SUDAM livestock projects.

TABLE 4.11

Mato Grosso and Brazil: Average Prices of Pastureland, 1966-75
(per hectare in current prices)

| | Mato Grosso | | | | Brazil | | General Price Index[a,b] |
| | Legal Amazonia | | State | | | | |
	Cr$	Index[b]	Cr$	Index[b]	Cr$	Index[b]	
1966	110.0	100.0	84.5	100.0	191.9	100.0	100.0
1967	106.8	97.1	113.5	134.3	223.0	116.2	128.3
1968	123.5	112.3	201.5	238.5	263.3	137.2	159.3
1969	158.3	143.9	216.4	256.1	284.4	148.2	192.4
1970	153.3	139.4	295.2	349.4	333.5	173.8	230.5
1971	325.0	295.5	394.8	467.2	419.2	218.5	277.6
1972	375.0	340.9	531.6	629.1	565.7	294.8	324.7
1973	337.5	306.8	928.3	1,098.6	998.5	520.3	373.8
1974	650.0	590.9	1,735.0	2,053.3	1,934.5	1,008.1	481.0
1975	2,058.3	1,871.2	2,661.0	3,149.1	2,718.0	1,416.4	614.2

[a]Wholesale prices (Conjuntura Econômica, column 2).
[b]1966 = 100.

Source: Fundação Getúlio Vargas (IBRE), Centro de Estudos Agrícolas, Conjuntura Econômica 28 (1974): 55.

northern Mato Grosso, investors who purchased average pastureland in this area in 1970 and who sold it in 1975 would have realized a gain of 504 percent on their initial outlay. (Pastureland held during the entire ten-year period [1966-75] would have yielded a lower, though still respectable, 308 percent in real terms.) Moreover, this return would have accrued to the landowner even if he produced nothing during the intervening period. Speculative profits of this magnitude surely contribute little to the development of rural Amazonia. They may even retard it by putting agricultural land out of the reach of small and medium farmers.

Ecological Factors

Despite repeated warnings by the Brazilian and foreign scientific communities, the recent occupation of Amazonia has proceeded with little regard to environmental considerations. Estimates of deforestation to data are imprecise but range as high as 25 percent of the original forest area. Some scientists have even predicted complete deforestation by the early twenty-first century.[23] Government development policies have undoubtedly accelerated this devastation, especially through their emphasis on improving overland access to the region and their encouragement of its human occupation. The SUDAM livestock projects have obviously played an important role in this strategy, though they should probably not be held responsible for a major portion of the environmental damage that has occurred. Nevertheless, the external diseconomies of deforestation must be weighed against any private merits these projects may have; failure to do so will result in gross overestimations of their social worth to both Amazonia and Brazil.

The Ecosystem

The natural environment of Amazonia is among the most complex in the world and is only now becoming fully understood. Although a remarkable number of ecosystems exist within the system, scientists differentiate between two major types: the várzea and the terra firme. The former comprises the floodplain of the Amazon River system, or about 1-2 percent of the total land area (60,000 square kilometers). It is the part of Amazonia subject to periodic innundations that leave behind rich alluvial deposits of mineral and organic nutrients. Because of this natural fertilization of the soil, the várzea provides excellent conditions for agriculture and livestock about six to eight months of the year. The agricultural possibilities of the terra firme, in contrast, are extremely limited, at least with the present state of technology. However, since almost 100 percent of the SUDAM-approved livestock projects have located on the terra firme, a more detailed discussion of this ecosystem is in order.[24]

It is a well-established fact that the climatic and soil conditions of a region are the prime factors determining its agricultural potential. On the terra firme, these factors are essentially negative. In view of the equatorial latitude and low altitude, it is subject to high, though stable temperatures, with monthly variations averaging less than 3° C. Annual rainfall is also high (generally exceeding 2,000 mm.) and irregular, falling in sudden, intense cloudbursts. In contrast to the várzea, the soils of the terra firme are most commonly latosols, poor in nutrients and moderately to highly acid. In spite of these inhospitable circumstances, however, it is typically covered by a dense tropical rainforest, occasionally interrupted by stretches of savanna (cerrado) and natural pastures (campos). The survival of this biomass depends on a delicate recycling process that takes place in the forest.

The crucial ingredient in this process is the thick forest canopy. This canopy absorbs about 25 percent of the daily rainfall and protects the forest floor from the erosion and ultraviolet rays that would otherwise destroy its thin layer of accumulated humus. Aside from rainwater, the principal source of nutrition for terra firme vegetation is the organic matter (for example, leaves, twigs, animal waste) that fall from the canopy. These nutrients are quickly absorbed by shallow, but well-developed root systems. In effect, soils are fairly irrelevant to the maintenance and growth of the forest, and mainly serve to support it in an upright position. An additional feature of the ecosystem is the extreme heterogeneity of the vegetation. This characteristic assures a balanced, noncompetitive utilization of the available nutrients and acts as a natural defense against animal and insect pests.

When terra firme forests are cleared for agricultural purposes, the intricate chain of events described above is broken and environmental degradation rapidly sets in. Soils become fully exposed to the vagaries of climate and lose any fertility they might have possessed through erosion and solarization. The prevalence of plant pests also increases as natural predators are deprived of their habitats. Crops planted by the traditional slash-and-burn method prosper during the first growing season, though sharp declines in yields are observed during the second and third years. After this point, the clearings are generally invaded by a stunted secondary growth (capoeira) and subsequently abandoned.[25]

The External Diseconomies of Deforestation

What has been the extent and nature of the ecological trade-offs linked to extensive livestock development on the terra firme? To address this question, one must first ascertain the extent of deforestation attributable to SUDAM projects. Unfortunately, this cannot be measured with a high degree of accuracy because of the problems of monitoring ranches located in more inaccessible areas. On the basis of original project specifications, however, a reasonable estimate would be no less than 30,000 square kilometers.* Though the area, deforested during the implementation of SUDAM projects, is insignificant in Amazonian terms (0.6 percent of the region), it roughly corresponds to the size of Belgium. Certainly, deforestation of this magnitude has entailed substantial social costs.

In accounting for these costs, one may consider the tremendous loss of timber. If we assume an average yield of 180 cubic meters per hectare, the total amount of timber actually cleared is around 540 million cubic meters, or over three and a half times the national production (wood and firewood) of 1974.[26] To be sure, some ranch owners have set up sawmills and profited from the sale of lumber, but this does not seem to be generally true.[27] In most cases, cleared timber is utilized only for basic infrastructure (fence posts, corrals, barns, housing), and the rest is burned. At the microlevel, this is often a rational decision since the price received for timber rarely exceeds the costs of transporting it from isolated rural areas to urban markets. Moreover, because of the heterogeneity of the forest, only a small part of the timber may actually have commercial value. In other words, to the rancher, the opportunity costs of burning felled timber approach zero.

The social costs of deforestation are obviously not zero. They include the value of lost timber plus the soil depletion that invariably accompany deforestation in tropical regions.† The costs of lost timber and soil depletion are difficult to quantify, but a rough estimate of the first may be obtained by multiplying the estimated volume of lost timber by its average market price. An assumed 80 percent loss during deforestation, in the case of SUDAM projects, amounts to 432

---

*This estimate was arrived at by adding intended pasture formation to the area reserved for installations, on projects approved through mid-1976. Since the process of deforestation takes an average of two to three years, this area will be effectively cleared by mid-1978 or 1979. By law at least 50 percent of the total land area of any project must be maintained in its natural state; it is assumed that this rule is being observed.

†We should rightfully add to this list the losses of wildlife, recreational benefits, scientific values, and esthetics. That the latter is a real social cost is evident to anyone who has traveled along the Belém-Brasilia highway.

million cubic meters of wood. At a conservative value of U.S. $2.39 per cubic meter—the average price received for firewood in Amazonia during 1974[28]—a total social cost of U.S. $1 billion is derived. This sum is more than twice the total investment realized by all livestock projects between 1966 and 1975.[29]

Moreover, if we accept the arguments of tropical ecologists, the erosion precipitated by deforestation should render much of land useless for the cultivation of crops after four or five years of use.[30·] In fact, the deleterious effects of soil depletion are already affecting the productivity of the livestock projects themselves. Field studies of functioning ranches within legal Amazonia have observed a progressively declining support capacity of artificial pastures planted in terra firme areas—from 2 head per hectare during the first year to 0.5 head per hectare during the third or fourth years. After this point, the support capacity declines at a relatively stable 5 percent annually.[31] On the basis of these findings, one must even question the projected gains in beef production asserted in project specifications discussed above.

In sum, a strategy of occupation and development based on extensive cattle raising is accompanied by important environmental costs that should be considered in any social cost-benefit analysis. The forests and soils of Amazonia can and should be made productive. It is by no means clear, however, that livestock represents the best possible alternative. Although this brief discussion has tried to call attention to the ecological processes and trade-offs linked with this mode of development, much more field research is needed before rational decisions can be made on future land-use patterns. In the meantime, however, "there is the danger of destroying the Amazon's comparative advantage in the very process of discovering and asserting it."[32]

The Question of Equity

Economists and planners are in general agreement that equity considerations should ideally constitute a part of any project evaluation; in reality, these considerations are either treated neutrally or simply ignored. To judge from the literature on social cost-benefit analysis, however, the justifications for this procedure are mainly methodological.[33] This methodological debate will not be taken up here, but the distributional implications of extensive livestock development are so significant that they should not be ignored. Our approach to this question falls between the two extremes of complete quantification and complete neglect; it consists of identifying and partially quantifying the relevant distributional factors. No particular weighting system is implied, although our observations are compared and contrasted with the stated goals of development policies for Amazonia.

The Dimensions

To approach the equity question, we first consider the system of land tenure resulting from SUDAM incentives and its implications for labor absorption and human occupation. In terms of the former question, only a cursory glance at the data show that SUDAM livestock projects have maintained or accentuated the concentrated pattern of landownership preexisting in Amazonia (see Chapter 3). At subsidized prices made possible by the fiscal mechanism and easy credit, less than 350 corporations have rapidly acquired 80,000 square kilometers of Brazil's agricultural frontier—an area about the size of Austria. Moreover, individual ranches all fall in the latifundio category, ranging from a low of 4,000 hectares to a high of over 200,000 hectares. The greatest frequency (143 projects) occurs in the 10,000-to-25,000-hectare interval, although landholdings larger than 25,000 hectares occupy over 60 percent of the total land area. This pattern of land tenure is, in itself, indicative of the skewed distribution of income and wealth likely to arise from the actual operation of these projects. However, its counterdistributional impact is further reinforced by the data on labor absorption.

In general terms, the relationship between farm size and employment is well recognized in the literature. Research in Brazil and other countries shows a strong inverse correlation between the two; that is, as farm size increases, the intensity of the labor input (as depicted by rising land-to-worker ratios) decreases.[34] The available data confirm that this rule also holds in Amazonia. According to the 1972 INCRA cadastral survey, the land-to-worker ratio rises progressively from 5 hectares per worker on properties of less than 100 hectares to about 200:1 on properties exceeding 100,000 hectares.[35] Hence, it follows that any policy that furthers a concentration of landownership does so at the expense of expanding rural employment opportunities.

This trade-off is particularly evident in the case of SUDAM livestock projects in which the average land-to-worker ratio is in the neighborhood of 500:1, or more than twice that observed in Amazonia on properties of over 100,000 hectares; and, if only pastureland is considered, the ratio still reaches almost 300:1. Moreover, it is probable that these ratios overestimate the real absorptive capacity of the projects. Although the data (based on project specifications) show about 16,000 new jobs being created by SUDAM enterprises, field studies report that a typical ranch in Pará is staffed only by an administrator and two or three cowboys per 1,000 hectares of pasture.[36] If this pattern were generalized, the real employment total would be about half (and the average land-to-worker ratio twice) that stated in the original project specifications.

Before discussing some implications of these land-to-worker patterns, two other factors merit attention: the nature of labor demand on livestock projects and the relationship of these large enterprises to subsistence farming. With respect to the first factor, it should be pointed out that labor requirements vary considerably and depend on a given project's stage of implementation. They reach their peak, however, during the first two or three years when land is being cleared and pastures planted. At these times, the number of available jobs is many times what it will be when the project reaches its operational stage.[37]

Temporary labor employed during the initial stages of project implementation is usually drawn from a pool of itinerant workers (peoes) who wander from ranch to ranch in search of employment. The recruitment of this labor is not usually performed by the ranch owner, but rather subcontracted to specialized brokers known as gatos. The gatos, in turn, recruit the bulk of their work gangs from among the ranks of displaced subsistence farmers—a practice common to all of Amazonia, but particularly along the Belém-Brasilia highway.[38] While the projects themselves are only partially responsible for this nomadic contingent (chiefly through their expulsion of squatters), they (and the gatos) appear to be the prime beneficiaries.

The basic cause of rural nomadism in frontier areas is the inability of traditional agriculture to support more than a small number of persons per hectare of land. It was suggested earlier that this lower limit on the land-to-worker ratio (usually reached after only two or three generations) arises from the adverse natural conditions prevailing throughout much of Amazonia. Institutional factors, however, are also to blame. Small farmers are denied the access to credit and technical assistance that could improve the productivity of their land,[39] and they are at a disadvantage when seeking legal titles to their land—the latter often being a requirement for receiving credit.

In many cases the only viable alternative to this predicament is migration, either to the cities or to other rural areas where livestock projects are locating or where virgin forest still exists. (When the migrant opts for the latter, the whole process begins anew.) Large enterprises typically fill the vacuum created by this emigration by acquiring and consolidating the land left behind.[40] With their superior access to credit and minimum labor requirements, moreover, they are able to raise the value (but not necessarily the productivity) of the land to levels unobtainable by a great majority of small farmers.

Some Implications

The processes described above have some important implications for the present and future development of Amazonia. First, it is clear that a frontier strategy based on extensive livestock can make only a limited contribution to both rural employment and fixed human settlement. Indeed, such a strategy must be considered as one of the major inconsistencies of recent regional development plans. While it may be argued that cattle raising represents the most efficient use of the land, it should be emphasized that the returns from this mode of development accrue to just a small (usually nonresident) minority.

To illustrate the potential impact of an alternative strategy, the additional employment that could arise from a more intensive use of the land was estimated. These estimates were based on the average land-to-worker ratios observed on "rural enterprises" in the states comprising legal Amazonia.* In order to arrive at a figure for potential employment, these ratios were applied to the area occupied by SUDAM projects. Admittedly, intrastate variations in agricultural potential render these calculations somewhat arbitrary; however, it is equally arbitrary to assume that land occupied by SUDAM projects is inferior to that occupied by "rural enterprises." The results of these calculations show potential employment to be over four times higher than that generated by livestock (Table 4.12). Moreover, if a farm family is assumed to average five members, the potential for total human occupation of these lands is 340,560 persons, as opposed to the 77,340 implied by the original project specifications. This difference should be considered an important opportunity cost of livestock development.

A second set of implications, partially deriving from the first, concern the relationship of extensive livestock to regional industry. If it could be demonstrated that the two are highly complementary, then the opportunity costs in terms of employment would be reduced. Although it is probably too soon to make a firm judgment on this question, the prospects are not overly bright. To begin with, it should be fairly obvious that livestock projects articulate few backward linkages with the regional economy—once implanted, they are practically self-contained. With their small labor forces (and consequent small payrolls), moreover, no appreciable demand is created for regionally produced consumer goods. Also, profits realized by the enterprises most likely flow back to the Center-South where they are distributed

---

*The "rural enterprise" is considered by INCRA to be more efficient and equitable than a latifundio (see Chapter 3).

TABLE 4.12

SUDAM: Actual and Potential Livestock Labor Absorption, by States
and Territories
(number of workers)

State/Territory	SUDAM	Potential	Difference
Rondônia	60	85	25
Acre	255	683	428
Amazonas	592	3,411	2,819
Pará	3,956	19,982	16,026
Maranhão	242	1,306	1,064
Mato Grosso	9,611	28,919	19,308
Goiás	752	13,726	12,974
Total	15,468	68,112	52,644

Sources: Instituto Nacional de Colonização e Reforma Agrária
(INCRA) Estatísticas Cadastrais/1 (Brasilia, 1974), p. 87; IPEA/
SUDAM/NAEA (unpublished survey).

to stockholders or reinvested in the main product line of the parent
corporation.*

The possibilities for forward linkages are more promising. In
this respect, livestock and regional industry should be mutually re-
inforcing. That is, as beef production increases, so should investment in related industries such as meat packing and leathers; and as
urban employment and incomes increase, so should the effective demand for beef. This is a chain of events that should be encouraged.
Two basic assumptions are made, however, which are not at all certain to occur in reality: first, that the induced investment will take
place in Amazonia and, second, that it will generate enough employment to significantly raise urban incomes. Investors (the majority
of which are Center-South residents) may, in fact, prefer to process
their livestock production closer to the larger urban markets of their
own regions. Even if all induced investment remained in Amazonia
(there is little evidence of this to date), however, it is doubtful whether
the net gains in urban employment would exceed 52,000—the total

---

*Since agricultural credit is obtainable at low or negative inter-
est rates, project owners are given an incentive to employ borrowed
funds, rather than retained earnings, for farm improvements.

needed to offset the losses in potential rural employment associated with the livestock projects themselves.

In short, SUDAM livestock projects should be awarded poor marks in the equity area. Since their direct employment of rural workers is insignificant, most income and all capital gains accrue to nonresident corporate entities. Some indirect ("trickle down") benefits may flow to regional urban centers through forward linkages, but this occurrence is by no means guaranteed. Most important, however, the livestock projects have preempted a vast portion of the agricultural frontier, a situation that is likely to perpetuate the concentrated patterns of land tenure, chronic rural poverty, and social violence that have long characterized Amazonia.

SUMMARY

By attracting capital from other parts of Brazil, the tax-credit mechanism administered by SUDAM and BASA has significantly raised the productive capacity of Amazonia. Fiscal incentives have also helped to diversify the regional economy by subsidizing the development of activities that either did not previously exist in the region or were of minor importance. Included among these activities are metallurgy, electronics, wood products, nontraditional chemicals and textiles, and livestock.

As a policy tool for regional development, however, the tax-credit mechanism has demonstrated several flaws. Some of these flaws are related to errors in administration, while others are related to the basic properties of the tax credit itself. In the first case, SUDAM committed the fundamental error of trying to establish an import-substituting industrial park in a region that has no aptitude for this type of model. Thus, considerable resources were squandered on projects demonstrating no real competitive advantage. Administrative problems also arose due to overzealous attempts to approve the maximum amount of projects possible. When the supply of tax-credit funds was unexpectedly reduced by the PIN-PROTERRA earmarking and by competition from sectoral agencies, SUDAM thus found it increasingly difficult to honor past commitments. Therefore, many approved projects were abandoned or had their implementations considerably delayed. In addition, it appears that SUDAM approved projects with little regard either to questions of vertical integration or to those of labor absorption.

Of course, the latter problem is essentially due to the capital-intensive bias of a development policy based on fiscal incentives. This bias is especially noticeable in the mining and livestock projects approved by SUDAM. While these new projects may raise the average income of Amazonia relative to other regions, their high capital-to-labor ratios will likely worsen the distribution of income prevailing within the region. Another problem created by the tax-credit mechanism is that of income retention. This aspect is built into any policy that seeks to attract extraregional capital to a peripheral region. It is exacerbated, however, when these resources are invested in capital-intensive projects—especially those of an enclave export nature. Transferring the benefits of the tax-credit mechanism to the population of Amazonia remains as one of the major unsolved problems of recent development policies.

NOTES

1. The basic premise of this strategy is that spatial income inequalities are a result of the concentration of modern productive activities in a few favored localities—in Brazil, the Center-South. Related to this premise is the hypothesis that untrammeled market forces only serve to reinforce or worsen these inequalities via the "backwash effects" emanating from dynamic centers. If the state intervenes in the market to promote investment in the poorer regions, it is reasoned, a new chain of "cumulative and causal" effects is set up leading to ever higher levels of income, employment, and welfare in the selected geographical areas. This point of view is persuasively argued in G. Myrdal, Economic Theory and Underdeveloped Regions (London: Methuen, 1965), esp. chaps. 3 and 4.

2. The literature on fiscal incentives for economic development was particularly extensive during the 1960s. The paucity of scholarly research on this topic in more recent years is perhaps indicative of the fiscal incentive's fall from grace among development economists. Recommended general works on this topic include two articles by G. E. Lent published in the International Monetary Fund Staff Papers: "Tax Incentives for the Promotion of Industrial Employment in Developing Countries" 28 (1971): 399–419; and "Tax Incentives for Investment in Developing Countries" 14 (1967): 249–321; P. Mendive, "Tax Incentives in Latin America," Economic Bulletin for Latin America 9 (1964): 103–17; and J. Heller and K. M. Kauffman, Tax Incentives for Industry in Less Developed Countries (Cambridge, Mass.: Harvard Law School, 1963).

3. The Brazilian system of fiscal incentives extends far beyond regional development. At present they are also utilized for inducing investment in selected sectors (tourism, forestry, fishing, and the like) and the stock market, promoting exports. A convenient summary of the system is R. I. Ávila, Os Incentivos Fiscais ao Mercado de Capitais (São Paulo: Editora Resenha Tributária, 1973).

4. There can be no doubt that regional fiscal incentives promote a misallocation of national resources. Recent research indicates that a shift of industrial capital from the Center-South to the North and Northeast results in a decline in real national income equal to 13 percent of the capital transferred. See C. L. Martone, "Efeitos Alocativos da Concessão de Incentivos Fiscais," in O Imposto sobre a Renda das Empresas, ed. F. Rezende, Série Monográfica, no. 19 (Rio de Janeiro: IPEA/INPES, 1975), p. 77.

5. For critical evaluations of the tax-credit mechanism in the Northeast, see N. Holanda, Incentivos Fiscais e Desenvolvimento Regional (Fortaleza: Banco do Nordeste do Brasil S. A., 1975); D. E. Goodman and R. Cavalcanti de Albuquerque, Incentivos à Industrialização e Desenvolvimento do Nordeste, Coleção Relatórios de Pesquisa, no. 20 (Rio de Janeiro: IPEA/INPES, 1974); and A. O. Hirschman, "Desenvolvimento Industrial do Nordeste Brasileiro: O Mecanismo do Crédito Fiscal do Art. 34/38," Revista Brasileira de Economia 21 (1967): 5-34.

6. For further information on the relevant legislative changes, see Ávila, op. cit., pp. 103-20.

7. J. A. de Almeida, Jr., et al., "Avaliação dos efeitos Gerados pela Política de Incentivos Fiscais Instituidos pela Lei no. 5.174, de 27-10-1966," mimeographed (Belém: Universidade Federal do Pará/NAEA/FIPAN-IV, 1976), p. 25.

8. See Goodman and Calvacanti de Albuquerque, op. cit., pp. 335-44; and G. E. Lent, "Tax Incentives for the Promotion of Industrial Employment in Developing Countries," op. cit., pp. 400-1.

9. A recent study (based on extensive interviewing) reveals that migrants following the Belém-Brasilia highway have not found industry to be a source of employment. However, the major barrier encountered by these persons has been their general lack of industrial skills. This finding would suggest that labor absorption could be increased (high capital-to-labor ratios notwithstanding) through greater use of on-the-job training programs. See J. Hebette and R. E. A. Marin, "Colonização Espontânea, Política Agrária e Grupos Sociais," mimeographed (Belém: Universidade Federal do Pará, NAEA, 1977), pp. 9-12.

10. For the local entrepreneurs' point of view on this question, see Centro de Indústrias do Pará, et al., Diagnóstico e Reivindicações das Classes Empresariais da Amazônia (Belém: Grafisa, 1971); and Assessôres Técnicos Ltda., "Situação Industrial no Estado do Pará: Análise e Soluções," mimeographed (April 1970).

11. See A. Villela and J. Almeida, "Obstáculos ao Desenvolvimento Econômico da Amazônia," Revista Brasileira de Economia 20 (1966): 191.

12. See A. O. Hirschman, The Strategy of Economic Development (New Haven, Conn.: Yale University Press, 1958), pp. 109-10.

13. The limited multiplier effects produced by mining enter-prises in Amazonia are discussed by M. T. Katzman, "Paradoxes of Amazonian Development in a 'Resource-Starved' World," Journal of Developing Areas 10 (1976): 453-54.

14. See Banco da Amazônia, S.A. (BASA), Desenvolvimento Econômico da Amazônia (Belém: Editora da Universidade Federal do Pará, 1967), pp. 182-84; and United Nations, Food and Agricul-ture Organization, Livestock in Latin America: Status, Problems and Prospects—II. Brazil (New York, 1964), p. 7.

15. Most of the following discussion is taken from Serete S.A./ SUDAM, Estudos Setoriais e Levantamento de Dados da Amazônia, vol. II-3, Setores Econômicos e Elementos da Política Setorial: Pecuária Bovina (November 1972), pp. 13-23.

16. The "slaughtering rate," a common measure of productivity, is defined as annual physical production (head of cattle) expressed as a percentage of the total herd. According to data gathered by the United Nations (FAO), the average rate for Brazil is an extremely low 9.3 percent. The rates in some other countries are: United States, 31.5 percent; Argentina, 25.3 percent; France, 17.3 percent; and Australia, 15.8 percent (see Conjuntura Econômica 28 (1974): 69).

17. See United Nations, FAO, op. cit., p. 28; and A. A. Santia-go, Pecuária de Corte no Brasil Central (São Paulo: Secretaria de Agricultura, 1970), chap. 1.

18. Serete S.A./SUDAM, op. cit., II-3: 124.

19. Ibid., vol. 4, Trabalhos Especiais, pp. 182-200.

20. This point is persuasively argued in two papers by C. C. Mueller: "Pecuária de Corte no Brasil Central: Resultados das Simulações com Modelos de Programação Linear," Texto para Discus-são, mimeographed, no. 29 (Brasilia: Universidade de Brasília, De-partamento de Economia, 1975); and Análise das Diferenças de Pro-dutividade da Pecuária de Corte em Áreas do Brasil Central," Pes-quisa e Planejamento Econômico 4 (1974): 285-324.

21. Serete S.A./SUDAM, op. cit., 4: 187.

22. United Nations, FAO, op. cit., p. 28.

23. This prediction is based on satellite photographs that show that 100,000 square kilometers of Amazonia were deforested during 1975 alone. See "Amazônia: O Verde que ainda Esconde um Areal Estéril," Jornal do Brasil, June 26, 1977, p. 7.

24. Much of the following discussion is taken from B. J. Meg-gers, Amazônia: A Ilusão de um Paraíso (Rio de Janeiro: Editora Civilização Brasileira, 1977), chap. 1.

25. A graphic example of this sequence is found in the Bragantina Zone of Pará, located to the northeast of Belém. Over the past 90 years, 30,000 square kilometers of virgin forest have been cleared in this area in successive waves of agricultural colonization. Today,

it is entirely covered by secondary growth and provides only subsistence levels of food production for its inhabitants. For more details, see E. G. Egler, "A Zona Bragantina no Estado do Pará," Revista Brasileira de Geografia 23 (1961): 75-103; and H. Sioli, "Recent Human Activities in the Brazilian Amazon and Their Ecological Effects," in Tropical Forest Ecosystems in Africa and South America, ed. B. J. Meggers, E. S. Ayensu, and W. D. Duckworth (Washington, D.C.: Smithsonian Institution Press, 1973), pp. 321-34.

26. The data on average yield are from A. Mesquita, "Subsídios à Política de Ocupação da Amazôia Brasileira," IPEA—Boletim Econômico, no. 6 (1975), p. 3. In this article, the author argues that the real natural vocation of Amazonia is forestry and not extensive livestock.

27. Because of their closer proximity to the Belém market and greater accessibility, SUDAM projects situated along the Belém-Brasilia highway have probably sold relatively more timber than those located in northern Mato Grosso. In fact, some ranches in the former region have apparently found lumbering to be a more lucrative business than livestock. See Hebette and Marin, op. cit., p. 17.

28. This represents the average price received in state, weighted by deforestation in state. Basic data are from IBGE, Anuário Estatístico—1976, p. 153.

29. This should be properly considered a total loss, since a tropical rainforest is not necessarily a renewable resource. Ecologists estimate that full regeneration may take as long as 100 years, and only when there is a nearby primary forest to provide seeds and wildlife. See R. J. A. Goodland and H. S. Irwin, Amazon Jungle: Green Hell to Red Desert? (Amsterdam: Elsevier Scientific Publishing Company, 1975), p. 111.

30. Of course, the cultivation of annual crops on the terra firme may not be very productive to begin with, except on scattered patches of fertile soils or under conditions of extremely low population pressure. Possibilities do exist, however, in the gathering of forest products (for example, fruits, nuts, resins, latex) and the planting of perennial fruit trees such as cacau, guaraná, açaí, coconut, and avocado. In the latter cases, the forest floor is partially protected and environmental damage is consequently lessened (see ibid., pp. 40-43).

31. Serete S.A./SUDAM, op. cit., 4: 182-83.

32. S. S. Panagides and V. L. Magalhães, "Amazon Economic Policy and Prospects," in Man in the Amazon, ed. C. Wagley (Gainesville: University Presses of Florida, 1974), p. 253.

33. See, for example, J. T. Bonnen, "The Absence of Knowledge of Distributional Impacts: An Obstacle to Effective Policy Analysis and Decisions," in Public Expenditures and Policy Analysis, ed.

R. H. Haveman and J. Margolis (Chicago: Markham, 1970), pp. 246-70.

34. See, for example, Y. Sampaio and J. Ferreira, Emprego e Pobreza Rural (Recife: Universidade Federal de Pernambuco/ PIMES, 1977); and W. R. Cline, Economic Consequences of a Land Reform in Brazil (Amsterdam: North-Holland, 1970).

35. Instituto Nacional de Colonização e Reforma Agrária (INCRA), Estatísticas Cadastrais/1 (Brasilia, 1974), p. 107.

36. Hebette and Marin, op. cit., p. 9.

37. The Suiá-Missú ranch (one of the largest approved by SUDAM), for example, employed about 3,000 manual laborers during its implantation stage; fixed employment on the same ranch is projected at 250. G. Müller et al., "Amazônia: Desenvolvimento Sócio-Econômico e Políticas de População," mimeographed (São Paulo: Centro Brasileiro de Análise e Planejamento, 1975), p. 2:60.

38. Ibid., p. 2:63.

39. In two urban centers along the Belém-Brasilia, credit facilities were found to be overwhelmingly geared to the needs of large landholders. Data from one city show almost 90 percent of total bank loans being allocated to ranches exceeding 1,000 hectares (see Hebette and Marin, op. cit., p. 19).

40. This process is further described in ibid., pp. 7-8; O. G. Velho, Frentes de Expansão e Estrutura Agrária (Rio de Janeiro: Zahar Editores, 1972), chap. 7; and D. E. Goodman, "Expansão de Fronteira e Colonização Rural: Recente Política de Desenvolvimento no Centro-Oeste do Brasil," in Dimensões do Desenvolvimento Brasileiro, ed. W. Baer, P. P. Geiger, and P. H. Haddad (Rio de Janeiro: Editora Campus Ltda., 1978), pp. 313-15.

5

Fiscal Incentives of Suframa

As indicated in previous chapters, the legal Amazon region is
by no means homogeneous in terms of population, economic structure,
resource endowments, infrastructure development, and other socioeconomic variables. Hence, the general program of fiscal incentives
administered by SUDAM almost immediately proved to be too inflexi-
ble a tool for promoting regionally balanced industrial and agricultural development. Eastern Amazonia, in particular, was perceived
as having important locational advantages (greater infrastructure development, a larger local market, closer proximity to major national
and international markets, superior natural resources, and the like)
vis-à-vis western Amazonia, and the bulk of private capital quite ra-
tionally flowed to this subregion (see Chapter 4). In recognition of
this initial imbalance in the intraregional allocation of investment
funds, the federal government subsequently passed legislation that
extended additional fiscal benefits to entrepreneurs willing to invest
in western Amazonia. Most important, the city of Manaus was desig-
nated as a "development pole" and was extended free-trade privileges.
Because of its favored position in the government's scheme for
developing the western Amazon basin, Manaus now appears to be in
the midst of a second boom. Like the rubber boom of the late nineteenth and early twentieth centuries (see Chapter 1), the recent surge
of economic activity has assumed an enclave nature with little apparent impact on the region as a whole. In many ways, however, this
new boom is quite different from that provoked by the rubber monopoly.
First, in contrast to the situation at the turn of the century, the boom
of the 1970s is not based on the exportation of a single primary product, but rather on the importation, manufacture, and sale of sophisticated industrial goods for local and national consumption. Second,
the recent industrial and commercial activity of Manaus is almost
entirely fiscally induced and not based on any apparent "natural" advantage the region may possess in these lines of production.

It is the purpose of the present chapter to analyze the nature of this new surge of economic activity on the city of Manaus and on western Amazonia. Although there are plans to develop an agricultural center in the vicinity of Manaus, recent quantitative and qualitative changes have been mainly confined to industry, commerce, and trade. Thus, the present analysis concentrates in these areas. Before turning to more detailed discussions of these sectors, however, it is useful to present a brief overall picture of the major fiscal incentive mechanisms that have precipitated this boom.

FISCAL INCENTIVE MECHANISMS

As noted in Chapter 4, fiscal incentives have been an important policy tool in postwar Brazil. They have been utilized not only for fostering regional development but also for stimulating tourism, commercial fishing, reforestation, and other activities. Legislation specifically designed for the development of western Amazonia is quite comprehensive and found at all levels of government. The following summarizes the most important of these laws.

Federal Mechanisms

During the 1964–66 period, less than 5 percent of total investments approved for SUDAM fiscal incentives was located in the western Amazon; in response to the concentration of investment in the eastern Amazon subregion, the federal government extended additional fiscal privileges to Manaus and, to a lesser extent, other areas of the western Amazon. The most important of this legislation is that which created the Zona Franca de Manaus (ZFM) in 1967 (Decree-Law 288 of February 27). According to this law (Article 1), for a period of 30 years, the ZFM is to comprise a zone of 10,000 square kilometers (Manaus and its environs) to function as "an area of free importation, exportation and special incentives, established for the purpose of creating an industrial, commercial and agricultural center in the interior of Amazonia." More specifically, industrial firms approved by the supervisory agency of the ZFM (Superintendência da Zona Franca de Manaus—SUFRAMA) are exempted from import duties on foreign components as well as from the manufacturers sales tax (IPI) on their assembly. When products utilizing foreign inputs are exported for sale in other parts of Brazil, the manufacturer pays an import duty reduced in proportion to the value added within the ZFM. Final goods leaving the ZFM are completely exempt from the IPI, although purchases in the "duty-free" local commerce are limited to U.S. $150 (f.o.b.) per person.

Subsequent legislation has extended some of the fiscal benefits of the ZFM to other parts of the western Amazon. In 1968, for example, federal legislation (Decree-Law 356 of August 15 and Decree 63,871 of December 20) established entrepôts of the ZFM in the cities of Porto Velho (Rondônia), Boa Vista (Roraima), and Rio Branco (Acre). Through this mechanism, a selected group of "first-necessity" items is permitted to flow to the non-Manaus population of western Amazonia free of federal taxes. Finally, the laws governing the ZFM were recently modified (Decree-Law 1435 of December 16, 1975) to exempt any firm from the IPI, provided that it is located in legally defined western Amazonia and it is engaged in the processing of regional agricultural products (excluding livestock).*

State and Local Mechanisms

Although federal legislation provides the most significant stimulus to industrial location, the state of Amazonas and the município of Manaus also concede fiscal relief to firms located in the ZFM. At the state level, legislation provides for the restitution of up to 95 percent of sales tax (ICM) collections from firms approved by the state development agency (Comissão de Desenvolvimento do Estado do Amazonas—CODEAMA).[1] This benefit runs for a period of not less than five years and does not apply to commercial establishments. The city of Manaus, in turn, exempts all firms and individuals from paying the local tax on services.

FOREIGN AND DOMESTIC TRADE PATTERNS: 1965-75

The original objective of extending fiscal incentives to the ZFM was to promote development through increased trade—both foreign and domestic. This section assembles the available trade data so as to reveal the impact of this legislation. A discussion of overall trends is followed by more detailed discussions of commercial relationships existing between the ZFM and the international, national, and regional economies.

Overall Trends

The fiscal relief granted to commercial and industrial interests located in the ZFM was expected to produce a rapid increase in the

---

*This same law also called for a minimum percentage of value added locally as a prerequisite for any industrial firm seeking the approval of SUFRAMA. (See the discussion of industry below.)

volume of merchandise entering and leaving Manaus. Trade statistics for the 1967–75 period appear to confirm this expectation. On the import side, the highest rates of growth have been experienced in international trade. In constant 1975 prices, foreign imports entering the ZFM rose from Cr$ 111.4 million in 1967 to around Cr$ 2.3 billion in 1975, an average annual growth rate of 46 percent (Table 5.1). Domestic purchases, although larger in absolute terms, grew at a somewhat slower 31.1 percent annually during the same period, from 290.1 million to Cr$ 2.6 billion. While foreign imports temporarily exceeded domestic purchases in 1968, the domestic share has varied between 55 and 65 percent since that date.

The data on products leaving the ZFM also reveal the impact of fiscal incentives. In contrast to the case of imports, the most rapid growth may be noted with respect to sales in domestic markets. In constant 1975 cruzeiros, the commercial value of these products rose from Cr$ 390.6 million in 1967 to over Cr$ 2.6 billion in 1975, an overall growth rate of 27 percent, which rivals that of domestic purchases. One would logically expect a high degree of correlation between the growth of purchases (international and national) and the growth of sales in domestic markets. Because of the restricted nature of the local market, few products (except for consumer durables) are actually retained in Manaus; what is retained is the value added when these imports are further processed in the industrial zone or sold to tourists in the commercial district.

Exports to foreign markets, in comparison, have practically stagnated since the mid-1960s, rising from Cr$ 147.1 million in 1967 to Cr$ 188.7 million in 1975. The ZFM's exports to foreign markets in 1975 accounted for only 6.7 percent of its total sales, as opposed to 27.4 percent in 1967.

The combined impact of these divergent annual rates of growth in total imports and exports (37 versus 23.1 percent) has been to transform the trade balance of Manaus from a generally surplus position in the pre-ZFM period to a deficit position in the subsequent years. This deficit has been financed by federal expenditures, inflows of private capital, and purchases by tourists in the local "duty-free" commerce. The deficit position of the ZFM has been most pronounced in its international balance, with its deficit equivalent to over 90 percent of its imports in 1975. Moreover, as a result of the ZFM's deficits in international trade, the balance of the entire Amazon region has turned sharply negative since 1967 (see Chapter 3). The deficit experienced in domestic trade, on the other hand, appears to have reached a peak in 1973, with the ZFM actually achieving a modest surplus in 1975.

TABLE 5.1

Manaus Free-Trade Zone: Foreign and Domestic Trade, 1965-75

(Cr$ millions, f.o.b.)

	Exports			Imports			Surplus (+) or Deficit (-)		
	Foreign (e1)	Domestic[a] (e2)	Total (E)	Foreign[b] (i1)	Domestic (i2)	Total (I)	e1 - i1	e2 - i2	E - I
1965[c]	162.6	536.3	698.9	100.0	533.3	633.3	+62.6	+3.0	+65.6
1966[c]	148.8	437.9	586.7	98.3	526.5	624.8	+50.5	-88.6	-38.1
1967	147.1	390.6	537.7	111.4	290.1	401.5	+35.7	+100.5	+136.2
1968	184.1	301.4	485.5	515.2	468.3	983.5	-331.1	-166.9	-498.0
1969	208.3	414.3	622.6	355.1	683.2	1,038.3	-146.8	-268.9	-415.7
1970	195.2	518.8	714.0	630.5	1,114.2	1,744.7	-435.3	-595.4	-1,030.7
1971	160.4	725.8	886.2	723.2	1,278.4	2,001.6	-571.8	-552.6	-1,124.4
1972	145.1	769.7	914.8	1,055.2	1,617.2	2,672.4	-910.1	-847.5	-1,757.6
1973	216.3	839.5	1,055.8	1,229.6	1,956.0	3,185.6	-1,013.3	-1,116.5	-2,129.8
1974	214.9	1,703.6	1,918.5	1,729.7	2,333.9	4,063.6	-1,514.8	-630.3	-2,145.1
1975	188.7	2,644.3	2,833.0	2,264.3	2,570.1	4,834.4	-2,075.6	+74.2	-2,001.4

[a]Excludes resales to entrepôts of ZFM.
[b]CIF.
[c]Data refer to state of Amazonas.

Note: Data in 1975 constant prices; the average 1975 exchange rate was Cr$ 8.126 = U.S. $1.00.

Sources: Superintendência da Zona Franca de Manaus (SUFRAMA), Anuário Estatístico (1975); Instituto Brasileiro de Geografia e Estatística (IBGE), Anuário Estatístico do Brasil (1967).

144

Foreign Trade

During the decade preceding the creation of the ZFM, foreign imports entering the port of Manaus were relatively insignificant in value and highly concentrated in a few product lines. In 1958, for example, over 92 percent of the total was accounted for by petroleum imported from Peru—the basic input to a local refinery, which, at the time, was western Amazonia's only major industrial enterprise (Table 5.2). Exports in this period were also highly undifferentiated and almost entirely confined to regional primary products such as Brazil nuts, rubber, manganese, rosewood oil, and jute.

With the advent of the ZFM, foreign imports have grown and diversified rapidly. As of 1975, almost 75 percent of the ZFM's foreign imports were accounted for by electrical and mechanical equipment, optical products and audio equipment, watches, precious stones and metals, jewelry, and textiles—all of which are important inputs for the new commerce and industry attracted by the fiscal benefits of the ZFM (see Table 5.2). The present export structure of the ZFM also reflects the nontraditional industrial activity generated since 1967, although over 50 percent of the total in 1975 was still accounted for by Brazil nuts, rubber, and wood products. While the chemical and textile firms located in Manaus have apparently been successful in placing their products in foreign markets, it is significant that firms in the equally important electronics sector have not. Whether the latter group of firms can attain the required levels of efficiency or even desire to compete in world markets are questions that, for the time, must remain unanswered.

When the foreign trade of the ZFM is compared with that of the country as a whole, it would first appear that the impact of the former has been negligible. Between 1967 and 1975, the imports of the ZFM averaged less than 2 percent of the Brazilian total and its exports less than 1 percent (Table 5.3). Considered in other ways, however, the impact of the ZFM has been much more important. As one would expect, commercial and industrial firms have not imported at random but have concentrated their purchases on products with the highest import duties. In 1974, for example, the ZFM accounted for the following percentages of total Brazilian imports of specific products:

	Percent of Total	Tariff Rate (percent)
Televisions	99	135
Polyester fabric	96	96
Radios	91	135
Men's apparel	88	105
Women's apparel	83	60
Stereo amplifiers	60	135
Loudspeakers	45	135

TABLE 5.2

Manaus Free-Trade Zone: Structure of Foreign Trade, 1958 and 1975
(current prices)

Product Category	Exports (f.o.b.)				Imports (CIF)			
	1958*		1975		1958*		1975	
	U.S.$ Millions	Per-cent	U.S.$ Millions	Per-cent	U.S.$ Millions	Per-cent	U.S.$ Millions	Per-cent
Vegetable products	4.58	73.8	9.01	36.2	—	—	1.72	0.7
Minerals, fossil fuels	0.37	6.0	1.11	4.5	6.15	92.5	4.20	1.7
Chemical products	0.25	4.0	5.22	21.0	0.03	0.5	5.56	2.2
Rubber, plastics	0.62	10.0	2.01	8.1	0.00	0.0	5.71	2.3
Wood and wood products	0.00	0.0	1.78	7.2	—	—	0.97	0.4
Textiles, clothing	0.07	1.1	3.11	12.5	—	—	22.15	8.9
Precious stones and metals, jewelry	—	—	0.20	0.8	—	—	17.81	7.2
Basic metals	—	—	0.01	0.0	0.04	0.6	15.45	6.2
Mechanical equipment	—	—	0.14	0.6	0.15	2.3	38.25	15.4
Electrical equipment	—	—	0.10	0.4	—	—	70.07	28.3
Transport equipment	—	—	0.56	2.3	0.20	3.0	8.22	3.3
Audio and optical equipment, watches	—	—	0.31	1.3	—	—	35.30	14.3
Other	0.32	5.2	1.30	5.2	0.08	1.2	22.34	9.0
Total	6.21	100.0	24.86	100.0	6.65	100.0	247.75	100.0

*Port of Manaus.

Note: Dashes indicate zero or no imports in category.

Sources: Ministério da Fazenda (SEEF), Comércio Exterior do Brasil (1957/58); SUFRAMA, Anuário Estatístico (1975).

TABLE 5.3

Manaus Free-Trade Zone and the Brazilian Foreign Trade Balance, 1965–75
(constant 1975 prices)

	Exports (f.o.b.)		Imports (CIF)		Balance	
	Brazil (Cr$ billions)	ZFM (percent)	Brazil (Cr$ billions)	ZFM (percent)	Brazil (Cr$ billions)	ZFM[a] (percent)
1965[b]	18.8	0.87	16.4	0.61	+2.4	2.6
1966[b]	23.4	0.64	20.1	0.49	+3.3	1.5
1967	20.4	0.72	20.6	0.54	-0.2	–
1968	23.8	0.77	26.3	1.96	-2.5	13.2
1969	29.4	0.71	28.7	1.24	+0.7	–
1970	28.9	0.68	34.4	1.83	-5.5	7.9
1971	34.0	0.47	42.5	1.70	-8.5	6.6
1972	44.6	0.32	53.1	1.99	-8.5	10.8
1973	62.2	0.34	70.4	1.74	-8.2	12.3
1974[c]	68.7	0.31	120.9 (91.7)	1.41 (1.42)	-52.2 (-23.0)	2.9 (4.6)
1975[c]	70.4	0.27	98.9 (73.8)	2.00 (2.34)	-28.5 (-3.4)	6.3 (45.3)

[a]ZFM trade deficit or surplus as percentage of Brazilian trade deficit or surplus; in 1967, the ZFM had a trade surplus and in 1969 a trade deficit.

[b]Data for ZFM refer to port of Manaus.

[c]Percentages in parentheses exclude imports of petroleum and wheat; data for 1975 in f.o.b. values, which are partially estimated.

Sources: IBGE, Anuário Estatístico do Brasil (1975); and Table 5.1.

Similarly high percentages are also noted with respect to other types of audio and photographic equipment, synthetic fabrics, clothing, and appliances.

The overall impact of the ZFM on the country's international balance of payments may also be appreciated by comparing its trade deficits with those of Brazil as a whole. During the 1968-73 period, the deficits of the ZFM ranged between 6.6 and 13.2 percent of the country's trade deficit (see Table 5.3). This may be contrasted with the situation in the two years immediately preceding the establishment of the ZFM when the state of Amazonas's surplus accounted for 2.6 percent (1965) and 1.5 percent (1966) of Brazil's trade surplus.

As Table 5.3 indicates, the nation's trade deficit worsened in 1974 and 1975, largely as a result of the rising costs of petroleum and, to a lesser extent, wheat imports. Since these two products represented a much smaller proportion of the ZFM's total imports than of Brazil's total, the former's trade balance was less affected by this occurrence. Hence, the deficit of the ZFM generally fell as a percentage of the national deficit in these years. If imports of petroleum and wheat are excluded from both balances, however, a different picture emerges, especially in 1975. In this year, stringent import-restriction measures were enacted by the federal government, although they did not apply to the ZFM.[2] Quite expectedly, nonpetroleum and wheat imports declined at the national level while those of the ZFM increased by over 30 percent. The final result was that the trade deficit of the ZFM (excluding petroleum and wheat) rose to over 45 percent of the total Brazilian trade deficit. Recent government attempts to remedy this serious conflict (to be discussed later) will probably alter the whole development strategy for the ZFM in future years.

Domestic Trade

As noted previously, Manaus's trade with the rest of Brazil has expanded markedly since 1967, with both purchases and sales achieving average annual growth rates exceeding 27 percent. This section considers the nature of this growth in greater detail through a description of the types of goods traded as well as of their geographical origins and destinations.

Table 5.4 illustrates the structure of domestic trade in the years 1966 and 1973. Contrary to what might be expected, the content of domestic purchases changed relatively little during this period, continuing to be dominated by durable and nondurable consumer goods. In 1973, for example, the most important individual goods entering the ZFM were (as percentages of the total): cigarettes, 5.5 percent;

TABLE 5.4

Manaus Free-Trade Zone: Structure of Domestic Trade, 1966 and 1973
(f.o.b. values in 1975 prices)

Product Category	Sales 1966[a] Cr$ Millions	Sales 1966[a] Per-cent	Sales 1973[b] Cr$ Millions	Sales 1973[b] Per-cent	Purchases 1966[a] Cr$ Millions	Purchases 1966[a] Per-cent	Purchases 1973 Cr$ Millions	Purchases 1973 Per-cent
Food, beverages, tobacco	6.1	1.4	5.3	0.8	123.4	23.9	310.8	15.9
Vegetable products	9.7	2.3	12.8	1.9	21.6	4.2	109.0	5.6
Minerals, fossil fuels	131.0	30.6	82.5	11.9	41.5	8.0	100.8	5.2
Chemical products	2.8	0.7	7.6	1.1	37.5	7.3	177.4	9.1
Rubber, plastics	92.4	21.6	124.2	17.9	13.4	2.6	62.9	3.2
Wood and wood products	4.3	1.0	1.4	0.2	1.0	0.2	16.1	0.8
Textiles, clothing	68.0	15.9	156.6	22.6	37.0	7.2	160.8	8.2
Precious stones and metals, jewelry	—	—	102.9	14.9	15.5	3.0	27.0	1.4
Basic metals	0.4	0.1	52.0	7.5	36.3	7.0	178.4	9.1
Mechanical equipment	2.2	0.5	29.4	4.3	14.5	2.8	153.5	7.9
Electrical equipment	0.7	0.2	18.7	2.7	35.6	6.9	112.7	5.8
Transport equipment	1.9	0.4	12.3	1.8	51.6	10.0	207.7	10.6
Other	109.3	25.5	86.5	12.5	87.8	17.0	338.9	17.3
Total	428.8	100.0	692.2	100.0	516.7	100.0	1,956.0	100.0

[a]Data refer to state of Amazonas; coastal shipping only.
[b]Excludes resales to entrepôts of ZFM.

Note: Dashes indicate zero or no sales.

Sources: Ministério da Fazenda (SEEF), Comércio de Cabotagem do Brasil (1966); SUFRAMA, Anuário Estatístico (1973).

medicines, 3.0 percent; sugar, 3.0 percent; powdered milk, 2.6 percent; and cement, 2.4 percent. Thus, it would appear that the increased volume of domestic purchases (at least to 1973) could be explained by population growth in Manaus coupled with generally rising incomes and the inability of local industry to satisfy the rising demands for these products. As of 1973, relatively little of what was brought into the ZFM from other parts of Brazil appeared to be destined for further processing by local industry; of the 15 most important domestic purchases in this year, only cement could be considered an industrial input. Between 1973 and 1975, however, domestic purchases in electrical equipment grew by about 50 percent in real terms, reaching over 11 percent of the total in the latter year. This phenomenon is no doubt an indication that the electronics firms in the industrial zone reached their regular production stages.

The geographical sources of the ZFM's purchases in the 1966-73 period have apparently changed to a greater extent than their structure. As Table 5.5 demonstrates, over two-thirds of all domestic purchases of the ZFM in 1973 originated in the Southeast. Within that region, São Paulo had become the dominant source of supply, accounting for almost four times the amount sold by its nearest rival, Guanabara (now part of the state of Rio de Janeiro). Of special importance is the relatively small and declining proportion of ZFM purchases originating in Amazonia, especially the western subregion. This observation would indicate that, so far, ZFM industry and commerce have developed few linkages with the regional and subregional economies. Furthermore, it is apparent that a significant portion of the potential multiplier effects emanating from new economic activity are lost through extraregional import leakages.

ZFM exports to other Brazilian regions continue to be dominated by the products of extractive agriculture (rubber and vegetable gums) and traditional industry (textiles of jute), although some new, locally produced merchandise may also be noted. Of this latter group, jewelry exhibited the most impressive rate of growth between 1966 and 1973, increasing from virtually no exports in the former year to a 15 percent share in the latter (see Table 5.4). Sales of basic metals, mechanical equipment, electrical equipment, and transport equipment also expanded rapidly during this period. Whereas in 1966 these four categories accounted for slightly over 1 percent of total sales, by 1973 they were accounting for over 16 percent. Unfortunately, detailed information on domestic sales in 1974 and 1975 is not available, and it is not possible to isolate the sources of the high rates of growth that characterized these years (see Table 5.1). It is almost certain, however, that a significant proportion of this growth can be attributed to the production of the electronics industry.[3]

The ZFM's principal domestic markets (other than the western Amazon) closely parallel the sources of its purchases. As Table 5.5

TABLE 5.5

Manaus Free–Trade Zone: Domestic Trade by Region and Selected States, 1966 and 1973
(f.o.b. values in 1975 prices)

Region/State	Sales 1966[a] Cr$ Millions	Sales 1966[a] Per-cent	Sales 1973[b] Cr$ Millions	Sales 1973[b] Per-cent	Purchases 1966[a] Cr$ Millions	Purchases 1966[a] Per-cent	Purchases 1973 Cr$ Millions	Purchases 1973 Per-cent
North	150.0	35.0	114.5	16.5	108.6	21.0	251.5	12.9
Pará	111.4	26.0	87.3	12.6	93.6	18.1	236.3	12.1
Northeast	47.7	11.1	60.5	8.7	72.7	14.1	274.6	14.0
Pernambuco	16.3	3.8	27.7	4.0	34.1	6.6	119.0	6.1
Ceará	11.2	2.6	5.8	0.8	24.1	4.7	86.0	4.4
South	56.8	13.3	68.9	10.0	9.2	1.8	129.5	6.6
Rio Grande do Sul	29.5	6.9	54.7	7.9	8.9	1.7	77.8	4.0
Southeast	174.3	40.7	441.2	63.7	326.3	63.1	1,292.6	66.1
São Paulo	154.6	36.1	331.6	47.9	164.9	31.9	926.9	47.4
Guanabara	11.2	2.6	77.0	11.1	158.7	30.7	257.0	13.1
Central West	—	—	7.2	1.0	—	—	7.7	0.4
Goiás	—	—	2.7	0.4	—	—	6.1	0.3
Total	428.8	100.0	692.2	100.0	516.7	100.0	1,956.0	100.0

[a]Data refer to state of Amazonas; coastal shipping only.
[b]Excludes resales to entrepôts of ZFM.

Note: Dashes indicate zero or no sales.

Sources: Ministério da Fazenda (SEEF), Comércio de Cabotagem do Brasil (1966); SUFRAMA, Anuário Estatístico (1973).

indicates, over 60 percent of its 1973 domestic sales were in the southeastern region, the majority of which were in São Paulo. When purchases and sales are considered simultaneously, it becomes apparent that in 1973 the ZFM was experiencing trade deficits with every major region and state in Brazil. In this year, the trade deficit with São Paulo alone (Cr$ 595.3 million at 1975 prices) accounted for almost half of the total deficit. Presumably, this situation tended to reverse during 1974 and 1975 as more of the ZFM industry reached the production stage and the local economy became more self-sufficient in consumer goods.

THE TWO STAGES OF DEVELOPMENT STRATEGY

During most of its ten years of existence, the ZFM has developed on the basis of imported final goods and component parts—the former destined for sale in local commerce and the latter for assembly in the zone's industrial district. When Brazil's foreign trade position worsened sharply in 1974 and 1975, however, this strategy came to be harshly criticized as being wasteful of foreign exchange and as constituting unfair competition to industry located in other parts of the country. Under increasing pressures to abide by import-restriction measures being adopted at the national level, SUFRAMA was thus obliged to alter its original modus operandi.

The "second-stage" strategy was put into effect in 1976 and will no doubt have a profound impact on the future pattern of economic development in Manaus and the western Amazon.[4] Since the ZFM is still in a state of transition, however, it is difficult to predict what these impacts will be with any degree of precision. The present section, therefore, is primarily concerned with the effects of the ZFM on local commerce and industry during the 1967-75 period (the "first stage"). On the basis of these observations, some hypotheses will be presented on the possible ramifications of the second-stage strategy.

Commerce

Due to Amazonia's traditional dependence on products imported from abroad and from other regions, the immediate impact of the ZFM was to drastically lower the prices of many goods relative to their pre-1967 levels.* What logically followed, via the "income ef-

---

*Since the rates of import duties and the federal manufacturers's sales tax (IPI) tend to vary inversely with a product's "essentiality,"

fect," was a major increase in consumer demand. This growth of sales volume, in turn, directly created new employment opportunities for the local population and also stimulated related activities such as banking, construction, and tourism. Of particular interest is the data on state sales tax collections, which grew over fourfold in real terms since the creation of the ZFM. Since industry is generally exempt from this tax, virtually all of this revenue growth is due to rising commercial sales.

The local commerce of Manaus received an additional stimulus in 1975 and early 1976 when import controls were established in other parts of Brazil. Since these restrictions did not apply to the ZFM, the prices of foreign goods sold in Manaus fell even further relative to those prevailing outside of the zone. As a result, the sales volume of "superfluous" items (taxed at rates of 37 percent or over) rose from U.S. $29.6 million in January and February 1975 to U.S. $54.6 million during the same two-month period in 1976.[5]

In recognition of this conflict with national policy, new federal legislation (Decree-Law 1455 of April 7, 1976), aimed at restricting the imports of the ZFM, was put into effect. This law retained the basic U.S. $100 limit on duty-free shopping, but assessed a tariff of 250 percent on any purchases above this amount. In effect, it completely removed the incentive for tourists to purchase "big-ticket" items such as sophisticated electronic and optical equipment. As a further deterrent to import expansion, federal legislation established an annual ceiling of U.S. $320 million on total ZFM imports, with the allocation of import rights among sectors and individual firms to be determined by SUFRAMA. Since the passage of this legislation, SUFRAMA has shown a clear preference for industry; during 1977, commerce was allocated only U.S. $76 million (23.8 percent) of the available import rights, while industry was allocated U.S. $200 million (62.5 percent). This distribution may be compared with that prevailing during the pre-import-restriction year of 1975 when commerce imported U.S. $94 million (44.9 percent) and industry imported U.S. $100 million (47.8 percent) of the U.S. $210 million total.

The cumulative impact of this legislation portends a significant decline in commercial activity. In the short run at least, this decline will cause unemployment and a stagnation of state tax revenues.*

---

the greatest relative price declines occurred in the area of consumer durables, that is, radios, televisions, cameras, and motorcycles.

*Data on 1976 sales tax collections already indicate a marked slowdown of the local economy. In real terms, revenues rose by only 2 percent during the year, versus the 27 percent growth rate attained

Whether the unemployment problem becomes serious will depend on the future pace of industrialization and the secondary sector's capacity to absorb displaced workers. Industry must also be expected to play a greater role in supporting state finances. With the sales tax exemptions of many industrial firms due to expire soon, this may come about automatically. Failure to renew the exemptions of marginally profitable firms, however, will undoubtedly provoke some bankruptcies and thus further erode local business confidence.

Industry

During its first stage of operation, the ZFM was highly successful in attracting new industrial firms. Between 1968 and 1975, 140 projects with a total investment of approximately Cr\$ 3.8 billion (U.S. \$468 million) were approved for the various types of fiscal relief provided by the state of Amazonas and by SUFRAMA. When in full operation, these projects are expected to provide employment for over 26,000 persons (Table 5.6). In addition, the majority of firms located (or locating) in Manaus have been approved for fiscal incentives provided by SUDAM. Among those locating in Manaus, several large firms in the metallurgical, chemical, food-products, and electronics sectors have also received approval for state and SUFRAMA fiscal incentives.* In fact, there is evidence to suggest that the creation of the ZFM has altered the spatial allocation of SUDAM investment funds, since a greater relative share of these funds have flowed to the western Amazon subregion since 1967. Because of the continued importance of large agricultural projects (mainly in Mato Grosso), however, western Amazonia is still allocated less than 20 percent of the total.

Investment attracted by the ZFM has not been evenly distributed among the various industrial sectors. Of the group of projects approved for state and SUFRAMA fiscal benefits, over 40 percent of the total investment and projected employment has been concentrated in

---

in 1975. Moreover, passenger-arrivals at Manaus airport rose by only 1 percent during 1976; during the previous 12-month period, they had increased by almost 16 percent. Taken together, these sets of data suggest a high degree of correlation between "duty-free" shopping and the relative importance of Manaus as a tourist attraction.

*When benefiting cumulatively from SUDAM funds and state and SUFRAMA incentives, firms are thus aided in acquiring both fixed and working capital. This, ceteris paribus, gives Manaus an advantage over other parts of Amazonia with respect to industrial location.

TABLE 5.6

Industrial Projects Approved by SUFRAMA, 1968–75
(constant 1975 prices)

Sector	Number of Projects	Investment		Employment	
		Cr$ Million	Percent	Number	Percent
Nonmetallic minerals	2	16.8	0.4	161	0.6
Metallurgy	10	309.4	8.1	1,737	6.6
Machinery	2	20.8	0.6	168	0.6
Electronics	25	755.1	19.8	6,861	26.2
Transportation equipment	11	227.2	6.0	1,473	5.6
Wood products	19	429.1	11.3	3,747	14.3
Furniture	1	3.8	0.1	90	0.3
Paper	2	11.0	0.3	161	0.6
Leather	1	1.0	0.1	99	0.4
Chemicals	9	292.9	7.7	1,058	4.1
Perfumery	1	48.5	1.3	77	0.3
Plastics	3	30.3	0.8	280	1.1
Textiles	5	830.1	21.8	3,883	14.9
Apparel	4	54.0	1.4	696	2.7
Foods	8	84.1	2.2	1,109	4.2
Beverages	5	59.6	1.6	468	1.8
Printing and publishing	4	20.3	0.5	273	1.0
Miscellaneous*	28	630.3	16.5	3,843	14.7
Total	140	3,814.5	100.0	26,154	100.0

*Includes product lines such as jewelry, toys, watches, optical equipment, and glassware.

Note: Excludes 22 projects whose approval was subsequently revoked.

Source: Calculated from unpublished data provided by SU-FRAMA.

two areas: textiles and electronics. The latter industrial sector is "nontraditional" and has only recently appeared in Manaus. Although there was a relatively important textile sector in Manaus before the advent of the ZFM (seven such firms existed in 1959), the larger approved firms in this sector have been predominantly of the nontraditional type, that is, engaged in processing synthetic fibers rather than jute.

This particular pattern of investment should not be surprising since both the "nontraditional" textile and electronics sectors are highly dependent upon tax-exempt raw materials imported from abroad. Elsewhere in Brazil, textiles and electrical equipment are generally high-tariff items. Therefore, firms specializing in these products may minimize their costs of working capital and thus enjoy an advantage over competitors located outside of the ZFM. A similar advantage results from the effects of exempting firms located in the ZFM from the federal manufacturer's sales tax (IPI). Since the rates of the IPI tend to vary inversely with a product's "essentiality," there is also a fiscal incentive to assemble high-tax, "nonessential" items (for example, television sets) in the ZFM on the basis of components manufactured in other parts of Brazil.

Finally, the sectoral allocation of investment in the ZFM may also be explained by the impact of transportation costs, for the distance between Manaus and its major markets in the South requires that a firm's fiscally induced cost savings more than offset its high transportation costs. If this latter situation is not the case, purchasers will either import the product directly or buy from firms within closer proximity. Therefore, the concentration of investment in such areas as electronics, luxury clothing, and jewelry is partially justified by the high value-to-weight ratios common to these types of products.

Firms for processing raw materials with low value-to-weight ratios (for example, wood, jute, rubber) have, however, located in Manaus in significant numbers. The primary reasons for this choice, as opposed to other locations in western Amazonia where these inputs originate, are the IPI exemption and the external economies (for example, electric power, port facilities, communications, centralized labor market, credit facilities) typically generated by urban agglomerations. With the IPI exemption now extended to all of western Amazonia, the geographical concentration of regional traditional industries should diminish somewhat, but only in those cases where the external economies offered by Manaus form a relatively unimportant part of a given firm's cost structure.

As a further consequence of the present pattern of investment, it seems clear that few linkages have developed with the local and regional economies. This hypothesis would, in turn, suggest a relatively low employment multiplier. With the exception of the jute and wood-processing industries, backward linkages are virtually nonexistent. Some "forward linkages" have been created with the local packaging industry (paper, cardboard, furniture), but, so far, these have not been significant in terms of total new investment and employment. The direct stimulation of commerce would seem to be a likely forward linkage of recent industrial activity, but local commerce has tended to rely on the sales of finished imported products rather than on locally produced goods. The latter are generally destined for southern Brazilian markets.

The second-stage strategy adopted for the ZFM industrial sector is aimed at correcting some of the distortions noted above through a reorientation of investment patterns and by exchange-conserving measures. While the latter objective is to be implemented in commerce through the prohibitive taxation of purchases above the U.S. $100 duty-free limit, it is to be achieved in industry primarily through a progressive substitution of foreign-produced inputs by those produced domestically. As required by law (Articles 1 and 2, Decree-Law 1435 of December 16, 1975), SUFRAMA will supervise this transition by establishing a series of "nationalization indexes" applicable to each product manufactured in the ZFM's industrial district. * These indexes will constitute a minimum requirement for any new firm at the time of its approval and will be applied to existing firms over a period of approximately 18 months.

Preliminary studies by SUFRAMA indicate that the nationalization indexes of firms already established in the ZFM vary considerably between industrial sectors and among the various products manufactured within a given sector. In general, however, one may note that the nationalization index tends to be inversely related to the degree of technological sophistication of an industrial sector or individual product. Thus, indexes range from less than 1 percent for some products of the electronics industry (that is, preprogrammed calculators) to 100 percent in industries engaged in the processing of regional raw materials (wood, Brazil nuts, vegetable gums). In recognition of these variations, SUFRAMA has established minimum nationalization indexes on a product-by-product basis, taking into account the types of difficulties likely to be encountered by firms substituting domestic for foreign components, such as technological incompatibilities, cost and quality differentials, and supply problems.

---

*Nationalization indexes (NI) are presently calculated by SUFRAMA on the basis of the following formula (value CIF, Manaus):

$$NI = \frac{MN}{MN + MI} \times 100\%$$

where MN = raw materials, component parts, secondary materials, and packaging of national origin

MI = materials, parts, and the like, of foreign origin.

In addition to the requirement of minimum nationalization indexes, the present industrial development strategy is also being implemented through a new set of criteria governing project approvals. This new system is much less complicated than that utilized by SUDAM and takes into account only four variables: intensive use of regional raw materials, favorable foreign trade balance, production of intermediate goods for ZFM industry, and production in sectors deemed high priority by SUFRAMA. (High-priority sectors include motorcycles and watches and exclude electronics.) For a given project to be approved, it must satisfy at least one of the four requirements.

The type of investment pattern that may emerge from the second-stage strategy is difficult to predict at this point, since the new guidelines for industry appear to be an attempt to simultaneously achieve national, regional, and local policy objectives. In general, it would seem that national interests have been most protected by the stage-two strategy, since the measures taken should effectively slow the further expansion of industries with a high import content. This prediction, however, refers only to new industries. It is possible that established industries will raise production in their highest import-content product lines, since import restrictions prevailing in the rest of Brazil should act to raise the domestic demand for such goods.

Regional ("non-Manaus") interests, on the other hand, have not been appreciably advanced by the new strategy since a firm may continue to utilize a minimum of regional inputs in its production process and still be approved by SUFRAMA. Thus, the continued enclave nature of the ZFM and the absence of any backward linkages with the regional economy is seemingly assured unless the IPI exemption is successful in attracting investment to other parts of western Amazonia. Finally, any attempt to promote the vertical and horizontal integration of industry may be frustrated by existing tax legislation, which discriminates against the sale of ZFM-produced intermediate goods in national markets. That is, the IPI exemption applies to all goods leaving the ZFM, but when a domestic firm purchases intermediate goods produced in the ZFM, it must pay the full IPI on them as they are incorporated in the final product. The success of the integration strategy is thus dependent upon the capacity of ZFM industry to create a components market large enough to generate sufficient economies of scale.

THE CITY OF MANAUS: SOCIOECONOMIC TRENDS

The stimulation of trade, commerce, and industry occasioned by the ZFM has obviously had a significant impact on regional population, employment, and income. Because of the enclave nature of the boom, however, most of the noticeable and measurable effects have been confined to Manaus, and the present section briefly surveys recent socioeconomic trends in this city.

Population and Employment

According to the intercensus estimate in Table 5.7, the city of Manaus (capital of the state of Amazonas) had a population of 388,811 inhabitants in 1975. Compared with that of the 1950s, population growth was especially rapid from 1960 to 1970, attaining an average annual rate of nearly 6 percent. Although this expansion has slowed somewhat during the 1970s, the population of Manaus continues to grow at over twice the rate experienced by the state of Amazonas as a whole. As a result, the proportion of the state population residing in Manaus has risen from 24.3 percent in 1960 to 35.7 percent in 1975. Although supporting data are scanty, it is probable that this centralization of the state population is largely attributable to migration in response to the economic opportunities created by the ZFM.[6] In this respect, a study conducted in 1971 showed that about 57 percent of the Amazonas-born population of Manaus arrived in the city after 1967.[7] In absolute terms, the same study estimated that approximately 23,000 new residents had entered the city between 1967 and 1971: 14,000 from the interior of Amazonas, 8,500 from other parts of Brazil (mainly Pará, Ceará, and Acre), and 300 foreigners. On the basis of these population movements, it seems clear that Manaus has acted more as a "pole of attraction" than as a "pole of radiation" since the establishment of the ZFM.[8]

In spite of this rapidly expanding urban population, it appears that both commerce and industry have been successful in absorbing the new workers. Comparison of the Demographic Censuses of 1960 and 1970 reveals that the active labor force grew from 44,844 to 86,852 workers during the past decade, at an average annual growth rate (6.8 percent) exceeding that of Manaus as a whole. A disaggregation of the labor force, however, reveals highly different rates of growth among the three major sectors. In terms of average annual growth rates, the most dynamic sector was industry (12.5 percent), which was followed by services (6.2 percent) and agriculture (0.9 percent). Even though employment in the tertiary sector grew at a much slower pace than the total, it continues to be the most important source of employment in Manaus. Consequently, growth in this sector accounted for 58.6 percent of the total growth of employment in the 1960-70 period as compared with 40 percent for the secondary sector and only 1.4 percent for the primary sector.

Although further data on employment in Manaus are insufficient, it is certain that the ZFM has acted to significantly lower the rate of

TABLE 5.7

Manaus and State of Amazonas: Population Estimates, 1950-75

	Amazonas		Manaus		Manaus/ Amazonas, Population as Percentage of Amazonas
	Population	Annual Growth (percent)	Population	Annual Growth (percent)	
1950	514,099	—	139,620	—	27.2
1960	721,215	3.5	175,343	2.3	24.3
1970	955,235	2.9	311,622	5.9	32.6
1975	1,089,747	2.7	388,811	4.5	35.7

Source: IBGE, Anuário Estatístico do Brasil (1976).

overt unemployment. Available data indicate that the rate of effective unemployment fell from 9 to 8.2 percent between 1968 and 1971—
a decline that is significant considering the rapid population growth
and particular demographic structure of the city.[9] For reasons discussed previously, commerce is unlikely to remain a growing source
of employment during the period of the second stage. If industry is
unable to absorb new additions to the labor force, the probable result
will be a rise in overt unemployment, the formation of a large, underemployed "informal" sector, or both.

Income

The total income of the state of Amazonas, and its sectoral
composition for the period from 1964 to 1974, also reflects the impact
of fiscal incentives. While the income of the state actually declined
in real terms from 1964 to 1967, the average annual rate of growth
since that date has been approximately 17 percent.* Since the annual
growth since 1967 has been most pronounced in the industrial and service sectors (20.5 and 18 percent, respectively), one can be certain

---

*It is probable that this overall growth rate is somewhat over-
stated due to the unrealistic treatment of agriculture in the state income accounts.

that most of this income has been generated in Manaus.* This contention is supported by a series of household surveys conducted during the late 1960s and early 1970s that found the average family income of Manaus had increased by about 50 percent in real terms between 1966 and 1973.[10] Because of the overall trade deficit of the ZFM and the fact that most of the new industry is not owned by local interests, however, it is evident that a significant proportion of the income generated in Manaus leaves the region through profit remittances and local purchases of goods produced by firms located in the South.

SUMMARY

On the basis of fiscal incentives, the ZFM has successfully attracted industry and commerce to western Amazonia. In doing so, average incomes and employment opportunities have been dramatically increased. The formation of local entrepreneurial ability and a modern industrial labor force have been important externalities of this process. Serious questions, however, may be raised about the economic efficiency and future prospects of this particular development strategy. The fiscal incentives essentially have created one commercial district based solely on the sale of imported merchandise to tourists and one industrial zone based on the assembly of components imported from abroad or from the south of Brazil. This basic strategy has created a number of conflicts and problems that will not be easily resolved even by the recent modifications of the ZFM.

First, the economic activity stimulated by the fiscal incentives has assumed an enclave nature with few real benefits spilling over into the hinterland. In fact, there is evidence to suggest that the ZFM has drained human and nonhuman resources from areas surrounding Manaus in direct conflict with the federal government's stated policy to physically occupy the frontier areas of Amazonia. So far, attempts to extend fiscal incentives to areas of western Amazonia outside Manaus have been unsuccessful as a result of persistent uncertainties as to the resource potentials of these areas as well as to problems associated with nonaccessibility and lack of basic infrastructure. One could thus argue that the ZFM has acted more as an urban development policy than as a compensatory subregional development policy as originally intended.

---

*According to unpublished estimates of the Fundação Getúlio Vargas for 1970, 98 percent of the state income from industry and 86 percent from services were generated in the Greater Manaus area.

Second, one may question the economic rationale of concentrating industrial development in sectors such as electronics and synthetic textiles for which the region has no apparent "natural," that is, nonfiscal, advantage. Although it is possible that these lines of production will become more efficient in the long run, it is debatable whether these firms will be able to compete with established firms in the South when the fiscal benefits of the ZFM expire in 1997. SUFRAMA has repeatedly expressed its desire to diversify the ZFM industrial park to take greater advantage of regional inputs, but this step will continue to be hampered by the general problems encountered in developing the hinterland.

Finally, any regional strategy adopted (especially in a developing country) that allows for free importation of foreign goods will almost inevitably conflict with industrialization efforts in other parts of the country as well as with international balance-of-payments considerations. The very threat of these conflicts, together with the legislative changes they might provoke, injects a degree of uncertainty that is not conducive to long-range economic and social planning. As we have seen, a deterioration in the Brazilian trade balance in 1974 and 1975 resulted in import-restriction measures that will undoubtedly transform the future growth and pattern of ZFM commerce and industry. At this point, however, one can only speculate as to what these transformations might be.

NOTES

1. Until 1975, industrial projects desiring fiscal relief from either SUFRAMA or CODEAMA were analyzed by the latter on the basis of a point system. This system took into account projected employment, value of investment, utilization of regional raw materials, complexity of production process, growth prospects, market conditions, and similarity to goods already produced in Brazil. Because of the method of weighting these various factors, special encouragement was thus given to large, labor-intensive firms. At the time of this writing, SUFRAMA had begun to analyze its own projects under somewhat different criteria. (See the discussion of "Development Strategy—Industry" in this chapter.) A complete description of the CODEAMA point system may be found in Comissão de Desenvolvimento do Estado do Amazonas (CODEAMA), Incentivos Fiscais para o Desenvolvimento (Manaus, 1974).

2. The most important of these measures was Decree-Law 1427 of December 2, 1975, which requires non-ZFM firms to deposit an amount equal to the f.o.b. value of their foreign imports in special blocked accounts. These balances cannot be withdrawn for 360 days

and earn no interest or monetary correction. A convenient summary of recent import restriction legislation may be found in "Importações: Etapas da Política de Controle," Conjuntura Econômica 30 (1976): 76-80.

3. Of the merchandise shipped by air in 1974 (equivalent to about 50 percent of total domestic sales), products of this industrial sector comprised over two-thirds. See IBGE, Comércio Interestadual, Exportação por Vias Internas: Amazônas—1974 (Rio de Janeiro, 1975).

4. Although not explicitly considered here, an integral part of SUFRAMA's second-stage strategy is the development of a 600,000 hectare agricultural district near Manaus. For more details on this topic, see SUFRAMA, Linhas Básicas do Distrito Agropecuário (Manaus, 1975).

5. Cited in "Em Manaus, Insatisfação," Gazeta Mercantil, May 13, 1976, p. 6.

6. The authors of a study on migration in Amazonia have calculated the relative economic attraction of various subregions by weighting the average salaries paid in local industry by the probabilities of locating employment in that sector. The results indicate that Manaus was almost ten times more attractive than the interior of Amazonas during the 1960-70 period. See M. de M. Moreira and J. A. M. de Carvalho, Migrações Internas na Região Norte, 2 vols. (Belém: Superintendência do Desenvolvimento da Amazônia, 1975), 2:97.

7. Comissão de Desenvolvimento do Estado do Amazonas (CODEAMA), III Pesquisa Sócio-Econômica (Manaus, 1972), pp. 44-45, 51.

8. This hypothesis is further discussed in J. Peres, "Zona Franca, Desenvolvimento e Estagnação," A Amazônia Brasileira em Foco 9 (1974): 79-83.

9. CODEAMA, op. cit., p. 95.

10. Not unexpectedly, the same studies revealed that family income had also become more concentrated during the same period; with the Gini coefficient rising from .445 to .490. This income concentration was even more evident on an individual basis in which case the coefficient rose from .444 in 1966 to .549 in 1971. See SUFRAMA, A Ação da SUFRAMA: Uma Avaliação Preliminar (Manaus, 1974), pp. 48-49; CODEAMA, I Pesquisa Sócio-Econômica (Manaus, 1973), p. 49.

6

Conclusions

As the preceding discussion has shown, recent government policies have already done much to surmount the challenges presented by Amazonia. Improved means of transportation and communication are ending its isolation; radar mapping and basic research are revealing its true natural resource potentials; diversified industry and agriculture are reducing its economic dependence upon a few forest products; and it is rapidly becoming settled through planned and spontaneous migration. In the final analysis, however, Amazonia is still a region in search of a balanced and coherent development policy. That is, while programs of the last two decades have ameliorated some of the region's traditional problems, they have inadvertently exacerbated others. These same programs have also created a number of new problems that are not likely to be resolved in the near future.

POLICY CONFLICTS AND QUESTIONS OF TIMING

Many, perhaps most, of today's problems are traceable to past pursuits of conflicting and mutually exclusive goals. The current difficulties of the Belém industrial park, for example, are in part due to the inconsistency of establishing improved means of access (principally through the national-integration highway system) while simultaneously applying a regional import-substitution industrialization model—a model that depends upon interregional trade barriers for its very success. Attempts to promote a more equitable intraregional distribution of economic activity through the creation of a free-trade zone in Manaus have also conflicted with the industrialization of Belém by effectively reducing the latter's potential market. Moreover, the expansion of economic activity caused by the zone has drained human resources from the sparsely populated interior of

164

western Amazonia and, therefore, has conflicted with the geopolitical goal of populating frontier areas.

One must also question the internal consistency of encouraging the human settlement of Amazonia while attracting private enterprise through a system of capital subsidies. The present analysis has shown that fiscal incentives have fostered an economic structure characterized by capital-intensive industries and land-intensive livestock ranches. Neither alternative has provided significant new employment. In fact, it can be argued that the proliferation of livestock projects has actually reduced future employment opportunities in rural areas by aggravating the land tenure situation. The fiscal incentive may also be criticized on the grounds that it is an inherently poor instrument for retaining income within regions. Since most investment capital is drawn from the Center-South, we are faced with the distinct possibility that most of the material benefits accruing from the development of Amazonia will eventually flow to extraregional interests.

Regional policies have also conflicted with those of a national scope. Efforts to improve the balance of payments and its negative impact on the Manaus free trade zone have already been discussed. Another case in point is the inconsistency of integrating Amazonia on the basis of highways during an era of increasingly scarce and costly fossil fuels. This latter conflict is especially unfortunate, given the abundance of alternative energy sources (that is, those derived from wood) suitable for powering fluvial transportation. In all fairness to planners, however, neither of these conflicts could have been perceived during the late 1960s when the respective regional policies were being formulated.

Other problems have arisen from errors of a sequential nature. Most important, it seems evident that the joint integration-occupation policy was embarked upon before a sufficient knowledge of the region's real comparative advantages was available. Thus, migrants have been settled in areas demonstrating no real agricultural aptitude, at least with the present state of technology. Similarly, many corporate cattle ranches have located in areas where this form of land use is of dubious validity. The result has been a continuation of chronic rural migration and poverty, as well as needless environmental degradation. It is hoped that the work of RADAM and the regional research institutes can provide regional planners with more precise and complete information upon which to base future land-use decisions.

THE TRAJECTORY OF DEVELOPMENT

For better or for worse, the medium-run trajectory of development seems inextricably linked to the export-enclave model; for a resource frontier like Amazonia, this may well be the indicated approach. The current favor enjoyed by the export-enclave model, however, brings to mind the French dictum, "Plus ça change, plus c'est la même chose." That is, although the commodities and details have changed, this approach to development is essentially the same as that followed at the beginning of the century. As such, it perpetuates, rather than resolves, many of Amazonia's traditional problems: dependence on international markets for primary products, control over economic decisions by extraregional interests, a skewed distribution of income and wealth, and chronic rural poverty.

A more general criticism of the export-enclave model is its preoccupation with generating "place prosperity"; that is, its major goal is to raise the aggregate product of Amazonia as rapidly as possible. While a "trickling down" of benefits to the regional population is a possible consequence of this approach, major improvements in the average welfare of poverty groups are by no means assured. According to one eminent regional economist, "Attacking human hardship and lack of opportunity solely through Place Prosperity might be like using a shotgun to kill flies."[1] Serious and complex problems still remain in Amazonia, especially those linked to agriculture and land tenure, employment, and environmental protection. It is doubtful whether policies based on capital subsidies to extraregional corporations can ever do much to resolve these problems.[2] In fact, such policies may even tend to aggravate them.

RECOMMENDATIONS

Of course, it is much easier to criticize than to suggest alternatives. The development of Amazonia is a perplexing topic for which there are no miracle solutions. In closing, however, several recommendations may be ventured. The first group of these is specifically directed at the serious problems encountered in rural Amazonia, while others are of a more general nature.

For various reasons discussed in the preceding chapters, public policies have not provided gainful employment for rural inhabitants, nor have they put an end to chronic migration. To help resolve these problems, some indicated avenues of action include intensified research on the agricultural potential of Amazonia, especially in the várzea areas; experimentation with low-technology development models stressing self-sustained forestry;[3] renewed efforts to ensure a just division of the public domain and a more efficient land-titling process; a reorientation of rural credit (preferably channeled through producer cooperatives) to provide relatively greater financing to small and medium-sized farmers; a restriction of planned colonization to areas selected for their agricultural aptitudes on the basis of RADAM soil surveys; and a reassessment of providing capital subsidies to the corporate livestock sector.

To improve the level of income retention in Amazonia, an increase in the taxation of mining enterprises should be considered. Moreover, the proceeds from such taxes should be distributed freely to states and municípios and not earmarked for expenditures benefiting the mining sector. A similar system could also be applied to the lumber industry, perhaps through a licensing system. In both the mining and lumber sectors, greater efforts should be made to ensure processing within the region, an option that is becoming more viable at this juncture as the enormous hydroelectric potential of Amazonia is finally being tapped.* In addition, all mining, forestry, and public-works projects should be required to submit an environmental impact study to appropriate authorities before implementation.

Finally, a greater role should be given to direct public expenditures as opposed to tax incentives. Public expenditures, by their nature, are more selective than tax incentives and can thus be more easily directed at specific problem areas like education, health, sanitation, and housing. Government expenditures could also be utilized to combat problems of urban unemployment and underemployment recently observed in Amazonia. In this respect, public employment and direct production subsidies to regional industry with idle capacity are interesting possibilities to consider. The latter could probably do much to improve labor absorption through correcting one of the major drawbacks of the tax-credit mechanism—the fact that it encourages the expansion of productive capacity (fixed capital) but does not guarantee that this capacity will be utilized.[4]

The underlying theme of all the above recommendations is that future policies should give more emphasis to the promotion of "people prosperity"; that is, there should be a greater preoccupation with raising the average welfare of the regional population—an approach that need not conflict with present attempts to increase the aggregate product. If this shift in emphasis does not occur, many Amazonians will be excluded from the fruits of their own region's development.

---

*According to the PDAM II, the hydroelectric potential of Amazonia (excluding the Amazon River itself) is around 62,000 megawatts, of which less than 2 percent (100 megawatts) has been harnessed so far. However, a 4,000 megawatt facility at Tucurui (on the Tocantins River, southwest of Belém) should be completed by 1982.

NOTES

1. E. H. Hoover, An Introduction to Regional Economics (New York: Knopf, 1971), p. 260.

2. This point is convincingly made in the classic article by R. E. Baldwin, "Patterns of Development in Newly Settled Regions," in Regional Development and Planning: A Reader, ed. J. Freidman and W. Alonso (Cambridge, Mass.: Massachusetts Institute of Technology Press, 1965), pp. 266-84.

3. Some of the available options are discussed in R. Goodland, H. S. Irwin, and G. Tillman, "Ecological Development for Amazonia," Ciência e Cultura 30 (1978): 275-89.

4. This point is further explored in F. Rezende, "Incentivos Fiscais, Acumulação de Capital e Emprego de Mão-de-Obra: Uma Contribuição ao Debate," Pesquisa e Planejamento Econômico 4 (1974): 111-18.

Appendix:
Sudam Projects—
Data Collection and Processing

The collection of basic data on SUDAM-approved projects was carried out by the Núcleo da Altos Estudos Amazônicos (NAEA) of the Universidade Federal do Pará, through a contract with IPEA/INPES. During this eight-month period, SUDAM provided both working space and full cooperation.

The original data were gathered from project specifications (pareceres) and transferred to questionnaires especially designed for this purpose. It was intended that all projects approved between 1964 and mid-1976 be included in our sample, although some may have been overlooked. In total, data were assembled on 563 firms: 180 industrial, 361 agricultural, and 22 in the basic services (education, energy, telecommunications, tourism, and transportation). At a later stage, it was decided to exclude all projects whose approval was subsequently revoked (caducos), requesting tax exemptions (isenções) only, and devoted exclusively to crops or extractive activities. The sample utilized in our analyses was thus reduced to 541 firms: 178 industrial, 341 agricultural (all livestock), and 22 in the basic services. Because of the relatively small sample, however, projects in the latter sector were not analyzed in depth.

Data processing was undertaken by the research-assistant pool of IPEA/INPES. During this stage, several methodological problems were encountered. First, an appreciable number of firms exhibited more than one approved project. In the majority of cases, these additional "projects" were merely "reformulations" (reformulações) of original financial specifications to adjust for inflation. In such instances, all financial data were taken from the most recent "reformulation." In the terminology of SUDAM, a project is considered to be any request for tax-credit funds and/or exemption from income taxes, import duties, and so on. This is true even in cases where the same undertaking is involved several times (usually through successive reformulations). Since we consider only the most recent reformulation, the terms project, firm, and undertaking are employed interchangeably in the text. The financial data were then inflated or deflated to 1975 prices utilizing the Fundação Getúlio Vargas general price index (Conjuntura Econômica, column 2) and attributed to the year of the first approval. This methodological choice, however, obscures the fact that total investment is realized over a number of years. Adjustments for this factor were utilized in the analysis and are described in the text.

A second methodological problem occurred when separating industrial projects new to Amazonia (implantações) from those previously in existence and desiring expansion and/or modernization (ampliações/modernizações). This separation was not deemed necessary in the case of livestock projects, however, as almost all were new to the region. Although this division was generally not difficult, some complications arose when new projects subsequently expanded or modernized. In all such instances, the entire project was classified as if it were new to the region.

A third problem arose due to the incompleteness of data on various projects. Generally, these statistical shortcomings were evident in the data on employment and value added. In some cases, improvement was achieved by utilizing data from the industrial cadastres of Pará and Amazonas. Unfortunately, no such subsidiary information was available for livestock projects. Thus, tabulations of "total employment" and "total value added," for example, are not really grand totals but rather totals for those projects on which this information was available.

A final, though extremely important, problem concerns data quality and reliability. In this respect, it should be stressed that the data represent only estimates of project designers based on conditions prevailing before the given project was undertaken. Since these initial estimates may not have coincided with subsequent operational realities, they should be interpreted with much caution. Furthermore, some exaggerations are to be expected in those cases (for example, employment creation) where higher numbers improve the chances of SUDAM approval. For instance, data on the employment generated by expansion or modernization projects are particularly suspect. It appears that project specifications refer to the total employment of the firm rather than the net employment gains (or losses) emanating from the projected expansion and/or modernization.

Bibliography

BOOKS AND MONOGRAPHS

Almeida, W. J. M. de. Serviços e Desenvolvimento Econômico no Brasil. Coleção Relatórios de Pesquisa, no. 23. Rio de Janeiro: IPEA/INPES, 1973.

_____, and M. da Conceição Silva. Dinâmica do Setor Serviços no Brasil. Coleção Relatórios de Pesquisa, no. 18. Rio de Janeiro: IPEA/INPES, 1973.

Andrade, A. de. Contribuição à História Administrativa do Brasil. 2 vols. Rio de Janeiro: Livraria José Olympio Editora, 1950.

Araújo, A. B. de; M. H. T. T. Horta; and C. M. Considera. Transferências de Impostos aos Estados e Municípios. Coleção Relatórios de Pesquisa, no. 16. Rio de Janeiro: IPEA/INPES, 1973.

Ávila, R. I. Os Incentivos Fiscais ao Mercado de Capitais. São Paulo: Editora Resenha Tributária Ltda., 1973.

Banco da Amazônia, S.A. (BASA). Desenvolvimento da Amazônia. Belém: Editora da Universidade Federal do Pará, 1967.

Benchimol, S. Amazônia. Manaus: Editora Umberto Calderão, 1977.

Bouhid, W. Amazônia e Desenvolvimento. Rio de Janeiro: SPVEA, Serviço de Documentação, 1961.

Camargo, J. G. da Cunha. Urbanismo Rural. Brasilia: Ministério da Agricultura-INCRA, 1973.

Cavalcanti, M. de B. Da SPVEA À SUDAM: 1964-1967. Belém: SUDAM, 1967.

Cavalcanti de Albuquerque, R., and C. de V. Cavalcanti. Desenvolvimento Regional no Brasil. Série Estudos para o Planejamento, no. 16. Brasilia: IPEA/IPLAN, 1976.

172 / FRONTIER DEVELOPMENT IN BRAZIL

Centro de Indústrias do Pará et al. Diagnóstico e Reivindicações das Classes Empresariais da Amazônia. Belém: Grafisa, 1971.

Cline, W. R. Economic Consequences of a Land Reform in Brazil. Amsterdam: North-Holland, 1970.

Collier, R. The River That God Forgot: The Story of the Amazon Rubber Boom. London: Collins, 1968.

Corrêa, L. de M. A Borracha e a II Guerra Mundial. Manaus: Edições do Estado do Amazonas, 1967.

Fonseca, C. A Economia da Borracha. Rio de Janeiro: Superintendência da Borracha, 1970.

Furtado, C. The Economic Growth of Brazil. Berkeley: University of California Press, 1968.

Goodland, R. J. A., and H. S. Irwin. Amazon Jungle: Green Hell to Red Desert? Amsterdam: Elsevier Scientific, 1975.

Goodman, D. E., and R. Cavalcanti de Albuquerque. Incentivos à Industrialização e Desenvolvimento do Nordeste. Coleção Relatórios de Pesquisa, no. 20. Rio de Janeiro: IPEA/INPES, 1974.

Graham, D. H., and S. B. de Holanda Filho. Migration, Regional and Urban Growth and Development in Brazil: A Selective Analysis of the Historical Record. São Paulo: Instituto de Pesquisas Econômicas, 1971.

Hebette, J. et al. A Amazônia no Processo de Integração Nacional. Belém: Universidade Federal do Pará, NAEA/FINAM, 1974.

Heller, J., and K. M. Kauffman. Tax Incentives for Industry in Less Developed Countries. Cambridge, Mass.: Harvard Law School, 1963.

Hirschman, A. O. Journeys toward Progress. New York: Twentieth Century Fund, 1963.

_____. The Strategy of Economic Development. New Haven, Conn.: Yale University Press, 1958.

Holanda, N. Incentivos Fiscais e Desenvolvimento Regional. Fortaleza: Banco do Nordeste do Brasil S.A., 1975.

Hoover, E. H. An Introduction to Regional Economics. New York: Knopf, 1971.

Langoni, C. G. Distribuição da Renda e Desenvolvimento Econômico do Brasil. Rio de Janeiro: Editora Expressão e Cultura, 1973.

Lodder, C. Distribuição de Renda nas Áreas Metropolitanas. Coleção Relatórios de Pesquisa, no. 31. Rio de Janeiro: IPEA/INPES, 1976.

Mata, M. da et al. Migrações Internas do Brasil. Coleção Relatórios de Pesquisa, no. 19. Rio de Janeiro: IPEA/INPES, 1973.

Meggers, B. J. Amazônia: A Ilusão de um Paraíso. Rio de Janeiro: Editora Civilização Brasileira, 1977.

Mendes, A. A Invenção da Amazônia. Belém: Universidade Federal do Pará, 1974.

Moreira, M. de Mello, and J. A. Magno de Carvalho. Migrações Internas na Região Norte. 2 vols. Belém: SUDAM, 1975.

Myrdal, G. Economic Theory and Underdeveloped Regions. London: Methuen, 1975.

Paiva, R. M.; S. Schattan; and C. F. T. de Freitas. Brazil's Agricultural Sector. Rio de Janeiro: Graphos, 1973.

Pereira, O. D. A Transamazônica: Prós e Contras. 2d ed. Rio de Janeiro: Editora Civilização Brasileira, 1971.

Rebelo, D. C. Transamazônica: Integração em Marcha. Rio de Janeiro: Ministério dos Transportes, 1973.

Reis, A. C. F. A Amazônia e a Cobiça Internacional. 4th ed. Rio de Janeiro: Companhia Editora Americana, 1972.

Robock, S. H. Brazil's Developing Northeast: A Study of Regional Planning and Foreign Aid. Washington, D.C.: Brookings Institution, 1963.

Sampaio, Y., and J. Ferreira. Emprego e Pobreza Rural. Recife: Universidade Federal de Pernambuco/PIMES, 1977.

Santiago, A. A. Pecuária de Corte no Brasil Central. São Paulo: Secretaria da Agricultura, 1970.

Silva, J. M. Oliveira e. A Sociedade Amazônica e o Problema Social da Desocupação e Subocupação. Belém: SUDAM, 1974.

Superintendência da Zona Franca de Manaus (SUFRAMA). ·A Ação da SUFRAMA: Uma Avaliação Preliminar. Manaus, 1974.

_____. SUFRAMA: Repercussões Sócio-econômicas de sua Atuação. Manaus, n.d.

Tavares, V. P.; C. M. Considera; and M. T. L. L. Castro e Silva. Colonização Dirigida no Brasil: Suas Possibilidades na Região Amazônica. Coleção Relatórios de Pesquisa, no. 18. Rio de Janeiro: IPEA/INPES, 1972.

Turnham, D. The Employment Problem in Less Developed Countries: A Review of Evidence. Paris: OECD, 1971.

United Nations. Food and Agricultural Organization. Livestock in Latin America: Status, Problems and Prospects—II. Brazil. New York, 1964.

Velho, O. G. Frentes de Expansão e Estrutura Agrária. Rio de Janeiro: Zahar Editores, 1972.

Villela, A. V., and W. Suzigan. Política do Govêrno e Crescimento da Economia Brasileira, 1889-1945. Série Monográfica, no. 10. Rio de Janeiro: IPEA/INPES, 1973.

Wagley, C. Amazon Town: A Study of Man in the Tropics. New York: Macmillan, 1953.

ARTICLES

"Amazônia: O Verde que Ainda Esconde um Areal Estéril." Jornal do Brasil, June 26, 1977.

Baer, W. "Regional Inequality and Economic Growth in Brazil." Economic Development and Cultural Change 12 (1964): 268-85.

Baldwin, R. E. "Patterns of Development in Newly Settled Regions." In Regional Development and Planning: A Reader, edited by

J. Friedman and W. Alonso, pp. 266-84. Cambridge, Mass.: Massachusetts Institute of Technology Press, 1965.

Becker, B. K. "A Amazônia na Estrutura Espacial do Brasil." Revista Brasileira de Geografia 36 (1974): 3-36.

Bhalla, A. S. "The Role of Services in Employment Expansion." In Essays on Employment, edited by W. Galenson, pp. 157-77. Geneva: International Labour Office, 1971.

Bonnen, J. T. "The Absence of Knowledge of Distributional Impacts: An Obstacle to Effective Policy Analysis and Decisions." In Public Expenditures and Policy Analysis, edited by R. H. Haveman and J. Margolis, pp. 246-70. Chicago: Markham, 1970.

Campos, R. de O. "La Rage de Vouloir Conclure." In Transamazônica, edited by F. Morais et al., pp. 103-31. São Paulo: Brasiliense, 1970.

Denevan, W. H. "Development and the Imminent Demise of the Amazon Rain Forest." The Professional Geographer 25 (1973): 130-35.

Egler, E. G. "A Zona Bragantina no Estado do Pará." Revista Brasileira de Geografia 23 (1961): 75-103.

"Em Manaus, Insatisfação." Gazeta Mercantil, May 13, 1976, p. 6.

Falesi, I. C. "Amazônia: A Terra é Pobre." Opinião, March 18, 1974.

Gall, N. "Letter from Rondonia." American Universities Field Staff Reports, nos. 9-13 (1978).

Gauthier, H., and R. Semple. "Tendências nas Desigualdades Regionais na Economia Brasileira, 1947-1966." Dados, no. 9 (1972), pp. 103-13.

Goodland, R.; H. S. Irwin; and G. Tillman. "Ecological Development for Amazonia." Ciencia e Cultura 30 (1978): 275-89.

Goodman, D. E. "Expansão de Fronteira e Colonização Rural: Recente Política de Desenvolvimento no Centro-Oeste do Brasil." In Dimensões do Desenvolvimento Brasileiro, edited by W. Baer, P. P. Geiger, and P. H. Haddad, pp. 301-37. Rio de Janeiro: Editora Campus Ltda., 1978.

_____. "O Modelo Econômico Brasileiro e os Mercados de Trabalho: Uma Perspectiva Regional." Pesquisa e Planejamento Econômico 5 (1975): 89-116.

Graham, D. H. "Divergent and Convergent Regional Economic Growth and Internal Migration in Brazil, 1940-1960." Economic Development and Cultural Change 18 (1970): 362-82.

Haddad, P., and T. A. Andrade. "Política Fiscal e Desequilíbrios Regionais." Estudos Econômicos 4 (1974): 9-54.

Hirschman, A. O. "Desenvolvimento Industrial no Nordeste Brasileiro: O Mecanismo do Crédito Fiscal do Art. 34/18." Revista Brasileira de Economia 21 (1967): 5-34.

Hoffman, R., and J. F. Graziano da Silva. "A Estrutura Agrária Brasileira." In Tecnologia e Desenvolvimento Agrícola. Série Monográfica, no. 17, edited by C. R. Contador, pp. 233-65. Rio de Janeiro: IPEA/INPES, 1975.

"Importações: Etapas da Política de Controle." Conjuntura Econômica 30 (1976): 76-80.

"Indios Posseiros." Jornal do Brasil, August 12, 1976.

Jornal do Brasil, July 30, 1971.

_____, September 29, 1975, p. 7.

_____, October 10, 1975, p. 30.

Katzman, M. T. "Paradoxes of Amazonian Development in a 'Resource-Starved' World." Journal of Developing Areas 10 (1976): 445-60.

Lent, G. E. "Tax Incentives for Investment in Developing Countries." International Monetary Fund Staff Papers 14 (1967): 249-321.

_____. "Tax Incentives for the Promotion of Industrial Employment in Developing Countries." International Monetary Fund Staff Papers 18 (1971): 399-419.

Martone, C. L. "Efeitos Alocativos da Concessão de Incentivos." In O imposto sobre a Renda das Empresas. Série Monográfica, no. 19, edited by F. Rezende, pp. 53-96. Rio de Janeiro: IPEA/INPES, 1975.

Meggers, B. J. "Environment and Culture in Amazônia." In Man in the Amazon, edited by C. Wagley, pp. 91-110. Gainesville: University Presses of Florida, 1974.

Melby, J. F. "Rubber River: An Account of the Rise and Collapse of the Amazon Boom." Hispanic American Historical Review 23 (1942): 452-69.

Mendes, A. "Amazônia: Primeira Grande Experiência Brasileira de Planejamento Regional." Revista do Conselho Nacional de Economia 14 (1965): 154-66.

Mendes, A. D. "Uma Nova Política de Valorização da Amazônia." Revista de Ciências Jurídicas, Econômicas e Sociais 1 (1963): 163-87.

Mendive, P. "Tax Incentives in Latin America." Economic Bulletin for Latin America 9 (1964): 103-17.

Mesquita, A. "Subsídios à Política de Ocupação da Amazônia Brasileira." IPEA—Boletim Econômico 6 (1975): 1-4.

Miyazaki, N., and M. Ono. "O Aviamento na Amazônia." Sociologia 20 (1958): 530-63.

Mueller, C. C. "Análise das Diferenças de Produtividade da Pecuária de Corte em Áreas do Brasil Central." Pesquisa e Planejamento Econômico 4 (1974): 285-325.

O'Brien, F. S., and C. Salm. "Desemprego e Subemprego no Brasil." Revista Brasileira de Economia 24 (1970): 93-115.

O Globo, July 7, 1971.

Panagides, S. S., and V. L. Magalhães. "Amazon Economic Policy and Prospects." In Man in the Amazon, edited by C. Wagley, pp. 243-61. Gainesville: University Presses of Florida, 1974.

Patrick, G. "Fontes de Crescimento na Agricultura Brasileira: O Setor de Culturas." In Tecnologia e Desenvolvimento Agrícola. Série Monográfica, no. 17, edited by C. R. Contador, pp. 89-129. Rio de Janeiro: IPEA/INPES, 1975.

Paula, R. D. de Garcia. "A Ocupação da Amazônia: Pelo Homem ou pelo Boi?" A Amazônia Brasileira em Foco 9 (1973-74): 61-87.

Peres, J. "Zona Franca, Desenvolvimento e Estagnação." A Amazônia Brasileira em Foco 9 (1973-74): 79-83.

Petey, B. C. C. de Mello. "Aspectos da Economia Amazônica à Epoca da Depressão (1920-1940)." Boletim Geográfico 31 (1972): 112-39.

Pimentel, L. "A Transamazônica e o Problema de Integração Social." A Amazônia Brasileira em Foco 9 (1973-74): 24-60.

Redwood, J., III. "Algumas Notas sobre Exportações e Desenvolvimento Regional." Pesquisa e Planejamento Economico 6 (1976): 431-59.

Revista Brasileira de Política Internacional 11 (1968): 1-214.

Rezende, E. "Estradas na Amazônia." In Problemática da Amazônia, pp. 383-405. Rio de Janeiro: Biblioteca do Exército Editora, 1971.

Rezende, F. "Incentivos Fiscais, Acumulação de Capital e Emprego de Mão-de-Obra: Uma Contribuição ao Debate." Pesquisa e Planejamento Econômico 4 (1974): 111-18.

Salm, C. "Evolução de Mercado de Trabalho, 1969/72." Estudos CEBRAP 8 (1974): 105-19.

Santos, R. "O Equilíbrio da Firma Aviadora e a Significação Econômica." Pará Desenvolvimento 3 (1968): 7-30.

Saunders, J. "The Population of the Brazilian Amazon Today." In Man in the Amazon, edited by C. Wagley, pp. 160-80. Gainesville: University Presses of Florida, 1974.

Senna, O. "Operação Rondônia, Assalto à Mão Armada." A Amazônia Brasileira em Foco 10 (1974-75): 65-81.

Sioli, H. "Problemas do Aproveitamento da Amazônia." A Amazônia Brasileira em Foco 10 (1974-75): 21-47.

_____. "Recent Human Activities in the Brazilian Amazon and Their Ecological Effects." In Tropical Forest Ecosystems in Africa and South America, edited by B. J. Meggers, E. S. Ayensu, and W. D. Duckworth, pp. 321-34. Washington, D.C.: Smithsonian Institution Press, 1973.

Tambs, L. A. "Geopolitics of the Amazon." In Man in the Amazon, edited by C. Wagley, pp. 45-87. Gainesville: University Presses of Florida, 1974.

Tolosa, H. C. "Dualismo no Mercado de Trabalho Urbano." Pesquisa e Planejamento Econômico 5 (1975): 1-36.

Villela, A., and J. Almeida. "Obstáculos ao Desenvolvimento Econômico da Amazônia." Revista Brasileira de Economia 20 (1966): 177-99.

OFFICIAL DOCUMENTS

Banco da Amazônia S.A. (BASA). Amazônia: Legislação Desenvolvimentista. Belém: BASA, Departamento de Estudos Econômicos, 1969.

_____. Relatório de 1974. Belém, 1974.

Castello, Branco H. de. Discursos—1965. Secretaria de Imprensa, n.d.

Comissão de Desenvolvimento do Estado do Amazonas (CODEAMA). Incentivos para o Desenvolvimento. Manaus, 1974.

República Federativa do Brasil. I Plano Nacional de Desenvolvimento (PND)—1972/74. Rio de Janeiro: Fundação IBGE, Serviço Gráfico, 1971.

_____. II Plano Nacional de Desenvolvimento (1975-79). Rio de Janeiro: Fundação IBGE, Serviço Gráfico, 1974.

Superintendência da Zona Franca de Manaus (SUFRAMA). Linhas Básicas do Distrito Agropecuário. Manaus, 1975.

_____. Termos de Referência para o Plano Plurienal da Zona Franca de Manaus. Manaus, 1975.

Superintendência do Desenvolvimento da Amazônia (SUDAM). Plano de Desenvolvimento da Amazônia: 1972-1974. Belém, 1971.

_____. 1º Plano Director; Triênio 1968/1970. 3 vols. Belém, 1968.

_____. 1º Plano Quinquenal de Desenvolvimento: 1967/1971. Belém, 1967.

_____. II Plano do Desenvolvimento da Amazônia: Detalhamento do II Plano Nacional de Desenvolvimento (1975/79). Belém, 1975.

Superintendência do Plano de Valorização da Amazônia (SPVEA). Política de Desenvolvimento da Amazônia: SPVEA, 1954-1960. 2 vols. Rio de Janeiro, 1961.

_____. Primeiro Plano Qüinqüenal. 2 vols. Belém, 1955.

_____. Programa de Emergência. Belém, 1954.

Vargas, G. "Discurso do Rio Amazonas." Revista Brasileira de Geografia. 4 (1942): 259-62.

STATISTICAL SOURCES

Comissão de Desenvolvimento do Estado do Amazonas (CODEAMA). I Pesquisa Socio-Econômica. Manaus, 1973.

_____. III Pesquisa Socio-Econômica. Manaus, 1972.

Conjuntura Econômica 28 (1974): 55.

_____ 30 (1976): 87.

Fundação Getúlio Vargas (IBRE). Sistemas de Contas Nacionais: Metodologia e Quadros Estatísticos. Rio de Janeiro, 1974.

Fundação Getúlio Vargas (IBRE)/SUDAM. Agregados Econômicos Regionais. 3 vols. October 1974-April 1976.

Instituto Brasileiro de Geografia e Estatística (IBGE). Anuário Estatístico do Brasil. Rio de Janeiro, 1954-76.

_____. Censo Agrícola. Rio de Janeiro, 1960-70.

_____. Censo Demográfico. Rio de Janeiro, 1920-70.

_____. Censo Industrial. Rio de Janeiro, 1960-70.

_____. Comércio Interestadual, Exportação por Vias Internas: Amazonas, 1974. Rio de Janeiro, 1975.

_____. Divisão do Brasil em Micro-Regiões Homogêneas—1968. Rio de Janeiro, 1970.

Instituto Nacional de Colonização e Reforma Agrária (INCRA). Estatísticas Cadastrais/7. Brasilia, 1974.

Ministério da Fazenda (CIEF). Anuário Econômico-Fiscal. Rio de Janeiro and Brasilia, 1968-74.

Ministério da Fazenda (SEEF). Comércio de Cabotagem do Brasil. Rio de Janeiro, 1958-62.

_____. Comércio Exterior do Brasil, 1957-1958. Rio de Janeiro, 1959.

Serete S.A./SUDAM. Estudos Setoriais e Levantamento de Dados da Amazônia. 4 vols. November 1972.

Superintendência da Zona Franca de Manaus (SUFRAMA). Anuário Estatístico. Manaus 1971-75.

Superintendência do Desenvolvimento do Nordeste (SUDENE). Estimativas do Produto e da Formação Bruta de Capital do Nordeste no Período, 1965-1972. Recife, 1974.

UNPUBLISHED

Almeida, J. A., Jr. et al. "Avaliação dos Efeitos Gerados pela Política de Incentivos Fiscais, Instituídos pela Lei no. 5.174, de 27/10/1966." Mimeographed. Belém: Universidade Federal do Pará/NAEA/FIPAM-IV, 1976.

Assessôres Técnicos, Ltda. "Situação Industrial no Estado do Pará: Análise e Soluções." Mimeographed. April 1970.

Costa, M. A. "Aspectos Demográficos da População Economicamente Ativa." Mimeographed. Rio de Janeiro: IPEA, 1968.

_____. "Aspectos Econômicos e Demográficos da Mão-de-Obra no Brasil, 1940/1964." Mimeographed. Rio de Janeiro: IPEA, 1969.

Hebette, J., and R. E. A. Marin. "Colonização Espontânea, Política Agrária e Grupos Sociais." Mimeographed. Belém: Universidade Federal do Pará, NAEA, 1977.

Magalhães, J. P. de A., and N. Kuperman. "Estratégias Alternativas para o Desenvolvimento da Amazônia." Mimeographed. Rio de Janeiro: Assessôres Técnicos Ltda., 1976.

Mueller, C. C. "Pecuária de Corte no Brasil Central: Resultado das Simulações com Modelos de Programação Linear." Texto para Discussão, no. 29. Mimeographed. Brasilia: Universidade de Brasília, Departamento de Economia, 1975.

Müller, G. et al. "Amazônia: Desenvolvimento Sócio-Econômico e Políticas de População." Mimeographed. São Paulo: Centro Brasileiro de Análise e Planejamento, 1975.

Reboucas, O. E. "Interregional Effects of Economic Policies: Multi-Sectoral General Equilibrium Estimates for Brazil." Ph.D. dissertation, Harvard University, 1974.

Redwood, J., III. "The Recent Evolution of Regional Income Disparities in Brazil." Texto para Discussão, no. 39. Mimeographed. Recife: Universidade Federal de Pernambuco/PIMES, 1976.

About the Author

DENNIS J. MAHAR is a loan officer with the Brazil Division of the World Bank, Washington, D.C. From 1975 to 1977 he was a senior economist with the Institute of Economic and Social Planning, Rio de Janeiro, where much of the research for this book was carried out. Previously, Dr. Mahar was a project specialist with the Ford Foundation and a faculty member of the University of Florida and of Pikeville College.

Dr. Mahar received his Ph.D., with a Certificate in Latin American Studies, from the University of Florida in 1970. He has published more than a dozen articles and monographs on Latin American development problems, with an emphasis on Brazil. His articles have appeared in such professional journals as Public Finance, Journal of Inter-American Studies and World Affairs, and Public Finance Quarterly.